SHADOW OF THE BRIDGE

SHADOW OF THE BRIDGE

The Delphi Murders and the
Dark Side of the American Heartland

ÁINE CAIN and
KEVIN GREENLEE

PEGASUS CRIME
NEW YORK LONDON

SHADOW OF THE BRIDGE

Pegasus Crime is an imprint of
Pegasus Books, Ltd.
148 West 37th Street, 13th Floor
New York, NY 10018

Copyright © 2025 by Áine Cain and Kevin Greenlee

First Pegasus Books edition August 2025

Interior design by Maria Fernandez

All rights reserved. No part of this book may be reproduced in whole or in part without written permission from the publisher, except by reviewers who may quote brief excerpts in connection with a review in a newspaper, magazine, or electronic publication; nor may any part of this book be reproduced, stored in a retrieval system, or transmitted in any form or by any means electronic, mechanical, photocopying, recording, or other, or used to train generative artificial intelligence (AI) technologies, without written permission from the publisher.

Library of Congress Cataloging-in-Publication Data is available.

ISBN: 978-1-63936-923-2

10 9 8 7 6 5 4 3 2 1

Printed in the United States of America
Distributed by Simon & Schuster
www.pegasusbooks.com

For Abby and Libby, who stuck together and solved the case.

Blood will drip from trees; stones will speak; nations will be in confusion; the movement of the stars will be changed.
—2 Esdras 5:5

CONTENTS

	A Note from the Authors	xi
	Introduction by Doug Carter	xv
Part One	The Crime: "It'll be okay"	1
Part Two	The Investigation: "I will want to kick you in the fucking nuts"	47
Part Three	The Suspect: "That's Bridge Guy"	121
Part Four	The Wait: "Just don't talk anymore"	183
Part Five	The Trial: "We've had this discussion a thousand times"	295
	Appendix	409
	Acknowledgments	411

A NOTE FROM THE AUTHORS

We started our podcast, *The Murder Sheet*, in 2020. Our first episode on Delphi was released on March 23, 2021. We were late. We had just moved back to Indiana. Laura Fleury encouraged us to look at this story of two girls who never came home from a walk in the forest. A listener named Michelle Roth did the same. We both recalled learning about the case when it first happened, and we wondered why answers were not yet forthcoming despite the fact that Libby German had managed to film the man accosting her and her best friend Abby Williams.

As we began to report on the case, we immediately got the strong sense that Hoosiers cared deeply about Abby and Libby. We came to find out that people the world over care about the girls. Before we released that initial episode, we went to see the area for ourselves. We traveled to Delphi and walked down the trail. We did not go on the bridge. We walked below, on the banks of Deer Creek. We stared up. The sight of that looming dark band cutting across the blue sky stuck with us. There was something mournful about that place.

Over the last four years, we conducted hundreds of interviews in this case. Some were ultimately aired on the podcast. Others were kept off-the-record. Some people did not mind having their names used. Others wanted their identities protected. Many of those talks were done in-person. Others occurred over the phone or video conferences. Some were one-off talks. Others were conversations that took place intermittently over the course of years.

We read and analyzed every single filing in the case of Richard Allen, as well as related cases. We relied on help from attorneys in Indiana and beyond to make sense of the happenings. We relied on tipsters and community members and anonymous sources to bring us information about rumblings within the case.

Due to a clerical error, we were able to get access to an interview between Kegan Kline and investigators and we published that. We attended all the pre-trial hearings in the case of Kegan Kline, as well as his marathon sentencing hearing. We also developed and maintained a lot of sources in Peru, Indiana, and Miami County.

After the arrest of Richard Allen, we became concerned that a number of court records were not being released to the public. We therefore took the step of filing into the case on June 8, 2023, to request that those records be made available. At the end of that month, Judge Frances Gull made public hundreds of pages of documents that had previously been sealed.

We attended all but one pre-trial hearing in the Allen case, traveling to both Delphi and Fort Wayne to do so. We also attended every day of Richard Allen's trial, from the start of jury selection on October 14, 2024, until the closing statements, and announcement of the verdict on November 11, 2024. We published detailed daily reports on the proceedings on our podcast, *The Murder Sheet*. We also covered the trial for the Franklin *Daily Journal*, a newspaper in Indiana's Johnson County. Both of us got into most hearings, and one of us got into all but one session of court. In each hearing we attended, we took extensive notes. We did not get seats for the verdict. We stood outside on the sidewalk and listened as the crowd erupted in cheers at the news of the conviction.

Covering the trial was one of the most difficult experiences of our professional lives. For reasons still unclear to us, Judge Gull personally intervened with the press consortium to insure that we would not be considered for press passes. As a result, we had to get in line outside the courthouse in the predawn hours to guarantee we would receive seats. Gull would not allow people to re-enter the courtroom if they left. That meant no food, water, or restroom breaks for anyone that wanted to keep their seat. A seat in the morning also would not guarantee a seat in the afternoon; an afternoon seat required standing in line once more. As a result, it was a month of dehydration and sleep deprivation. Brinkmanship ensured that trial observers started getting in line for court earlier and earlier, ultimately standing in line for the morning session as soon as the afternoon session ended. Our coverage of the trial would not have been possible without the support of loyal—and much appreciated—listeners who were willing to stand in line for us and hold our spots while we caught a few hours of sleep.

At the time we prepared this book, no transcripts of the trial proceedings had been made available. Our coverage of the trial is based on our own observations as well as the detailed notes we took at the time. All of the dialogue and observations included in this book come from source interviews, available court documents, which are listed in the Appendix, or our notes from the courtroom. We have strived to be as accurate as possible, but in the event we have made errors, we take full responsibility for those.

Once the gag order lifted, we were able to talk to more people. Despite repeated requests on our part, defense attorneys Andrew Baldwin, Bradley Rozzi, and Jennifer Auger did not speak with us for the book. We strived to include the perspectives of the people who lived this case.

The city of Delphi has long been cast as a haunted place. A place touched by darkness. That is true. The loss of Abby and Libby has changed the city. But it is important to remember that it is a real city, a place where real people live.

The story is a gutting one. Two children lost their lives because a selfish man held his own sexual gratification above their lives. There is nothing more sordid and low than that. The recesses of the bad behavior on and off the internet, the ways that the inhumane amongst us prey on those in pain, is disgusting and soul-deadening to behold.

But this is also a story about hope. It was an honor to watch a case unfold that ultimately saw the victims rise to become the heroes—we do not believe this case would have been solvable without the actions of Abby and Libby.

It was an honor to bear witness to the kindness and warmth of the people of Delphi and Carroll County and Peru and Miami County, as well as the courthouse staff and the deputies. We are grateful to have seen firsthand the efforts of the law enforcement officers and prosecutors who never stopped working and searching for answers and the families of the girls who lost so much.

It was an honor to see the dedication of those who worked on the case, who thought of Abby and Libby constantly, who took the case to heart, who remain shattered to this day, who will never forget.

We will never forget them, we will never forget Delphi, we will never forget the families, and we will never forget Abby and Libby.

INTRODUCTION

BY SUPERINTENDENT DOUGLAS G. CARTER (RETIRED)

INDIANA STATE POLICE

Having served as the Superintendent of the Indiana State Police for twelve years, I received bad news about people, events, or violent crimes nearly every day. All of the reports were troublesome and mattered very much, but two specific events rocked my soul and the souls of many others. I specifically remember the events surrounding the death of four young sisters that tragically died in a house fire in Flora, Indiana in November of 2016. Keyana, Keyara, Kerriele, and Kionnie's lives were taken by a cowardly arsonist that I know one day will be held accountable. Then Abby and Libby, two girls in Delphi, were discovered dead after going for a walk in the woods on a beautiful winter's day in February of 2017. Both of these crimes occurred in Carroll County, Indiana, which is a small rural community that resembles every small town in America.

I am often asked about how I dealt with such tragedy for nearly forty years. I believe that even though there is an enormous amount of darkness in our world—there is way more light. The light, while sometimes hard to see, in the aftermath of the murder of Abby and Libby was the people. I wish you all could have witnessed what went on behind the scenes of this investigation for nearly eight years. The hope, desire, and commitment for a resolution; the compassion and empathy during times of perpetual criticism; and the absolute refusal to give up, no matter the setback, were extraordinary examples of extraordinary people. Those that stayed the course are owed a debt of gratitude that can never be repaid.

The citizens of Delphi and Carroll County overwhelmed me with their courage, service, and sacrifice. From day one, they stood with us and cared for us—bringing us food when we were hungry and a kind word when we needed support. The families of Abby and Libby inspired us all and, even though I know they were often frustrated, they stood strong. I am so grateful for the friendship we have formed, and our bond will last forever. They felt unimaginable grief that altered their lives forever. I will never forget how they stood up in the sentencing hearing and talked about how their lives have been changed and how they will never be the same. They conveyed their grief in a manner that was beautiful in some kind of mysterious way and for a moment it seemed like time stood still.

My primary responsibility was to my team, the many other law enforcement agencies, and, initially, a narrow focus on the Delphi community. Over time though, this investigation began receiving global attention which challenged our messaging strategy, collaborative efforts, and management of the enormous amount of information. I was so fortunate to represent and stand with some of the most courageous, professional, committed, and unselfish law enforcement professionals for more than eight years. Thank you seems so insignificant, but I mean it with every ounce of my being.

While there were literally hundreds of law enforcement personnel involved in this murder investigation, a few of them deserve to be specifically referenced. Lt. Jerry Holeman was, and continues to be, the adhesive that kept the case together. He committed his entire existence to the murder of Abby and Libby and set a standard for the Indiana State Police in managing a complex and long-term investigation. Detectives Vido, Rector, Harshman, Harper, Buckley, Burgess, Cecil, Bunner, Chapman, Olehy, Datzman, and Page for bringing their technical skills and commitment throughout the entire investigation even during the ups and downs. The ISP

Forensic Laboratory system is represented by really special people. Melissa Oberg, Stacey Gosnell-Day, Stacy Bozinovski, Nikki Benson, and Renee Troxel who offered expertise in DNA, Firearm examination, Intelligence analysis, and managing an enormous amount of evidence and documentation. These men and women along with many others confront the worst the world has to offer to make life better for the rest of us—THANK YOU!

I routinely spoke to Lt. Holeman and other involved members of the ISP after the murders occurred. Strategic decisions were made, and I support every one of them. While we are all human, of course unintentional mistakes were made, but the decisions were pure and were never about hiding the truth or protecting anyone. I will never apologize for doing what we believed was right even if it was not popular—period! Some members of the online community tried so hard to break us based on their own theories and, while I appreciated the attention to this case, the efforts were generally subjective, opinion-based, and not helpful to the outcome.

Over the years, we just kept going—every day, every week, month, and year. We shared a core belief that one day accountability would come. On the surface it might have looked like some of the law enforcement personnel who investigated this case didn't have a lot in common. There certainly was not any group think, and we oftentimes had different ideas or approaches. Much of the accountability organically came from the multitude of agencies participating on either a daily, as needed, or part-time basis. Sheriff Tobe Leazenby and now Sheriff Tony Liggett from the Carroll County Sheriff's office were there from the very start. The US Marshals Service, FBI, and officers from dozens of agencies participated as they could especially early on. Kathy Shank volunteered all of her time from the very beginning until the end and sure played a critical part in the conviction of Richard Allen. Kathy Shank volunteered literally thousands of hours since the very beginning and never left. What an amazing example to all of us. She became a dear friend to many and her knowledge, memory, and commitment proved to be a critical piece that led to the arrest of Richard Allen.

Nick McCleland, the Carroll County Prosecutor, Steve Mullin, Jim Luttrull, and Stacey Diener were amazing and were the architects of the prosecutorial strategy. One common theme was that this case would be solved if we kept at it no matter the barriers or how strong the headwinds were.

That very theme led to the arrest of Richard Allen in October of 2022. Not long after he was incarcerated, Judge Frances Gull issued a gag order prohibiting people involved from publicly talking about this case to protect due process and the constitutional rights of the defendant. The State sure respected and complied with the order of the court, but the defense sure did not. The defense attorneys continued to perpetuate a false public narrative inferring a hidden conspiracy and the officers involved were corrupt and not trustworthy. I fought back my intense desire to respond, but because of the gag order I simply could not. It was brutal and like watching your child get off the bus every day with a black eye and knowing there is nothing you can do to stop it.

Journalists from major news organizations all over the world covered the case. There were many organizations that I developed relationships with, and they tried to report facts and share common interests while being fair and balanced. I came to trust, care for and confide in the two-person team of Áine Cain and Kevin Greenlee. There were times they were critical of the law enforcement strategy and of me personally and there were times I disagreed with them, but they were always respectful, fair, and came to their position with deliberation and care. They came into this case with an open mind and followed the evidence and facts along the way. Both cared deeply about this case and even during the trial were in line outside the courthouse at 2 A.M. to get a seat in the courtroom for the day. Over time, I have come to sincerely respect how deeply they care about Abby and Libby, their families, and the people of the Delphi community that have lost so much.

I am going to carry this case with me until my dying day. I will always recall the incredible investigative collaboration I observed behind the scenes, and the determination and discipline of the investigative team to ensure that one day there would be justice for Abby and Libby. Because of the gag order, the true story has never been completely shared, and I worried it never would be. I am grateful to Áine and Kevin for bringing the truth to the public.

Every single person involved in this case will always remember it. They will carry the load and bear the scars forever. But then they will do what they always do. They will get up and go to work prepared to do it all over again, to work cases we may never even hear about, to go once more into the darkness to bring light and hope to those who need it the most.

For a lot of people it may feel like this case is over, but for the families and the Delphi Community it will never be over or ever end—not as long as they live.

PART ONE

THE CRIME

"It'll be okay"

CHAPTER ONE

Only the brave walked the bridge.

Abandoned years ago, the Monon High Bridge loomed in the woods of Delphi, Indiana, marking the end of one of the paths on the local trail system. Narrow and hulking and hovering sixty-three feet above Deer Creek, the railroad bridge long ago decayed into a ruin of rusting trestle and rotten ties. But to some in Delphi, crossing the High Bridge became a ritual test of courage. The kids of the small Indiana city often ventured out there just to show they could.

Liberty German knew that. The fourteen-year-old had done it before. She could recall rushing forward along the rickety old train ties, persevering despite the whistling wind and the water that glinted through the gaps in the boards. Now, she would take her best friend, thirteen-year-old Abigail Williams, to the High Bridge. The two girls sat on the floor of the garage at Libby's house. The night before, Libby's family had hosted Abby for a sleepover. The girls spent part of the evening hanging out with Libby's older sister, Kelsi, and her friends. Together, Libby and Abby ate pizza and garlic knots, watched a scary movie, filmed themselves getting up to silly antics, and then hopped on social media to chat with boys. The girls got to stay up late even though it had been a Sunday night. The winter had been warm in Indiana. Delphi Community Middle School, where both girls were in eighth grade, had canceled classes that Monday to balance out the heap of unused snow days.

On the morning of February 13, 2017, the girls slept in late. When they rose, Libby's father, Derrick, made them a breakfast of banana pancakes. Libby lived with her grandparents on the outskirts of Delphi. Her father and older sister lived there too, three generations in one home.

In some ways, Abby had become more like a sister to Libby than a friend. That was despite the fact that Libby was outspoken where Abby was shy. Libby was certainly garrulous and protective, but she was also logical and thoughtful, a source of support and advice for her friends. And Abby could be more talkative and assured in the presence of those she knew and trusted. She loved thrills too, especially riding roller coasters. The girls had personalities that complemented rather than contrasted. Where Libby went, Abby followed. And where Abby went, Libby followed. Libby's family even brought Abby along on a spring break trip to Florida.

Both girls belonged to the volleyball team and played the saxophone in band. Libby had recently convinced Abby to join her on the softball team that spring. If Abby also opted to take up soccer and swimming, then the best friends would be perfectly matched in terms of extracurricular activities. In the halls of the middle school, they always stuck together. All their teachers knew that calling Libby would often also summon Abby, and vice versa. That afternoon, Libby would lead Abby across the High Bridge. They would make it to the other side together. That was the unspoken plan.

But Libby did not say anything about crossing the bridge to her grandmother, Becky Patty. She only asked to go with Abby to the trails. Then she cuddled the family's new fluffy black-and-white puppy, Tucker.

That day, Libby donned a fringed shirt splattered in tie-dyed swirls, along with gray sweatpants and her black Nike tennis shoes. Libby wore her dark blonde hair cropped short. Abby wore blue jeans, tennis shoes, and a red shirt. Her reddish-brown hair was tied up in a bun.

At her desk, Becky looked up from a heap of paperwork and considered Libby's request. She ran a home appraisal business out of an office in the garage. It was a true family business, with Becky's children Derrick and Tara pitching in. The office certainly reflected that. On one of the walls of the garage, a line marked Libby's height back when she was only four feet and one-and-three-quarter inches. With her large blue eyes, wavy blonde hair, and small figure, fifty-seven-year-old Becky looked far younger than most grandparents. She had originally made a bargain with the girls. If they helped her sort away papers into her filing cabinets, she would pay them for their trouble. That afternoon, they could even take their earnings and all go shopping for clothes together.

But now, Libby wanted to go to the trails instead. Becky was fine with that. The seat of rural Carroll County, Delphi was a city with fewer than three thousand residents. Delphi had its own share of problems like anywhere else, largely owing to methamphetamines, but it was a safe community. Becky told the girls that if they could get a ride to and from the trails, they could go. So when Kelsi popped into the garage to say she was heading out, Libby jumped to her feet.

"Can you take us to the trails?" she asked.

Kelsi agreed. Becky reminded her younger granddaughter that she also needed to arrange a ride home. Libby knew exactly what to do. She pulled out her phone and dialed Derrick. He was out of the house now, on his way to the nearby city of Frankfort, a city about a half-hour to the southeast of Delphi. He was going there to photograph houses for Becky's company.

Libby got Derrick as he was halfway to his destination. She asked him to pick her up at the trails. Derrick said yes, he could swing by in about two hours. He had dropped Libby off at the trails before, so he knew where to go. Father and daughter did not set up an exact meetup time. Instead, Derrick said he would ring or text Libby once he was close to the trails. The girls would then walk to the trailhead for the rendezvous.

Becky watched Libby and Abby scramble after Kelsi. A thought struck her. The air would be chilly. It was sunny out, but it was still February, after all. She told Libby to take a jacket with her.

Libby paused in the doorframe. The last words she ever said to Becky were, "Grandma, it'll be okay."

Kelsi knew the way to the trails. She and Libby had walked them plenty of times together. With her pale blonde hair and blue eyes, Kelsi resembled Libby. She was three years older, a junior in high school. Still, the German sisters were close.

That day, Kelsi had her own plans though. She declined the invitation to accompany Abby and Libby. She wanted to spend time with her boyfriend, Chase, then head off to her job at the local Dairy Queen. She loaned Abby a gray sweatshirt, while Libby took along her new black swim team sweatshirt.

In the rearview mirror, Kelsi could see her sister extend her arm for a selfie. Sitting behind Libby, Abby was gazing straight ahead at the moment her friend snapped the picture. The song "Heathens" by Twenty One Pilots droned on the car radio.

The entrance to the trails was across from the Mears family farm in Delphi. Residents called it the Mears entrance. More driveway than parking lot, the space could fit about two vehicles.

At 1:38 P.M., as she pulled up to the Mears entrance, Kelsi got a call from Chase. As she chatted with her boyfriend, the doors popped open, and the two girls rushed toward the trail. Abby and Libby disappeared into the trees.

The afternoon was strangely warm for February. Still, only a few hikers were out and about on the trails while the girls were there. On the walk to the High Bridge, Libby snapped pictures and sent messages to friends.

Her iPhone was her social lifeline. She spent quite a lot of time on the photo-based apps Instagram and Snapchat, even using the latter to message friends. Snapchat was popular with the teenagers because it erased sent pictures within seconds, barring a well-timed screenshot.

Abby did not have a phone yet. But she had a work-around. Libby had added Abby's fingerprints to her iPhone's system, so her friend could access it with ease.

Social media was not just for friends though. It was also Libby's means of contacting her new crush. Anthony was slightly older, maybe a high schooler. Libby had met him online. He had connected with her and a bunch of her friends on Instagram and Snapchat. Born in Alaska, Anthony had grown up in Indiana, but he also took regular trips to Los Angeles and New York City. Instagram revealed that the traditionally handsome Anthony had suntanned skin, floppy brown hair, and blue eyes. He styled himself with a modern twist, sporting gleaming white teeth, stud earrings, and ink to spare. Twin birds swooped down his collarbone, above a row of Roman numerals. Text on his shoulder urged observers to "Stay positive."

For such a young guy, Anthony seemed to be doing well. One of his Instagram photographs depicted bands of hundred-dollar bills piled high on a granite countertop. Screenshots of online shopping carts on Gucci's website revealed not-yet-finalized orders for gabardine slim pants, a silk bomber jacket, and a monogrammed backpack, totaling over ten thousand dollars. Another image showed the red steering wheel of a Ferrari.

Libby eagerly told her friends about Anthony. Here was a cute boy who was interested in her, who loved to hear what she had to say, who thought she was beautiful. He asked her for risque pictures. She declined to send them, but the attention was flattering. Perhaps one day he would take her away on one of his luxurious trips. That would be a real adventure.

Abby had a boy she liked too. Logan Holder was from Logansport, a larger city that was a twenty-five-minute drive to the northeast. Dark-haired and lanky, he was a high schooler. He and Abby had only met in person once or twice. By grade school rules, though, that was enough to be considered at least a burgeoning relationship.

Abby and Libby were both at that age where crushes and romance and boys were taking on a new urgency. Adolescence brought with it awkwardness and anticipation and immense confusion. Being liked by a crush could imbue a kid their age with a real sense of value and belonging.

On the trails, the girls walked close together. Their heads were bowed. They were deep in conversation. They barely noticed the middle-aged woman passing them on the trail.

Libby and Abby kept moving. They soon reached the end of the gravel trail. What lay before them, cutting past the treetops, was the High Bridge itself. A thirteen-hundred-foot relic of rail's golden age, the first portion of the bridge spanned Deer Creek, a tributary of the Wabash River. Pictures tended to flatten the Monon High Bridge, making it appear wide and stable. Photographs could never capture the creaks and groans and rotten springiness of the wooden planks. Libby and Abby stepped over the orange barricade and onto the first ties.

A strange little man watched them cross onto the bridge. The girls might be eighteen or nineteen, or they might be eleven. Their ages did not matter to him. This was his chance. He had been waiting for what felt like a long time, lurking on the trails, watching for women and girls. But in another way, he had been lying in wait all his life, craving a chance to do exactly as he pleased.

The man followed behind the girls.

The High Bridge stretched far above the sea of dead trees. Clambering atop the bridge's third platform, Libby aimed her phone at her best friend. Abby faced north, away from the gravel trails they had just traipsed along.

She had her hands jammed into her pockets. Her eyes were lowered. The ground was so far below her feet.

Being high up did not bother Libby. Beneath the afternoon glare, she took the picture. She did not turn the lens on herself. Satisfied with her photograph of Abby, she selected an artsy filter and posted it to her Snapchat.

A shadow appeared at the end of the bridge. The speck of darkness must have looked so small at first, just a smudge between the endless gray of the forest and the bridge. But a figure would emerge in short order. A man ambled across the bridge. He kept his hands close to his hips, perhaps stuffed in his pockets. He wore light, baggy jeans—cuffed in a way that revealed his short stature—and a navy jacket. An outfit common enough throughout Delphi and the rest of rural Indiana. His body type was hard to make out beneath the heavy clothing, but it looked average enough from afar. He was white, from the looks of his pale skin. Something dark circled his hips. A fanny pack, a tool kit, a belt holster, or an undershirt poking beneath the jacket. It was unclear.

From a distance, there appeared to be something brown atop his head. A skullcap fitted tight, perhaps. His face remained vague. His mouth seemed to be masked by a covering of some kind. By the time he got close enough to the girls for them to make out such details, it was far too late.

Libby was unsettled. She held up her phone like she was photographing Abby. But she ended up capturing the man's strange movements starting at thirteen minutes past two o'clock. In her phone, he remained a blurry enigma forever moving closer. As he neared Abby, he quickened his pace. The man frightened the girls. But they had nowhere to go. The only escape was to jump.

"Is he right here?" Abby called. Her voice was a high-pitched cry, like it got whenever she was excited or nervous. "Don't leave me up here."

Libby never left her friend. She chattered on, her nonchalant tone concealing an undercurrent of anxiety. Both girls were sniffling. The man was almost upon them. Perhaps if the girls behaved normally, he would leave them alone. "This is the path." Libby swung her phone around so it captured the gravel and the brush that lay before them. Then, Libby saw something. Under her breath, she said something about a gun to Abby. "There's no path going there, so we have to go down here," she said.

The man stood before the girls. He held a gun. He stared at them, eyes pale and bulging, and said, "Guys."

"Hi," one of the girls said. They must have felt trapped there, between the bare trees and the blue winter sky.

The little, lumbering man spoke to the girls again. "Down the hill," he said.

Down they all went.

CHAPTER TWO

The High Bridge blocked out the sun as Brad Weber rumbled beneath it in his white van. Every workday, he took that same route home. His parents owned the house in the woods where he stayed. The Webers lived at the very end of a road that extended from 625 West. Some called it the Weber drive. It was truly more of a private driveway than a proper street. The remote access road ran right under the Monon High Bridge.

Driving the Ford van was one of two minor alterations Weber made to his usual routine that day. He was a Subaru man through and through. Weber had worked at Subaru of Indiana Automotive, the assembly plant in Lafayette, for decades. Normally he drove his Subaru to work. Today was different because he had needed to haul a trailer for a friend, and the van had the necessary hitch. His white van was unencumbered now. He had dropped that trailer off earlier in the day.

The other change was that Weber had clocked out of the plant slightly early. He worked the first shift. That day, he had clocked in at 5:41 A.M., nineteen minutes before his scheduled start. Normally he clocked out at 2:30 P.M. That day, he left at 2:02 P.M., scanning his badge at the turnstile. Usually, it took Weber about twenty to twenty-five minutes to drive home.

With his graying hair and eyebrows that naturally rounded upward, the fifty-year-old was not just a Subaru man. He operated his own line of ATM machines around Indiana as a side business. He could be blunt and even fiery. He was rather literal-minded. He did not like the trespassers that frequented his family's property, and often called local law enforcement to shoo them away.

On Weber's journey through the trees, he saw no one.

But someone saw him.

Derrick German hurtled toward the bridge. It was 3:11 P.M. He was driving back from work, along Delphi's winding roads. He knew Libby and Abby were likely trudging back from their adventures in the woods, or even waiting for him at the trailhead, faces red from the chilly air.

Through his windshield, Derrick could see the refurbished red trusses of Wilson Bridge soar overhead. He was crossing Deer Creek. He was close. He called Libby and waited to hear his daughter's voice. She might be giggling with Abby over some joke, or else breathless from the hike and eager to head home. But the phone rang on, and Libby never answered. Derrick kept driving. He pulled into the parking area and drove up to the trailhead. Libby and Abby were not there. Derrick called his daughter again. No one picked up. That did not make sense. Libby was not careless. She had asked for a pickup. She would have known to keep an eye out for his calls and texts.

Derrick waited. He heard nothing. He saw no one. The trees were bare, white branches raised to the sky. Derrick got out of his car and began walking down the path. After a few minutes, he found himself at a three-way intersection. To his right, the trail would lead to Freedom Bridge, a new pedestrian bridge spanning the Hoosier Heartland Highway. To his left, two trails sprawled off, deeper into the forest. Trail 501 led to the decaying Monon High Bridge. Trail 505 ran to the banks of Deer Creek.

Derrick saw an elderly man with wild white hair and a droopy mustache of the same color strolling toward him, emerging from Trail 501. David McCain was a longtime Delphi resident. A nature-lover who frequented the trails and sat on civic boards, the seventy-two-year-old had arrived sometime after 3:00 P.M. He snapped photographs of fence posts and oak trees as he walked.

Derrick asked him if he had seen two girls.

McCain said he had not.

Derrick decided to follow Trail 505. The path sloped downhill, taking him to the edge of the water. Deer Creek babbled along, streaked blue from the clear skies. The High Bridge loomed above Derrick, a rusty ruin. There was no sign of the girls anywhere.

Becky's phone rang around 3:30 P.M. She was still in the garage, working with Tara. She picked up. Her son, Derrick, was the caller. He was at the trails trying to find Libby and Abby. The girls were missing.

Derrick asked Becky to try calling Libby while he searched. She agreed. After the call ended, she began ringing her granddaughter. So did Tara. Libby never responded. Around 4:00 P.M., Tara drove off to the trailhead to meet her brother.

Becky remained behind in her otherwise empty home. She called her husband, Mike. She called Kelsi. She told them to head to the trails.

Becky hung up. The path ahead was clear. She needed to get to the trails and meet up with her family. She needed to contact AT&T to see if they could provide her with location information for Libby's phone. She needed to alert Abby's mother, Anna.

Becky was scared for Libby. All sorts of disturbing scenarios sprang to her mind. Like most teens, Libby carried her phone with her constantly. The iPhone must have died, or else some technical issue was preventing calls and texts from going through. In the event of an accident, Libby may have even dropped her phone. Depending on the circumstances, the device could have been lost under piles of leaves, or dents in the forest floor, or beneath the rushing waters of Deer Creek. Then there was the possibility of injury. Libby or Abby might have tumbled down a steep hill or plummeted into a ravine. If one girl was hurt, the other one would likely want to stay with her friend. That idea frightened Becky the most. Libby hated pain. Even as a teenager, she was terrified of needles. Once, at a routine doctor's appointment for school shots, she panicked so badly that she ended up hiding under the examination table. Becky had been ushered out of the office as the doctor held a screaming Libby so the nurse could inject her. If she was hurt in any way, she would probably feel so scared.

But there was no time for fear. Becky felt she ought to focus on what she could control. Her family had been alerted and mobilized. Together, they would convene at the trailhead and scour the woods. Becky knew they would search until they found the girls.

The High Bridge frightened Kelsi. She had once crossed over with Libby, but she had not been able to complete the trek by walking. Kelsi ended up on her hands and knees, crawling over the rough boards. She had felt ridiculous watching her younger sister effortlessly maneuvering over the ties. Libby had always been the brave one.

But now Libby needed Kelsi to be brave. The High Bridge offered the best vantage point to look down upon Deer Creek and the surrounding forest. And the girls had definitely been there. After dropping them off, Kelsi saw a picture of Abby on the bridge posted to Libby's Snapchat account. So the High Bridge was a good place to start.

Kelsi took off, leaving solid ground and walking onto the bridge. Glancing down, she watched the creek trickling by. She was not alone. Cody Patty—the son of one of Becky's half-brothers—was Kelsi and Libby's uncle. The Pattys had adopted and raised Cody as their own. The twenty-nine-year-old had been at work all day, and he had arrived at

Becky's house just before she headed out to join her family in the woods. He had hopped in the car with her, and they had driven to the trails, leaving the vehicle in a ditch when they found the parking area full.

Together, Kelsi and Cody reached the southern side of the railroad bridge. Beyond the end of the bridge, they could see a hill plummeting down into a private driveway. Amid their trek, they saw no one, no signs of the girls. No flash of colorful fabric glimpsed between the trees, no sunlight caught in strands of blonde hair.

Kelsi screamed her sister's name. Cody followed her lead. Standing there, the two called for Libby and Abby for about half an hour. When they fell quiet, the forest was silent, aside from the occasional rustle of fallen leaves. Nobody answered them.

Kelsi pulled out her phone and called Libby. The call seemed to go through. Kelsi listened to the ringing through her own phone's speaker. Libby never answered. No corresponding chimes echoed from the forest either. A cold hush seemed to fall over the whole woods.

One could not see clear across the Monon High Bridge. It was simply too long. So Kelsi and Cody walked until they reached the bridge's end. At the edge, where wooden ties gave way to dirt and gravel, they turned to the southwest. The drive eventually led to the house where Abby lived. Perhaps the girls had gone that way. Above them, the sun sank in the winter sky.

The man looked as if he had just slaughtered a hog. His dark jacket was so caked in mud and dirt that it appeared tan. Blood, red and fresh and glistening, drenched his legs and boots. He walked west, toward Delphi. The orange sun blazed low in the sky.

Sarah Carbaugh watched him as she eased her little red Saturn along 300 North. The road was a cement ribbon running beneath Deer Creek's snaking route. It cut clear across Carroll County, from the town of Camden to the Hoosier Heartland Highway. The road was so narrow it could barely accommodate two large pickups going in opposite directions. So Carbaugh got close.

She slowed the car down. The pedestrian was on the opposite side of the road, but she did not want to risk losing control and hitting him. Staring through her car's window, she saw a middle-aged man with a scruffy little beard circling his lips and chin. He seemed to wear a lot of layers for a day so warm. Carbaugh glimpsed a brown sweater peeking up around his neck, light blue jeans, and a hat. In the thirty seconds she saw him, she noted his eyes looked slightly effeminate. The strands of hair sticking out from underneath his hat appeared curly.

Carbaugh lived near the High Bridge, and frequently walked the trails with her unfriendly dogs. As a kid, she had walked on the High Bridge. The last time, she became so scared that she ended up crawling all the way back. Thinking about the terrain around the trails, Carbaugh imagined that the muddy, bloody man had fallen while attempting to traverse some of the rocky bluffs and steep hills. That seemed far more likely that an impromptu pig butchering or a backwoods altercation.

Still, she was not about to stop her car and give the man a ride. Letting a stranger into one's car went against plain common sense.

Besides, the man gave her a weird feeling. He looked as if he was trying to be stealthy. Her car passed within three feet of him, but he seemed determined to not look at her at all.

So Carbaugh drove on. As she passed him, the man hunched his shoulders and kept his head down. Curled into himself, he just kept shuffling along. He behaved like a man who did not want to be seen.

CHAPTER THREE

By five o'clock, Libby's family had tried everything. They had searched the trails themselves, devising and assigning routes to cover the most ground. They had called, texted, and screamed through the trees. Becky had even tried to pinpoint her granddaughter's location using technology. A week earlier, after complaining about her device freezing, Libby had done a factory reset on her phone. Somehow, that had made it impossible for Becky to pull up her location data. Becky called AT&T's customer service department asking for help as she walked the trails. She told the woman on the other end of the line that two girls were missing in the woods. Her granddaughter was out there, possibly lost or hurt.

The AT&T employee said the only way for Becky to legally trace the iPhone was to locate it and download an app—which would of course be impossible, given that the phone had disappeared along with Libby.

"Don't you understand?" Becky asked. "I don't have her phone."

In the end, nobody pinged Libby's phone.

With no other options, the family called law enforcement for help. But Becky knew there was one more person she needed to contact. She had been unable to get in touch with Anna Williams, Abby's mom. Somebody needed to tell the woman that her only child was lost.

"I'm going to Anna's house," she told her family. "I've got to get ahold of Anna."

Alone, Becky returned to the car she had abandoned in a ditch. She drove to Anna's house, but Anna was not there. A member of Anna's family came to the door instead. Becky left a message with the relative, then drove toward the bar where Anna worked part-time.

Becky's phone rang, but it was Mike, not Anna. Her husband had news. The police wanted the families to all gather at the police station. Becky took in that information and kept driving. She was nearly through town when her phone rang again. In the middle of her shift, Anna was returning her call. She had screened the number but became alarmed after getting three calls back-to-back.

Becky told Anna that the girls were missing. She had allowed them to go for a walk on the trails. Now, no one could find them.

"I don't know what these girls are up to, but I'm sure it's not that big of a deal," Anna said.

Deputy Mitch Catron was almost at the end of his shift when he got the call about Libby and Abby. He worked days for the Carroll County Sheriff's Office and was due to drive home at six in the evening. At 5:17 P.M., dispatch called to advise him of a gentleman named Mike Patty who was reporting two kids missing. The girls had last been seen at the trails that afternoon, and they might have even gotten onto the High Bridge.

The sky was darkening as Catron pulled his cruiser onto North 625 West. He parked and got out beneath the bridge.

Then he returned to his cruiser and drove onward. Kids goofing off sometimes wandered onto the Weber property. Catron had once even responded to a call about a few miscreants messing with the family's chicken coop. Catron drove up to the Weber house, got out of his cruiser, and knocked on the door. After a pause, Brad Weber appeared. The man looked sleepy, like he had just woken up from a nap. Catron told him two girls had gone missing from the trails. Weber gave the deputy permission to search his family's land. Catron walked around. He heard nothing. And in the dimming light, with so many trees crowding around, there was only so much he could see.

Unlike Catron, Steve Mullin just missed the call. The police chief of Delphi had clocked out at half past five, a few minutes after the Pattys rang the county dispatch. He was already at home when his radio buzzed with a call about two missing girls.

Concerned, Mullin got back in his car and headed to the sheriff's office. On the drive, his phone kept going off. Civilians—friends, family, and neighbors—were texting him about Abby and Libby.

The trails were the domain of Sheriff Tobe Leazenby and his deputies. But when Mullin arrived at the sheriff's office, he offered any support he could. He started off by calling school officials to get a list of the girls' friends. Perhaps they had gone off with a larger group and lost track of time. A more realistic possibility was that one or both girls were stuck somewhere, injured. Either way, Mullin did not suspect anything nefarious.

The bespectacled, soft-spoken Mullin resembled a professor more than a seasoned law enforcement official. Unlike many in his field, he even refrained from swearing. He was a religious, churchgoing man who put his faith in God. But he had served in law enforcement since 1983, doing stints at both the Delphi Police Department and the sheriff's office. Mullin was well-known as a compassionate, understanding officer, but one who was firm about enforcing the law.

The Delphi Police Department was not the only agency to assist the Carroll County Sheriff's Office. The Delphi Fire Department also took a leading role, with chief Darrell Sterrett at the helm. Deputies and firefighters began pouring in from nearby counties too. Officers from the Department of Natural Resources even stepped in.

Going from the sheriff's office, Mullin followed Leazenby to the fire department. Bald with a dark mustache and a booming, resonant voice, Leazenby had been the sheriff since 2014. He was confident about finding the girls. Children and the elderly disappeared sometimes in the county. Both groups had the tendency to wander off, for different reasons. Older adults might be dealing with health issues and confusion. Little children might get turned around and lost. And teenagers sometimes ran away or headed to a friend's house without giving sufficient notice. Leazenby prided his office on finding the missing and bringing them home safe, every single time. He believed the girls would be home soon.

Tony Liggett waited in the darkness of the dispatch room. Screens glowed on the walls. In Carroll County, the sheriff's office and jail were crammed into one building. The dispatch room separated a long, bright hallway of cells—each with thick, colorful doors—from the rooms crowded with desks and filing cabinets.

Liggett was there to book an accused child predator. The suspect was due to turn himself in on a warrant. Liggett had worked that investigation—one of his first. He had only recently been promoted. Others in the office sometimes called Liggett "Junior"—short for "Junior Detective."

So he ended up in the dispatch room when the call came in about the two missing girls.

When his suspect arrived, Liggett booked him. Once that was done, he learned that the girls were still missing. He got on his computer to see if he could help. He found that Abby did not live far from the High Bridge. He drove out to her house but saw no one.

At the Delphi police station, the families of the girls convened to file missing persons reports and provide law enforcement with more details on the disappearances.

Mike Patty also made an extra trip back to the house to collect Libby's remaining electronics. He grabbed iPads, iPods, and computers, then brought them in for law enforcement to review.

Kelsi spoke to investigators at length. She had been the last person to see the girls. She also opened up her phone and showed the police Libby's Snapchat story, a collection of her latest pictures. The first photo was an artsy shot uploaded at 2:05 P.M. It showed the Monon High Bridge stretching out into the far distance. The planks looked bleached as bone thanks to the stark filter Libby had selected. Two minutes later, she had posted a Snapchat of Abby strolling along, looking down through the bridge. As late as 2:07 P.M., the afternoon had been proceeding as planned for the girls.

As she sat at the police station, Kelsi hovered over her phone. She reached out to different social media accounts that Libby had been communicating with online, messaging each profile in quick succession. Most belonged to Libby's friends. One account was called @anthony_shots. Kelsi barely looked at the profile's picture. She asked a few questions, trying to figure out if the person had any information on where Libby might be. Satisfied the person knew nothing, she moved on to the next account. Then Kelsi forgot about the boy who said his name was Anthony.

Becky took to social media as well. At 6:57 P.M., she posted on her Facebook: "Ok everyone I need help!!! Libby and a friend are missing. They went to walk the trails around high bridge today, and we have had no contact for the last 4 hours. She is not answering her phone. If anyone knows anything, please call the Carroll County police department."

Other family members took note and published similar cries for help. Libby's mother, Carrie Timmons, who lived in Kentucky, was one of those relatives. Comments began to pop up with condolences and offers of help. Soon, word spread across Delphi. Two young girls had vanished in the woods, and their families needed to find them.

Mostly, Liggett remained in the sheriff's office that night, conducting research, answering calls. He did leave once more, heading out to the gym at the old middle school. The local school system still hosted basketball games there, and they drew a crowd. Some of the officers wondered if the girls might have gone out there to attend the game with friends. Liggett did not know the girls. He did know teenagers, though. He could imagine his younger son Cole going off to the trails and then heading to a game without checking in. Cole was a good kid, a skater with a bit of a mischievous personality. But teenagers could make mistakes.

When Liggett arrived, he made his way to the main door of the gym. There, he ran into Mike Patty. The two men talked briefly. Then, Mike descended the stairs to the gym below. Liggett went upstairs to the concession stand. He found a crowd there, milling about, chatting and waiting to purchase drinks and snacks. He saw plenty of kids. But Libby and Abby were not there.

Soon enough, the waiting got to be too much. Becky remained at the station through the evening to answer questions from law enforcement officers. But Mike Patty continued to conduct his own search. People let him know about groups of girls they saw wandering. After he left the basketball game, he drove around, seeking his granddaughter and her friend, or at least a whisper about where they might have gone. Other relatives of the girls set out into the cold to join up with scores of neighbors, along with the county deputies, firefighters, and Department of Natural Resources officers. All around the forest and surrounding fields and roads, the searchers tramped across the twilight and into the night. Drones twinkled in the sky above.

Anna Williams went along with one of the volunteer search parties. Together, they trekked along the banks of Deer Creek. Only thirty-three, with an expressive, sensitive face and her daughter's reddish-brown hair, Anna was not a Delphi native. She had grown up in Michigan. A single mother, she juggled two jobs to support Abby. That night, she was surrounded by people braving the cold to help find her daughter.

The girls had only been missing for a few hours, but some already feared the worst—that the girls had slipped into the water and drowned, that they were gone. Some of these whispers reached Anna—and she pushed back. She told the searchers they were not looking for bodies.

Before heading out into the forest, Anna had hurried back to her house to grab Abby's jacket. She wanted to wrap her daughter in something warm and familiar the moment they were reunited.

One of the searchers that night was a man named Pat Brown. Dark-haired with a silvery white beard and thick glasses, Brown lived a little over a mile from the High Bridge. He had known Mike Patty since high school, and he had a daughter the same age as Kelsi. He gave Mike a call after his wife saw a post on social media asking for help with the searches. The sky was dark by then, but Brown drove out to meet his retired friend Tom Mears at the cemetery by the trails. Among the graves, they spoke and decided to drive off and call on another man who lived nearby, seventy-seven-year-old Ron Logan.

Logan owned thirty-eight of the acres of scrubland and pasture bordering the trails. He had lived on his land for decades. He rambled around in a white Ford F-250. He was not supposed to, though. He had lost his driving privileges due to his drinking habits. His white hair formed a widow's peak, and he sported a prominent white mustache.

Mears and Brown knocked on his door and asked him if he had seen any trace of Libby or Abby. A deputy had been by earlier to ask the same question. Logan told them he had not seen the girls.

After that, Mears and Brown surveyed the dark woods, with all its slopes and ravines. Brown thought that anyone navigating in the dark might easily break a leg along the rugged terrain. They watched the glowing flashlights bob through the woods.

Carroll County Deputy Darron Giancola had the night off, but he was out there looking with the others. Close to midnight, he parked his car along the Weber drive and followed a group of firefighters and civilians. The procession reached the High Bridge. Then the beam of Giancola's flashlight caught something strange. Amid the earth that sloped from the end of the bridge, he could see a slide of leaves with bare dirt exposed, like somebody had slipped down. Giancola pointed it out to one of the firefighters. But the girls were not there, so the searchers moved on.

Hours passed, and the girls remained lost. None of the searchers wanted to say it out loud, but everyone realized that the chances of a happy reunion were growing increasingly remote.

Around midnight, law enforcement called off the official search. There were safety concerns and liability issues to consider. But scores of firefighters, deputies, and civilians stayed out, well after the sanctioned search concluded. Some stayed in the woods until after two o'clock in the morning. Others lingered even longer. They found nothing. Leazenby did not know what to make of it. He had been sure that the girls would be located, either in the woods or goofing off at a friend's house. A man who always strived for optimism, he felt frustrated and confused.

Meanwhile, Mike Patty picked up Becky, and dropped her off at home. On the chance Libby and Abby made it back there on their own, somebody needed to stand watch. Becky waited for hour after blurry hour. She walked around her quiet home. She did not sleep. Libby never came home. She and Abby were still gone. The night outside was so dark. Libby was afraid of the darkness. The girl was nervous just to descend into the family's finished basement, often asking Becky to accompany her. Becky would point out all the light switches on the walls, telling her, "Libby, there's lights all the way down. You'll never be in the dark." Becky knew that Libby and Abby had not carelessly run off. There was no way her granddaughter would be out so late. There were no light switches to illuminate the deep, dark woods. That night, there were only flashlight beams cutting through the blackness, flickering in the trees, shining in the swirling waters beneath the bridge.

CHAPTER FOUR

When the sun rose on Valentine's Day, the official search resumed. By midmorning, an American Red Cross disaster relief truck sat in front of the city's fire station. Nearby, somebody planted a lawn sign stuck with blue tape. Its big red letters called for volunteers.

Dozens of Delphi residents heeded the call, largely thanks to posts that spread on social media. Civilians flocked down Union Street and clustered outside the city's fire station. Donning jeans and flannels and jackets, they huddled up and awaited orders. Mullin was one of the officials who greeted the volunteers at the fire station. He gave the searchers his phone number and told them to call him if they found anything. Brown was one of those volunteer searchers. He entered Mullin's number into his phone. He did not even realize the man was the police chief.

Like so many of his fellow Delphi residents, Brown had taken the day off work to help with the search. After picking up a can of Skoal for his wife and dropping his daughter off at school, he ended up meeting with Tom Mears at the Stone House Restaurant that morning. Then they headed to the fire station together to get their search assignments.

By this time, the media had picked up on the case of the missing girls. A few news briefs had gone out in the early hours of the search. Leazenby had told reporters then that there was no sign of foul play. But now that dawn had broken with no sign of Libby or Abby, journalists from a range of local and regional stations were sent to cover the ongoing mystery. Camera operators mingled in with the crowds, filming neon-jacket-clad search party leaders as they passed along instructions to the volunteers. Groups of searchers were sent into town to look for the girls. Others were told to search deep in the woods, far away from the places either girl would have gone willingly.

First Sergeant Jerry Holeman had flowers on his mind as he filled out reports at the state police post in Lafayette. He had procrastinated on his Valentine's Day plans. His fail-safe was to take an early lunch break, buy a bouquet and a card, and take it all to Nicole, his wife of twenty-six years, at the hospital where she worked as a nurse. Standing over six feet tall, Holeman's authoritative bearing and dark close-cropped hair attested to his service as a Marine. Around the time of the Gulf War, he had been deployed all around the world. But he grew up in White County, which hugged the northern and western borders of Carroll County, and now served that area as an officer with the Indiana State Police.

Just before he could leave around half past ten, Holeman got a call from Captain David Kirkham, the Area I Commander. Kirkham's domain included Lafayette, as well as the posts in Lowell and Peru.

"Do you know about these two missing juveniles?" Kirkham asked.

Holeman said he did. Driving in to work, he had heard the report on his radio around 7:30 A.M. Holeman had immediately called Leazenby and offered him assistance. The sheriff declined for the time being, noting that they had plenty of search party volunteers. "They're not asking for any assistance at this time."

"Well, they're asking for a helicopter," Kirkham said. "And if we're going to send the helicopter, you need to get boots on the ground."

So Holeman called in Sergeant Steve Buckley and Detective Jay Harper. He told them about the helicopter. "We need to go to Delphi and see what's going on."

Holeman and Buckley were both pretty new in their roles. Holeman had taken over as the district investigative coordinator in July. He ran all investigations, including roadside ones. Buckley had taken on Holeman's old job, and now led the squadron of detectives focused on investigations. They came up together as troopers a few months apart. Meanwhile, Harper was a senior detective with plenty of experience in major investigations.

The state police officers drove to Delphi, where they discovered a crowd around the fire station. The street swelled with fifty to a hundred volunteer searchers. Holeman parked and looked for somebody with the Carroll County Sheriff's Office. He found Kevin Hammond. Holeman had worked drug cases with him, and they had even busted a few meth labs together. A detective with the county, Hammond had lost the 2014 sheriff's election to Leazenby. There was no bad blood between the two men though. With Hammond was another sheriff's detective, Tony Liggett. Bald and mustachioed, he projected a certain intensity.

"We're getting beat up over not doing an Amber Alert," Liggett told Holeman.

The sheriff's detectives had tried to set one up. But the disappearance of Abby and Libby did not qualify for an Amber Alert because there was not enough descriptive information or evidence that they had definitely been abducted. Holeman said he would call the Indiana Intelligence Fusion Center to see about putting out an alert with looser criteria.

Overhead, the state police helicopter took flight. The chopper hovered above the woods of Delphi. Somewhere among the trees, the girls were waiting to be found.

Once again, Kelsi crossed the High Bridge. With three volunteers, Kelsi then walked along the trail that snaked directly below the bridge. She could occasionally hear other groups of volunteers trudging through the brush or hanging back to smoke a cigarette. The midday sun glimmered through the railroad ties far above her, and she walked along the bars of light and shadow. Nearby, she could hear yet another group of searchers clambering through the woods.

Then, a voice cried out. One of the searchers had found a shoe. Somewhere, perhaps from the opposite bank of the creek, a man yelled out a question: What kind of shoes had the girls been wearing? Kelsi knew Libby had worn her black Nike tennis shoes. She called out the details. She realized the other searchers had no idea that she was Libby's sister.

Jake Johns and Shane Haygood had followed the creek all day. Starting in Delphi's Riley Park, they walked upstream along the banks until they reached the High Bridge. The trek took them four hours.

Dark-eyed with dark scruff and a ring of tattoos around his bicep, Johns worked at a propane delivery company. His wife, Jennifer, did part-time work for Becky at her appraisal company, so he knew Libby's family. When his boss gave the workers the day off to look for the girls, he grabbed Haygood and they got to searching. They knew they were looking for a tie-dyed shirt. Haygood kept his eyes on the water, and Johns kept watch on the ground.

They saw the colors as soon as they emerged from under the bridge. Warm hues—yellow, orange, and pink—and a bright blue. The tie-dyed shirt was in the creek, sodden and hung up on some reeds. Near it was a black Nike shoe. Haygood and Johns wore boots that only went up to their ankles, so they did not wade into the waist-deep water. Instead, they cried out to a local firefighter they spotted nearby on the banks. The firefighter tried to ring other first responders, but he could not get a signal on his phone. Haygood managed to put in a call to Tom Mears, though, to let him know about the discovery.

Reception problems aside, sound carried well in that part of the forest, near the bridge. Others heard about the shirt and the shoe. Soon, Haygood and Johns were shouting back and forth with the searchers in Kelsi's group. The forest became loud with voices.

Haygood pulled out his phone, called Pat Brown, and told him about the garments. Brown was in a group on the opposite side of the creek. Earlier in the day, Brown had checked a cave in the side of a nearby hill, only to find the whole system had collapsed some time ago. Then he got a call from Tom Mears, letting him know that Johns and Haygood had seen something in the creek. So Brown and his group headed that way. On the way down, they ran into Becky's sister Melissa, and she joined up with them.

Along with firefighter Ben Mears, Brown kept moving forward toward the creek, ready to rendezvous with the other searchers. As he got closer, Brown could hear Haygood and Johns, and they could hear him. Dry leaves crackled on the ground, and sticks snapped as they moved closer. But neither group could see one another across the creek.

Brown stepped into a shallow indentation near the edge of the water. He saw pale skin against the fallen leaves. Two forms lay there on the forest floor, about five feet away. Brown froze. He thought they must be discarded mannequins. Then he saw the blood. He was looking at the bodies of Libby and Abby.

"We found them." Brown's voice carried through the woods. "We have found the bodies."

Sobbing, Melissa ran from the scene. Standing on the opposite bank, Johns, Haygood, and the firefighter listened to Brown's voice ringing through the trees. He sounded shocked.

Kelsi heard the shouts too. She wanted to go to her sister. One of the other women from her search party grabbed hold of her before she could sprint across the creek.

"We need to call the police," Brown said. He managed to do so himself, ringing the number Mullin had given him. The scene at the fire station, the surge of hope and determination from all the volunteers, felt like a thousand years ago now.

Brown told Mullin he found two bodies near the creek, not far from the cemetery.

Then he stood watch, with his back to the bodies. He wanted to make sure nobody got too close to the girls.

Murmurs spread fast across the wandering bands of searchers. Becky saw Pat Brown's wife take a call, only for her face to go ashen. Then her own sister Melissa staggered toward her, up the hill.

Melissa was crying. "I'm so sorry." She refused to say more; she only kept repeating that she was sorry.

Becky did not understand until she saw the coroner's van rolling toward her. The girls were dead.

CHAPTER FIVE

The girls waited in the woods. They grew cold in the night, beneath a cloudy sky and a waning moon. Deer Creek flowed by. The girls were on the north bank, just a few feet from the water. The earth around them was slightly depressed, forming a shallow bowl. The girls were not visible from the other bank. The shape of the earth concealed them from view until one got close. Throughout the morning, the calls of the searchers went unheard in the little hollow.

Hauling in all his equipment, Buckley set up at the Delphi police station. He was a digital media recovery specialist. He could download all the pertinent data off of cell phones or computers. He could help break open any devices the girls left behind. That morning he was trying to get into Libby's iPad. A few of her relatives had offered up possible passwords. Now he was employing different tools and software.

All across the room, law enforcement officers and other first responders talked and coordinated and worked.

Mullin was on the phone. Then he stopped talking. He looked up. "They found them."

The room went quiet. Nobody asked any questions. Mullin did not have to say anything more. His tone of voice was enough.

One by one, Buckley, Liggett, and the others stood and walked from the room. They got in their cars and drove out to the cemetery in a line, like a funeral procession.

After the discovery of the bodies, authorities told the searchers to go home. Police did not say the girls were dead. They did not need to. The searchers who had been with the girls' family members already knew. Everyone else who had not heard yet was ordered away. The civilians staggered back to their cars, eyes red from the cold and the implications.

Doug Carter was standing in his office in downtown Indianapolis when the phone rang. He picked it up and learned that two bodies had been found near Deer Creek in Carroll County. Just earlier that day, his officers had briefed him on the search.

As the superintendent of the Indiana State Police, Carter was used to getting bad news every day. He had started out his career as a trooper, and later became sheriff of Indiana's Hamilton County before then-governor Mike Pence put him in charge of the state police. Carter was the first to say he had never worked as an investigator, but it fell to him to support the state police through their investigations—the grueling and high-profile ones in particular.

Not long ago, there had been another such case in Carroll County. An unknown perpetrator had set a devastating arson fire in Flora, claiming the lives of four young girls, all sisters: Keyana Davis, Keyara Phillips, Kerriele McDonald, and Kionnie Welch. State police had taken on that investigation several weeks in. Their deaths haunted Carter, and he had gotten to know Carroll County better through that case.

Now he was heading back. Carter hurried outside and got in his Dodge Charger. As superintendent, he mostly eschewed drivers. He raced up to Delphi himself. He wanted to find out what was going on.

Holeman was trapped. Somebody told him that two bodies had been found. He needed to get to the crime scene. But his car was blocked in. He ended up grabbing a ride with FBI special agent Rich Davies. They drove out together to the cemetery.

In the ravine, they found the state police district lieutenant, Tom McKee, there with Deputy Drew Yoder and Giancola. Descending further, they met a group of men and women who were searchers. They had found something horrible. Some of them were crying.

"Where are the girls located?" Holeman asked them.

The searchers gestured. But Holeman saw nothing but Tippecanoe County divers in the water. One of them recognized him and called to him, pointing out all the articles of clothing in the creek.

"Okay, well we're going to try to get the scene secured," Holeman called back.

McKee and Trooper Larry Mote Jr. wound crime scene tape around the trees and started a crime scene log. Anyone who did not need to be there cleared the area.

Buckley and Hammond made their way down the hill. They met with Holeman and called up Liggett too. The ravine loomed over them as they spoke about the case.

"What do you guys want to do?" Buckley asked.

"Do you guys want this case, or do you want to let the state police run with it?" Holeman asked.

"You take it," Liggett said.

Hammond was more hesitant. "Ah, we better ask the sheriff."

Holeman called Leazenby and asked him if Carroll County wanted to keep the case.

The sheriff paused. "Well, are you guys going to leave us?"

"No," Holeman said. "We're not going to leave you."

Sergeant Brian Olehy was on his lunch hour when he got the call from Hammond. Hearing from a county detective was no surprise. A bespectacled man with a slightly world-weary demeanor, Olehy had been with the state police for decades. He had done just about everything. District patrol operations in northwest Indiana. Casino gaming enforcement up in Gary. The investigation into the death of Indiana Governor Frank O'Bannon. The ISP public information office, as an assistant commander. Finally, he became a crime scene investigator in the Indiana State Police Laboratory. He was the lead CSI at the Lafayette post.

Most of the cases he worked on came from local agencies. That morning, Olehy had been vaguely aware of two girls missing in Carroll County. Hammond told Olehy they had been found. Hammond had only just learned the news himself, and he had not even been out to the bodies. He said Carroll County would need help to document the crime scene and determine cause and manner of death.

Olehy got in his well-equipped CSI van and headed from Lafayette to Delphi. As he drove, he called up Sergeant Jason Page and Sergeant Duane Datzman. Page and Datzman were the lead CSIs at the Peru and Lowell posts, respectively. Olehy asked them to head over to Delphi. He had known and worked with both men for years. They had come up together as CSIs around the same time. They all considered themselves disciples of Dean Marks. Largely regarded as the father of CSI work within the state police, he had been a mainstay in forensics since the early nineties.

Pulling into the cemetery, Olehy could see the swells of searchers. He met up with Hammond. Together, the two men made their way from the cemetery to the woods across the street.

Every crime scene was unique. But just approaching this one would prove to be a challenge. The area around Deer Creek, with its sharp ravines, was a bit of an aberration in flat north-central Indiana. Olehy quickly realized there was no chance of getting a vehicle down there. To access the spot where the girls lay, Olehy and Hammond had to descend a steep embankment. Olehy did not have too much trouble with the slope. The waters of Deer Creek glinted through the trees. Olehy could see two pale forms lying on the forest floor.

The girls were in a floodplain, thick with fallen leaves and branches. Only select personnel were allowed to approach the nightmare in the clearing. The crime scene investigators needed to be able to work without contaminating valuable evidence.

When Datzman and then later Page arrived, the three investigators conferred with one another. All three men had worked hundreds and hundreds of crime scenes between them. They chose their path to the bodies carefully, selecting a route they felt would destroy the least amount of potential evidence, where the killer and victims were unlikely to have trod. The CSIs marked the way with yellow rope.

Libby was naked, lying beneath a tree. Her face, neck, and hands were smeared with blood. Her head was tilted to the side. Her left arm stretched out, reaching. A large branch lay across her left shoulder, nearly touching her cheek. Sticks crisscrossed her body, laid across her throat, shoulders, and thighs, forming an irregular shape about her torso. On the trunk of a nearby tree, about four feet from the ground, there was a smear of blood.

Abby lay to the right of her friend. She wore Libby's black-and-yellow Delphi Swimming sweatshirt, and a pair of damp, unzipped blue jeans. Her neck was cut. Her elbows were bent. Hidden within the sleeves of the too-big garment, her hands rested on her chest. Three small branches intersected over her left arm.

Both girls were cool to the touch, and stiff, in a state of full rigor. No insects buzzed around them. No signs of predation from coyotes. That was not surprising for February in Indiana.

The three CSIs were not the only ones near the scene. Beyond the bodies, in the waters of the creek, divers still searched for more evidence. The FBI's Evidence Response Team (ERT) swung by much later. Olehy asked them to collect the items the divers found. Sergeant Jim Cody, the lead CSI at the Putnamville post, arrived to scan the landscape with a lidar device and take the soaked clothing found in the creek. Putnamville boasted a drying room superior to that in Lafayette. Olehy and the other CSIs wanted to prevent mold and mildew from growing on the evidence.

Other law enforcement figures like Holeman, Buckley, Davies, Hammond, and Harper hung back. The journey down had been a difficult one. They had each scaled a cattle gate, crossed a field, and then clambered down a huge slope. The investigators were mostly in suits and ties. The February day was warm for winter, but the detectives were still underdressed for the chill in the air. On the few occasions when it became necessary to scale the hill again, they had a hard time making it up to the top. Many would need to take a break on a slight plateau that jutted out from the slope.

Since his time in the Marines, Holeman had seen quite a few corpses. He had witnessed bodies torn apart by explosions in war, a shotgun suicide that blasted a man's head off, and a car wreck that had ripped a person's torso in half. They all looked fake to him. To him, most dead bodies resembled living people with makeup slapped on to look pale.

Holeman got within thirty feet of the girls. He saw Abby first. Her injury was less visible. She appeared to be wearing wet clothing that was far too baggy for her. Then he saw Libby. Her throat had been slit several times. What Holeman saw made him angry. All those who came close to the scene, who became involved in the case, became angry. They had all seen death, gruesome killings, horrible accidents. But this crime was brutal. A killer had slaughtered two children and left them to grow cold in the woods. But that was a feeling that had to pass so the work could begin. There was so much to do.

Buckley called his girlfriend and said he would not make it home in time for a Valentine's Day dinner. She asked no questions.

Trooper David Vido did not know what was going on. When he signed on for his mid-shift, he was just told to head straight to Delphi. The twenty-five-year-old called around to try to figure out what was going on. Dark-eyed and thin, Vido had worked at the Lafayette post since 2014. There, he found himself providing scene security. Something awful had happened. Investigators would need plenty of space. He parked his car to block off the road, at West 300 North and North 575 West. Sitting inside, he watched officers dragging equipment toward the scene. The stream of people flowed in and out of the woods for hours.

Olehy snapped on one pair of gloves, and then another. He liked to be careful. The CSIs would come to dub the immediate area around the bodies "Ground Zero." Once again, they made their way single file along a path that looked undisturbed, that did not look promising as far as yielding evidence.

Since the three members of the CSI team had worked together before, they fell into an easy rhythm. They went from the least intrusive tasks to the most intrusive tasks. Their two primary goals were to document the scene and collect possible evidence.

Datzman focused on taking pictures at the edges of the scene, moving closer and closer in a spiral. Later, he soared up in the state police helicopter for aerial pictures.

Page was the artist of the group. A graduate of Indiana University's Herron School of Art, he knew about the rule of thirds and how to photograph a scene in a way that told a story. He sketched the scene out in a diagram, drawing outlines of the bodies, branches, bloodstains, and trees from a bird's-eye view. At some point, he headed back to his truck to grab a ladder. That heightened vantage point better allowed him to capture the overhead layout of the scene.

Occasionally, the other detectives nearby would call out observations—the clothing swap, possible shoe prints. They pointed out evidence for the CSI team to look at. The CSIs would listen, but they did not need guidance.

The leaf fall obscured much of the blood. They found one large pool and several smaller pools. Libby was covered in it. Abby seemingly was not, although they found later that her sweatshirt was saturated with blood. Some reddish splotches on nearby trees were just naturally pigmented bark. Others were smears of blood.

Alternative light sources could provide an even more comprehensive view of the blood. Olehy and Page set up a device, and blue light shone down on the scene. Datzman's eyes went to the ground. Something was glittering there. He shone a flashlight and saw the headstamp of a cartridge peeking up through the leaves, between the two girls. It looked intact, and ever so slightly pressed into the ground.

There was no chance it had come from one of the three CSIs. As state police officers, they were all permitted to carry weapons. But none of them had firearms that took .40-caliber ammunition. Two of them did not even have weapons on them that day. Datzman never carried his gun to crime scenes. The holster would poke at him when he knelt to work. Olehy had left his firearm behind because he knew he would need to descend a steep slope. Nor could it be traced back to any of the other investigators at the bottom of the hill. When the CSIs mentioned the cartridge, they asked if anyone was carrying a gun that took .40-caliber ammunition. Nobody was.

The CSIs photographed the cartridge and placed it in a paper bag.

Then it was time to process possible evidence on the bodies. Judging from the bloodstains, both girls had been killed in the clearing. First, the CSIs set aside the sticks. They had no blood on them. Mossy and crumbly, they were all clearly fallen branches. None of them had clean edges. The killer had likely picked them up right off the forest floor. The CSIs systematically documented and set them aside.

Working on one body at a time allowed them to avoid distractions. The CSIs focused on Libby. Olehy ran a series of swabs over parts of her body. He searched for areas that were not coated in blood. All the places the killer might have touched her and left skin cells. He paid attention to Libby's left wrist. The position of her body and the barely visible trail of blood in the leaves indicated that the killer had dragged Libby by her left arm to where she lay. When the swabbing was done, the CSIs moved her to a fresh sheet and wrapped her up. Finally, they placed her in a body bag. The body bags were then sealed shut with tape and marked with Olehy's initials and an identifying number.

Next it came time to examine and move Abby. They collected a strand of hair from her hand. The CSIs rolled her over. They found a Nike shoe beneath her. Olehy noticed something else. One spot was black. It did not look like soil.

"Oh," he said. "Hey. Something here."

Still holding up Abby's rigored body with one hand, he reached with the other for the spot on the ground, even blacker than the dark earth. Olehy's fingers found a phone, nestled amid the leaves.

Becky thought the police needed help. So when the investigators asked to talk to the family members, everyone complied. They were in shock. The reality that Libby and Abby were gone seemed impossible.

The investigators separated the girls' relatives. They talked to them one by one. Some of the more pointed questions barely hit the grieving interviewees.

The investigators took a hard look at Derrick. Libby's father struggled with an addiction over the years. He ended up getting involved with methamphetamine, even becoming a low-level dealer. When police caught up with him in 2014, he did not snitch out his associates. After a probation violation, he took the punishment and went to the Westville Correctional Facility. There, he received treatment to help him overcome his addiction. When he got out, he stayed clean and focused on caring for his daughters.

Quickly, investigators determined a few key facts about the men closest to the case. Mike and Cody Patty were both at work that afternoon. The pictures Derrick had taken for Becky placed him in Frankfort. There was no evidence that Derrick had reverted back to the drug world. Nor was there any indication that Libby was targeted over her father's past.

One after another, the relatives drifted from the interviews. Years later, Becky realized they had all undergone a series of subtle interrogations. The police started their investigation with a look at those closest to Abby and Libby, and found nothing.

The air grew colder as the investigators talked about what needed to happen. Holeman and Buckley coordinated troopers and detectives. Hammond and Liggett listened to the findings the CSIs occasionally called out. They all considered the resources they would need. They were all on the phone.

Holeman and Buckley also spoke with one another. Other agencies were offering resources, manpower, whatever they needed. That was all starting to pour into Delphi.

A well-known figure joined them. Guided by Harper, Doug Carter had earlier visited the bottom of the hill. That was before the bodies had even been moved. The CSIs did not want him or anyone else to approach though. They were adamant and vocal about protecting the scene. The superintendent stood and stared. The whole woods pulsated with a fresh darkness. The sight was hard to take, the horror of the two pale bodies atop the blanket of dead leaves. Lingering at the bottom of the hill, the other investigators made arrangements to meet the following day. Carter realized straight away that the state police would need to play a big role in the investigation.

In time, Leazenby joined him on the hill. Carter encouraged him to take as much help from the state police as possible.

"We're going to do it together," he said.

Leazenby understood that the state police had vast resources his county could never match. Holeman had assured him that the state police were not out to take over the case. Leazenby believed him. The sheriff knew and trusted the troopers and detectives at District 14 in Lafayette. But he believed the case rightfully should stay with the county. A faithful Methodist, Leazenby recognized that he might be guilty of the sin of pride. But a killer had spilled the blood of children on Carroll County soil. He would not abdicate responsibility. He imagined that a former sheriff like Carter might understand that.

Carroll County would keep the case, but the state police would work it with them, side by side, all the way.

That first day, Carter walked the path the girls walked. Up on the High Bridge, he felt such fear. The bridge swayed slightly as he walked. Carter wondered if the whole thing would collapse beneath him. Like so many before him, he ended up crawling the whole way back.

A thought came to Carter's mind out on that bridge. A stranger passing through would not just happen upon the place. There were even people within Delphi who seemed unaware of the High Bridge. The killer was probably not an outsider.

As the sky darkened, Holeman felt grim but confident. The crime scene was complex. He thought there would be plenty of clues and evidence. The way most cases went, good leads popped up in a matter of days. He imagined they would have someone in jail by the end of the week. The detectives remained there throughout the afternoon and into the night.

The CSI team worked for hours too. Darkness fell. Olehy, Page, and Datzman each left well after ten at night. The bodies were gone by then. The clearing was left empty. Blood still soaked the ground and the leaves. On the other bank, Giancola stood vigil until dawn.

Page and Datzman returned to the scene the next day with metal detectors and chemicals meant to render blood more visible. Olehy did not accompany them. Instead, he drove nearly ninety miles to the west until he reached the Terre Haute Regional Hospital. So did Hammond and Liggett. There they met Dr. Roland Kohr, a physician with a snow-white mustache and many years of experience. Kohr had served the region as a forensic pathologist for decades.

Abby's autopsy came first. She suffered only a single wound to the left side of her neck, a cut about two inches in length and an inch deep. That had partially opened up her left jugular vein. Based on the edges of the wound, the killer had likely inflicted it from right to left. Because the injury involved a vein, the bleeding out was slow. Abby could have held on for five or ten minutes. She had no defensive wounds, no bruising, no other incisions, although her arms and hands were frozen in an almost pugilistic attitude. Kohr noted one odd thing. While Abby's body bore no obvious ligature marks, there were two faint lines across her face. A mark ran between her chin and lower lip, and another dipped below her chin. Kohr determined that the lines were left perimortem, around the time of her death. He thought the markings resembled the edges of duct tape, but no adhesive residue had been left behind.

Libby's injuries were more extensive. Kohr found four, or maybe five, separate incisions across her throat. Her left and right carotid arteries and her left jugular vein were completely severed. At least two incisions overlapped, and the abrasions told the forensic pathologist that the killer had drawn the knife back and forth several times across Libby's throat. Kohr noted that the girl had suffered a cerebral edema, or swelling of the brain. That was evidence that Libby could have lived five to ten minutes with her throat cut. She also had no defensive wounds. Yet something about the injuries to Libby bothered Kohr. They did not resemble injuries from a classical serrated blade, but they were serrated-like.

Blades can be serrated—with a jagged edge, like a saw—or non-serrated, and they can cause different patterns in wounds. One of Libby's wounds had a serrated-like pattern. But it was not a classic appearance of a serrated pattern, as the telltale marks were spaced at a distance. Kohr thought it was almost like the handle area of the blade caused the strange appearance of serrated-like marks. Kohr wondered to himself what kind of weapon could make such wounds.

Neither girl bore signs of injuries from sexual assault. Kohr completed sexual assault kits for both girls for DNA analysts to scrutinize.

When it came time to identify the bodies, Mike Patty volunteered. He wanted Anna, Becky, and the others to remember the girls as they were when they were alive. So he met with coroner Jordan Cree's deputy and father Jay Dee. Cree showed him photographs of the bodies. Mike confirmed that they belonged to Libby and Abby. He thought about the last few minutes of his granddaughter's life, and how much both girls must have suffered before they died.

That afternoon, Leazenby and the Lafayette post's public information officer Kim Riley held a press conference. They announced that the bodies had been identified as the two missing girls. Journalists wanted more information about the causes of death, but authorities kept quiet. Such details could help police quickly dismiss false confessions from disturbed attention-seekers. The murder of children tended to stir up a lot of darkness.

PART TWO

THE INVESTIGATION

"I will want to kick you in the fucking nuts"

CHAPTER SIX

The men who would become some of the main investigators met in Delphi's city council room above the police station. The group gathered around a large table. They would eventually be called Unified Command. That was a term borrowed from the FBI, represented there by special agents like Davies and Mike Peasley. In a complex multiagency case, the FBI would bring in stakeholders from various law enforcement organizations to make up Unified Command, a centralized group tasked with running an investigation. The earliest Unified Command in Delphi consisted of Davies, Peasley, Holeman, Harper, Liggett, Hammond, and Mullin, with county prosecutor Robert Ives and his deputy Jerry Bean often showing up to discuss the case as well. Big decisions were going to be made as a group.

Almost immediately, Unified Command lost its room with the grand table. They moved to a nearby room with a cluster of smaller tables, in the part of the building that was still under construction. They established an interview room and designated an area for the investigators working on phone extractions and other technological processes. In the big open space, Unified Command set up the first set of dispatchers working the phone lines. Detectives would hover over the dispatchers, poaching what they considered the hottest and most exciting tips until the higher-ups barked at them to knock it off.

When the police unlocked Libby's phone, they found the face of her killer. Brian Bunner, a sergeant and a digital forensic examiner, managed to open the device. Libby's phone yielded chilling clues. Before her murder, Libby managed to capture forty-three seconds of audio and video. As she moved her phone about, the image jumped around in a jerky motion. Mostly, she captured the gravel-strewn ground. In the background of the video, for an instant or two, the detectives spotted a man in a blue jacket, his head down, moving rapidly across the Monon High Bridge toward the two girls.

Investigators listened to the girls speak. Their voices sounded scared. They heard the man speak to them. They heard a metallic click that sounded like a gun racking.

That was all; after that, the short video ended.

Faced with a terrifying situation, both girls had shown remarkable bravery. Libby recorded the footage. Abby managed to hide the phone with her body. They had stuck together until the end.

Police knew the video likely captured the appearance and voice of the killer. But they did not want to send the perpetrator running. So when they released a screenshot from the video to the media at close to 7 P.M. on February 15, they did not explain its provenance. They instead told reporters they viewed the unidentified man as a witness, and they only wanted him to come forward about what he might have seen that day.

All around the country, viewers stared into the blurred face and projected their own memories of specific features. Someone somewhere gave him the nickname "Bridge Guy," and it stuck. More importantly, tips about the man's identity began to roll in.

Investigators scoured Libby's online activity. There were even more clues on her social media. Police found Libby's communications on Snapchat and Instagram with @anthony_shots, but the account looked fake. Anthony did not seem to be a real person. He looked like a lure for teenage girls.

The CVS shift manager had a story to tell. On February 16, 2017, he called the Delphi tip line. He had something very important to share. Dispatch was inundated with tips. The dispatcher, a volunteer, took the man's information. But something went wrong. Somehow, the man's surname got swapped with the name of the street he lived on. The CVS shift manager's tip was recorded under a false name.

A flood of state police troopers poured into Delphi to investigate the murders, and the agency had no way to get them hotel rooms or even buy them food or water. Carter did not want his investigators to have to worry about such things, so he resolved to fix the problem himself. He put in a direct call to Governor Eric Holcomb. Within eight hours, the agency had a purchase card to buy food, water, and lodgings. Carter brought in special operations planners to coordinate further. Soon enough, they had more food than they even knew what to do with. The families of Delphi came forward with plate after plate of chicken and noodles, lasagna, and practically every type of pie known to man. Farmers, local business owners, church groups, and Old German Baptist Brethren in their traditional dress pitched in. Carroll County was determined to do everything to support the people investigating the murders of Abby and Libby.

The population of Delphi seemed to swell in the wake of the murders. Newcomers crowded the restaurants. Unfamiliar, out-of-town cars jammed the streets.

A good number of the strangers were press. Some worked for regional outlets based in Indianapolis and Chicago. Others were national reporters looking to put their own spin on the case. Camera technicians paced about, shooting interviews and B-roll to capture the haunting bareness of the woods, obvious bursts of law enforcement activity, and images of a small Indiana city in mourning.

New faces from local, county, state, and federal law enforcement also arrived in force. Agencies were sending as many people as they could spare to help find out who killed Abby and Libby.

One volunteer that the police had to turn down was Mike Patty himself. Tired of feeling so helpless and wanting to be useful, Libby's grandfather asked for the sheriff to deputize him. The police said no. They could not have a relative of one of the victims working the investigation. But the detectives respected Mike's dedication. They could imagine themselves doing the same thing if a tragedy befell their families.

Unable to sit by, Mike gathered his friends. Long after the crime scene was released and the surrounding forest cleared, the men marched through the fallen leaves. They were desperate to find a clue tying back to the killer. They touched nothing but planted little flags when they discovered something of possible note. By the time they were done, they left behind a trail of little fluttering flags, but nothing further came of the search.

Brad Holder met with investigators on February 17, 2017, the day after someone filed a tip claiming he was a white supremacist with a creepy online presence. After arriving at the Delphi Police Department, he sat down with two investigators—FBI Special Agent Adam Pohl and Sergeant Christopher Gootee of the Hammond Police Department, an agency based in a city over eighty miles to the northwest of Delphi.

Holder readily admitted his own indirect personal connection to the case. His son Logan was friendly with Abby. That slim link was enough to warrant interest from the police. Holder and his son quickly cooperated with every request. The teenager even turned over his phone to the police.

Gootee and Pohl quizzed Holder about his connection to Delphi. He did not live there. He only traveled to Delphi on the weekends to see his Army buddy, Patrick Westfall. They had served in Afghanistan together. With five or six others, they had started an Ásatrú "tribe" that met each Sunday at Westfall's house. In the United States, those who practiced Ásatrú worshipped the old gods of North Germanic tradition and practiced a folkish form of heathenry that excluded non-whites. The specific beliefs of Holder's tribe remain unclear. An enthusiastic convert, Holder posted images on his Facebook account associated with Ásatrú, including a picture of his own hand-carved runes and a separate image showing two women lying covered in branches on a forest floor.

During those weekend trips, Westfall's son and Logan would go off together to play basketball at Delphi's Wabash and Erie Canal Park. Holder imagined that his son would text or call Abby when they were in town. He told the investigators he had the sense that Abby and Logan Holder only ever met once in person.

Holder proved to have a solid alibi for the time of the murders. That afternoon, he was at work at Waste Management in Buffalo, Indiana, over half an hour away from Delphi. He clocked out sometime after two o'clock, and then checked into the Logansport gym, Workout Anytime. The girls had been abducted at 2:13 p.m. Investigators needed to find a man with more than a few off-putting Facebook posts.

Betsy Blair saw Bridge Guy. On February 17, just four days after the murders, she sat down with Master Trooper Taylor Bryant of the state police to share her story. Blair was a slim, middle-aged woman with glasses. She frequented Delphi because she liked to walk loops on the city's trail system.

While walking there on February 13, she spotted a man standing on the Monon High Bridge, from about fifty feet away. It was the man in Libby's video. She was sure of that. Blair estimated the man she saw to be around twenty years old and white, with curly brown hair and a medium build.

After seeing him, Blair turned back in the direction of her parked car. As she hiked that way, she saw two girls she later realized were Abby and Libby heading toward the High Bridge. Other than their killer, she was likely the last person to see them alive.

As Blair carefully described the man she had seen, Bryant sketched out an image of a young man with a prominent chin, a turned-up nose, wavy hair, and narrowed eyes.

The public would not see it for another two years.

CHAPTER SEVEN

Olehy brought the cartridge discovered at the crime scene to DNA analyst Stacy Bozinovski at the state police laboratory in Indianapolis. She was unable to collect any trace evidence from it.

The cartridge was then passed on to Melissa Oberg, a forensic firearms examiner who had spent years at the state police laboratory. She got the cartridge last because she was sure to destroy any possible trace evidence it might yield.

In most cases, examiners were looking to see if they could find sufficient agreement between fired bullets. But the Delphi case was different. She just had a cartridge, a single unit of ammunition, made up of a case, primer, and the bullet within. It was unspent, unfired. However, Oberg was seasoned. She had examined cycled, unspent cartridges before.

Most likely, the killer had racked a firearm and then racked it again, perhaps ejecting the cartridge by accident. Plenty of gun owners carried their firearms with an empty chamber for safety reasons. When the killer racked his gun on the bridge, the chamber may have been empty.

Oberg began her process. First, she assessed the evidence, from the packaging inward. She was looking for broken seals, biological material, anything that could have contaminated or damaged the evidence.

Opening up the packaging, she found that the cartridge from the scene was a Smith & Wesson, nickel, with visible marks on the head and side, and a few random gray scratches. In the cases of such ammunition, Smith

& Wesson was not the brand, but instead designated a type of bullet. The cartridge's headstamp read Winchester 50. On the cartridge's head, there looked to be ejector marks, along with extractor marks on its rim. It did not appear to be weathered, as it might have looked had it been out in the elements for some time.

Next, Oberg assessed the evidence for weight, the direction of the twist, and other class characteristics. In forensic firearms science, class characteristics refer to the features that define specific types of tools. They can result from design factors determined prior to manufacture. So a gun locker full of Glocks would share class characteristics, design factors determined prior to the manufacturing process. Then there were subclass characteristics, which came about during the manufacturing process but affected numerous firearms and could not be used to identify a specific gun. But each Glock could have any number of tiny differentiations on its extractor claw and ejection pin. Those imperfections or irregularities were the individual characteristics. A forensic scientist could observe those, mull over the similarities, and reach an opinion as to whether a particular round had been cycled through a particular gun.

Relatively new federal standards in forensic science demanded Oberg dispense with any over-the-top conclusions. Because she was unable to test every gun in the world, she would be unable to make the scientific claim that the firearm was a "match." A growing critical community wanted to go further. They argued that all forensic firearms analysis was suspect and unscientific, and that such information ought to be tossed out of court altogether. Forensic experts, however, argued that while the field was due for improvements, forensic firearm examination still had considerable merit.

Oberg herself remained a proponent of forensic firearms analysis. A small, dark-haired woman who spoke with a calm voice, she was confident in her abilities. In all her years at the lab, in either her case work or the proficiency examinations she completed, she had never made an identification that the examiner verifying her work disagreed with. And when examiners checked one another's work, they never knew their colleague's conclusions. Oberg was sure that by relying on her expertise and years of experience, she could examine the cartridge's characteristics. Once she had a suspect's firearm, she could cycle another cartridge and look for sufficient agreement of individual marks between the two so that she could give an opinion on whether both had gone through the same weapon.

Investigators realized they needed to keep the existence of the cartridge a carefully guarded secret. If word about it leaked to the press, then the killer might discard the gun somewhere—and police would forever lose a crucial chance to link the murderer to the scene of his crime.

The detritus of the brutal crime came to the Indianapolis state police laboratory in carefully sealed packages. Bozinovski examined it all. She was a seasoned analyst with a delicate voice and a head of wavy brown hair kept in a meticulous middle part.

Bozinovski was looking for DNA profiles—specifically, the DNA profile of the offender. Typically, a killer's blood or semen made for the best source of DNA. Touch DNA, or sloughed-off skin cells, was the poorest source. But she would strive to find anything she could.

After taking swabs, Bozinovski would start out with the extraction process, which involved adding chemicals to a possible sample that could break open cells and release DNA. She would then extract and measure that sample of DNA. If she found the quantity was high enough, she could start a polymerase chain reaction with an electric current that allowed her to copy the DNA.

She went over all the garments. The sweatshirt, the shoes, the pants, the underwear. The CSIs and the dive team had recovered everything, aside from Libby's underpants and a single sock. Those had either been taken as trophies by the killer, or else washed away down Deer Creek. When the clothing that had been recovered from the water dried at Putnamville, she went over all of that too.

A DNA swab from Derrick confirmed that the hair found on Abby almost certainly belonged to one of Libby's close female relatives. That made sense, given that Abby was found wearing Libby's clothing. There was no investigative relevance there.

Testing the kits done by Kohr, Bozinovski found no evidence of sexual assault. The girls' bodies contained minimal amounts of trace male DNA. But it was in such scarce amounts that its presence could be explained by living near a man or boy.

Bozinovski found very little evidence. Most of the clothing was dirty, damp, or soaked from the creek. Water washed away and diluted DNA evidence. Items like the shoes were filthy, caked in dirt and plant material. That inhibited DNA evidence too. And then, of course, there was the blood. In the hierarchy of DNA, blood was powerful, overwhelming. A sea of blood from a victim was sure to drown any trace amount of offender skin cells.

She did discover some unidentified male DNA though. And it did not show any kind of familial link to either victim. The tiny sample could very well belong to the killer.

CHAPTER EIGHT

On February 18, 2017, Lieutenant Dan Dulin happened to grab one of the many unassigned lead sheets. It memorialized a tip from a CVS shift manager who had a story to tell police.

Just a few days into the investigation, tips were pouring in fast. The Department of Natural Resources officer was one of the many law enforcement officials volunteering with the case. Dulin had been out of town when the girls vanished, but as soon as he returned on February 16, 2017, he headed to his first briefing. He knew the area very well, and many of the other officers working on the investigation.

That morning, Dulin reviewed his lead sheets and called the shift manager who claimed to have information. He asked if they could meet at the tipster's home, or else the command center. The shift manager balked at both, offering instead to head over to the Save A Lot grocery store parking lot, right near the CVS.

There, the shift manager told Dulin he had been on the trails the day of the murders, arriving at around 1:30 p.m. and leaving around 3:30 p.m. He said he parked at what he called the "old Farm Bureau building." No such building existed. Afterward, he walked to the Freedom Bridge. He drifted high above the cars speeding down the highway. As he strolled, he kept his eyes on his phone, watching his stock ticker in particular. He ran into a few other witnesses that Dulin might want to follow up with. There were three girls. One was tall, with brown or black hair. On the back of the lead sheet, Dulin scribbled a reminder to identify the three girls. The lieutenant held the man's phone and wrote down the device's unique mobile equipment identifier.

The interview took about ten minutes in total. Dulin recorded other interviews on his phone, but he did not record that one. The shift manager went back to CVS. Dulin took an hour to write down all of his notes. He made certain to correct dispatch's error and fixed the man's name before he turned in the lead sheet. He wrote that the lead required further follow-up. He did what he was supposed to do. Then he got back to work. He forgot about the shift manager. That was unfortunate.

The shift manager was not a witness. He was not a tipster. Dulin had been talking to the killer.

Before Libby and Abby were buried, the community was invited to say goodbye. The families scheduled a joint public viewing at Delphi Community High School at 4:00 P.M. on February 18. To prepare for it, Libby's family wanted to get copies of some of their favorite pictures of her; they wanted to display them at the event so the community could see happy moments in her life.

To get the photographs developed, the family went to the local CVS. The photo technician there—a small, paunch-bellied shift manager—told Libby's grieving relatives he would not charge them for the pictures. He held the photos of Libby—joyful, safe, and very much alive—in his hands. Then he passed them on to the family.

CHAPTER NINE

It was incumbent upon Unified Command to get a handle on the case. Investigators had streamed in from all over. The help was vastly appreciated. But the reality was a managerial nightmare.

Long-haired, grubby undercover guys were causing a stir by knocking on doors around the city, scaring the locals. Some officers would meticulously document their work. Others would fail to properly corroborate and verify leads, then just move on to the next thing. Files and tips and information sometimes failed to get to the right people. In one technological mishap, an officer had forgotten to turn the key that switched off the Delphi police station's interview recording system—and as a result of that oversight, months' worth of interviews were recorded over and lost, forcing investigators to go back and reinterview some people. Mullin insisted that he would take the blame for that incident, as it occurred in his department. Maintaining order was hard, even with Unified Command in play. Not everyone was willing to take feedback or criticism from investigators who were not their supervisors.

Striding into the room for briefings, Holeman would sometimes get cantankerous. "Look, I don't care who solves this. But we've got to do it the right way."

The right way meant carefully documenting and reporting back about leads. Holeman suspected that a few personnel were more focused on cultivating their favorite theory than working on a team. The investigation resembled an unruly pack of hunting dogs more than a highly drilled army. Holeman became concerned that some officers were seeking glory at the expense of paperwork and proper procedures.

"Hey, first person to make an arrest," he would say, "I'll buy you all the beer you can drink and all the liquor you want." Then Holeman would pause. "But if you guys start leaking information, I will want to kick you in the fucking nuts."

The female troopers and detectives would laugh at that. Holeman was not really planning to start attacking fellow officers. But the case was a delicate thing.

The momentum in the beginning was tremendous. But Carter worried about the investigators. He saw the detectives working hard. Some were only getting three hours of rest a night. In those early weeks, Carter would find himself arguing with troopers and detectives who refused to go home after working for thirty-six hours straight. He resolved to help them take care of themselves.

When the superintendent heard that Holeman wanted to cancel some long-standing concert plans and instead spend that time on the case, he stepped in. Not only did Carter order Holeman to go to the concert, but he also arranged for Carter and his wife to have a fancy dinner beforehand.

The incident taught Holeman something about leadership and taking care of people. A few weeks later, he forced the detectives under his command to go to the spa.

The detectives did not let up though. And more people continued joining the case. One was Vido. He and other state police troopers were asked to head to the command center and run tips. By that point, the investigation was based out of a building that once headquartered the local rural electric membership cooperative, known locally as the old REMC building.

Inside the center, officers from all kinds of agencies bustled in and out of the big, open office space. The place was furnished with a jumble of tables and phones for investigators to use while running down tips, and the center always seemed stocked full of food, office supplies, and equipment for handling evidence.

Newcomers sat through a brief presentation about the facts of the case. A lot of officers griped about that introduction. The presentation felt vague. They wanted more details. There was a real sense of secrecy about the investigation. Those in the inner circle, including Holeman, Buckley, Harper, Liggett, Hammond, would often retreat to closed-door meetings. But Vido thought the rank-and-file had plenty of facts to work with.

In the mornings, pastors from the local churches would say a quick prayer over the group. Then a daily briefing would commence. Vido would show up and grab a stack of lead sheets—as many as seven at a time—and work to close each out. Each sheet was a summary of a lead printed on a piece of paper and stapled to a folder. Vido found most subjects he encountered were very cooperative and eager to clear themselves. Some were easy to rule out. A subject might be able to provide a timesheet or a video, proving they were at work on the day of the murders. Other times, whenever a subject was home sick or lacking any sort of obvious records establishing their location, clearing them became an arduous process. After the investigative process was done, Vido would complete his report and provide a summary explaining either how he cleared the subject, or how he was unable to do so. Lead sheets that fell into the latter category were marked as requiring further follow-up.

When he was done, Vido would drop the sheets off with an officer to input. Then he would grab a new stack, and start over.

Not all of those who worked the case were law enforcement officers. One civilian volunteer who came in early was retiree Kathy Shank. She had been vacationing in Florida when the murders happened. She saw a breaking news alert on her phone and learned that two children from Carroll County were dead in a double homicide.

Kathy Shank had grown up in Flora and lived in Delphi for years. She knew Ives, the county prosecutor. She had worked for decades as a case manager with Carroll County's welfare office, later rebranded as the Department of Child Services. In cases of neglect and abuse, she was unrelenting. The safety of children had to always come first. Working with law enforcement, she would keep up the pressure for them to act. Early in her career, she might get some eye rolls from law enforcement officials who saw her as pushy. Ultimately, though, they learned to take her concerns seriously.

When Kathy Shank joined as a volunteer, she went to work as a receptionist. A tiny woman with short brown hair, she would greet the tipsters who came into the building and refer them to the next available detective. A killer had preyed upon two children in Carroll County. As far as Kathy Shank was concerned, retirement could wait.

Others did not have the luxury to stick with the case forever, though. Early on, Vido had met the relatives of Libby. Standing at the end of their driveway, he talked to them. He saw they were in such pain. He told them he would not give up seeking answers. When he was eventually reassigned to his typical responsibilities along with other troopers, that search came to an abrupt halt. Vido felt he had broken his promise.

Ultimately, the fix that helped with all the tips came from the FBI. They did not just bring their people. The Bureau introduced one process to the Delphi case that eased some of the organizational burden. Operational Response and Investigative Online Network was the agency's crisis management system. Known as ORION, it shared its name with the mythical hunter.

The system allowed the investigators to better file and sort all the information. There were some issues, of course. For instance, ORION was sensitive about names. Tossing in an extra initial or a middle name could throw things off. But it was far better than the alternative. With the sheer number of leads, investigators were quickly working toward burnout. But ORION could not improve the quality of the leads themselves.

The earliest tips were the most helpful. People who had been at or near the trails stepped forward. One group of four girls had run into a mysterious man on the trails. Others came forward to say they saw nothing unusual on the trails that day. Citizens called in information on specific individuals. The sexual offenders in the area were put under special scrutiny. None of those tips panned out, but police were able to solve at least one Peru cold case based on those reach-outs. A small number of tips came from unhelpful cranks as well. Self-proclaimed psychics and tarot card readers wasted time and resources. But that was to be expected in such a high-profile case.

At the end of the day, investigators were seeking to prove the elements of the offense and secure probable cause for searches and arrests. Some leads started out promising, but they all fell short in the end.

As time went on, the tips degraded. Most of the diligent people with something relevant to say had already provided their information. So that left the portion of the population who thought watching *CSI* and *Law & Order* gave them special insight. They provided investigative suggestions instead of calling about suspicious people. For example, they advised police to investigate nearby sexual offenders, canvas for surveillance footage, try to swab for DNA profiles, and employ genetic genealogy to solve the crime. One common piece of advice was for the police to get ahold of the Bridge Guy for an interview or a polygraph examination. One tipster was enamored with the idea of shooting up the guy on the bridge with sodium pentothal, to force him to tell the truth. They did not seem to realize that the police needed to identify Bridge Guy first.

Police felt those tipsters were at least well-meaning, but their advice was useless. Investigators had already tried or were working on all the angles the "tipsters" had thrown out.

But the vague calls and emails were the most frustrating. Liggett found himself going through thousands of tips where the caller simply said they found a man's Facebook profile and thought he vaguely resembled Bridge Guy. These tipsters had no connection to their quarry. Their targets were often not even from Indiana and had no known connections to the state.

Liggett was baffled. The video was so blurry that plenty of people could resemble Bridge Guy. Nobody even knew how tall the man was, although several investigators suspected he was a shorter man. Scattershot internet sleuthing was unlikely to do anything other than waste time. He imagined some of the callers were just after the reward. Thanks to donations from Pat McAfee, the retired Indianapolis Colts star, and Jim Irsay, the football team's owner, the fund had increased to $200,000.

Other messages were still vaguer.

"Oh, I saw a guy at a Walmart," a tipster might say. "Looked just like him."

"Okay," Holeman would reply. "Where?"

"Oh, I don't know. He got in a blue truck with a partial plate."

"Oh, okay. What state?"

"Well, shit, I don't know."

Holeman would try to keep his cool. What was he supposed to do with such scant information? He bet the crack detectives on fictional police procedurals could triangulate the call and figure out a way to hack satellite cameras and zoom in on the exact coordinates of the elusive blue truck. But that was not how real-life policing worked.

There was a certain mob-like mentality to tips too. When internet sleuths or locals discovered that a person had talked to the police, they would bombard investigators with even more tips on that person, even if they had no connection to the specific individual.

Some of the tips were actively malicious. These people were largely attempting to use the case as a cudgel to harm others in their life. Rifts between relatives, spouses, or neighbors could result in a call to the tip line. One common scenario that played out was a woman would call in, telling police that a certain man was the killer. Investigators would track the man down. Inevitably, those men would have alibis. Sometimes they were not even in the state of Indiana. Invariably, it would turn out that the tipster shared children with her target, and the man she accused owed her substantial child support payments. Police were being used as warning salvos in all kinds of messy interpersonal drama. The upside of those kinds of calls was that some of those men had outstanding warrants. Investigators showed up at a few houses, only to find an indoor marijuana grow or an active methamphetamine operation. Police ended up arresting at least twenty of them.

They were solving crimes. Just not the crime they wanted to solve.

Then came the truly nonsensical tips. These were from hoaxers who did not take the murder of two children seriously, or otherwise disturbed individuals. Sometimes tipsters called in drunk and rambled. Other people told the police that they saw things nobody else could see. Bridge Guy had a puppy tucked inside his jacket, or a little monkey clinging to his back, presumably to charm and lure the girls. Or perhaps a racoon had been biting his face. Tipsters urged police to find the Sasquatch family living under the High Bridge. Those mythical creatures presumably witnessed the kidnapping, and it would behoove detectives to study their language for an interview. Others claimed inaccurately that a group of Potawatomi—an Indigenous people who originally lived in Indiana before the United States government forced them down to Kansas—resided in the forest and could provide help. Investigators once received a lead claiming that aliens abducted and killed the girls. Assuming the person was talking about undocumented immigrants, police ran them down, only to find the lead actually referred to real, genuine extra-terrestrials.

Law enforcement could not simply block out the noise. There was no telling what might be important. Psychics were all frauds, but what if they ran into one trying to pass off guilty knowledge as clairvoyance? So they had to read through everything and take the calls that came in. They had asked for the public's help, and they had to deal with the consequences.

Meanwhile, members of the public became frustrated that police were not releasing more information on the case. Some tipsters would write letters, expressing bitterness about never hearing back about their worthless tips. They did not seem to fathom that the information they provided did not at all fit the facts of the case, or that investigators had more important things to do than personally updating them. In such instances, the act of submitting a lead was more about attempting to establish an inside line into the case than about handing over valuable information. A certain segment of the public viewed the murders as an opportunity to pose as sleuths, and they were hurt when the police did not play along.

CHAPTER TEN

The neon lights of Las Vegas shone down on the Klines. Kegan Kline and his father, Tony, had journeyed there from their home in Peru, Indiana—leaving very shortly after the murders of Abby and Libby. But even in Sin City, Kegan's mind remained on what had happened back home.

On his iPhone, he looked up articles on the Delphi murders. He checked the post about the case on the FBI's website. He looked up whether internet protocol addresses could be gleaned from social media accounts. He researched how much information gets stored on internet servers.

Again and again, Kegan returned to the voice Libby had recorded on her phone. In the quiet of his hotel room, or over the chimes and bells of the casino floor and the din of the Strip, he listened to the three words spoken by the Delphi killer: "Down the hill." He played the recording six times. Then he deleted his search history from February 10 to February 15.

Kegan opened his Snapchat app. He logged in under the name @anthony_shots. He put together a few messages. Then he sent them to Libby, a girl he knew to be dead.

The @anthony_shots account stuck out to police. To detectives, Anthony did not appear to be a real person. He looked like a decoy, calculated to draw in teenage girls like Libby.

A predator had seemingly wormed his way into Libby's social circle. Some of her friends came forward to share their interactions with the account.

"O.M.G. what happened?" Anthony wrote to one of Libby's friends.

The friend explained that Libby had been murdered.

Anthony expressed shock. "Yeah, we were supposed to meet but she never showed up."

Detectives subpoenaed Instagram, Snapchat, and Comcast. Records revealed IP addresses linked to Jerry Anthony, or Tony Kline, of Peru, Indiana.

The Klines returned to Indiana on a Saturday. The air in Peru must have felt especially cold coming back from the dry desert heat. The Klines were not alone in their little white house on Canal Street for long. They barely had time to unpack. Peering through a window, Kegan saw a line of police cars. He wondered if Immigration and Customs Enforcement agents were coming to bust a neighbor.

Instead, a SWAT team crashed into the Kline house around half past noon, followed by personnel from the FBI, ISP, and other law enforcement agencies. A mobile command unit—a big blue-and-white truck—pulled up nearby. State police presented their warrant.

Tracy Kunstek and Andrew Willmann took the lead on the raid. Willmann was a special agent with the Indianapolis office of the FBI. He was known to speak to groups of parents about the dangers posed by online child predators. Kunstek was a seasoned detective with the Indiana State Police. She worked on a few cases based on tips from the National Center for Missing & Exploited Children.

About an hour into the raid, the two investigators got their chance to talk to Kegan Kline. Police hauled him out of the house. He was brought into the truck and asked to sit down with Kunstek and Willmann. After hearing his rights, he still agreed to talk with them. Over the course of the interview, Kunstek ended up building a rapport with Kegan. He focused on her more than Willmann, during the interview and for years afterward. She was kind. She seemed invested in helping him. She was motherly, he thought.

In the beginning, Kegan played the role of a baffled young man with nothing to hide. Sure, he owned a white iPhone 5c. But he was not a pervert. He never created any fake social media accounts or talked with any underaged girls. Willmann and Kunstek told him he was a child predator, that he had stalked and killed Abby and Libby.

Unbeknownst to Kegan, the investigators before him were not the only ones digging into his crimes within the metal walls of the command unit. In a separate compartment, Internet Crimes Against Children specialists were triaging his seized electronic devices, working as swiftly as possible to locate and identify any child sexual abuse materials (CSAM) within his files. They pulled out all the disturbing images they could find.

Kunstek and Willmann confronted Kegan on the CSAM. Faced with all of that, Kegan admitted he had a problem. He claimed he had only created the accounts six months ago, for the express purpose of catfishing underage girls.

As @anthony_shots, he would trawl Instagram to find young girls, and then contrive ways to lure them onto Snapchat—with its automatically disappearing posts—for more intimate communication. Kegan would quickly screenshot and save any photos he liked to his phone's gallery. He estimated he had probably talked to fifteen underage girls, getting pictures from each one.

Kegan told the investigators he was "fucked." He mulled over his regrets, revealing to the detectives he planned on running away from his father in Vegas. Now he wished he had.

But he still denied killing Libby and Abby.

Willmann and Kunstek suggested Kegan take a polygraph test. He acquiesced and was transported to the ISP's Peru post. There, he met with Sergeant Matthew Collins. Hooked up to the polygraph machine, Kegan again admitted to a host of grave crimes. He estimated he had received a hundred sexual pictures from children. On his command, they sent him pictures of their genitals and breasts, and photographed themselves masturbating. Kegan would himself masturbate to those images. But again, he insisted he had no knowledge of the murders.

At 7:30 P.M., the polygraph exam ended. Kegan was unhooked from the machine.

Investigators confronted him. They said he had flunked the polygraph. Kegan began to panic.

But nothing happened.

He was not charged with murder. He was not even hit with any counts around his CSAM collection. The mobile unit chugged off down Canal Street, taking with it Kegan's CSAM-laden devices, including two Apple iPhones, an Apple iPod Touch, two Samsung Galaxies, and a Nextbook Tablet. Nobody would think much about those devices for another two years. Investigators lost interest in Kegan Kline almost as quickly as the lead cropped up.

On the very day of the raid, FBI Special Agent Bob Ramsey even took the extraordinary step of publicly clearing Kegan to the Lafayette *Journal & Courier*. Kegan told investigators he and his father were in Vegas on the day of the murders. In fact, they had departed Indiana after the killings. But investigators seemingly believed Kegan, and nobody had thought to verify his claim. And while investigators could see that Libby had been in contact with Kegan through his Anthony persona up until right before the murders, Snapchat had erased most of their communications. There was no direct evidence tying him to the murders. So Kegan walked, despite his cache of CSAM.

Dazed, Kegan was dropped off at his home. Tony was beside himself. Police had barged into his home. They had taken his son and their dog,

Cujo. Kegan's grandfather Jerry also swung by to help clean up after the raid. Three generations of the same family stood in the home. The Kline men wept.

That night, Kegan Kline went into the kitchen. He ran his hand along the top of the microwave, quickly finding his Apple iPhone 5c—the single device the police had somehow not been able to find. This was the device he had used to communicate with Libby.

Kegan needed to make a few adjustments.

At 9:19 p.m., he uninstalled and deleted Snapchat. Then at 10:14 p.m., he uninstalled and deleted Instagram. The following day, at twelve past one, Kegan uninstalled and deleted MeetMe, then redownloaded Snapchat. On February 27, at 9:48 a.m., Kegan cleared his Safari browser history and website data. At 1:28 p.m. that afternoon, Kegan once again removed his Snapchat. Only then did he turn his phone in to the Peru post.

He thought he had erased all traces of his contact with Libby.

CHAPTER ELEVEN

Ron Logan had always felt proud of his acres and acres of land—the rolling hills, the woodlands, the pastures where his ponies grazed.

The clearing where the girls died belonged to him, although it was across the creek and well away from his home. It was not long before police began looking at him as a possible suspect. Before the Delphi murders, the Navy veteran had a history of reckless and intoxicated driving, which had led to some legal troubles. After the murders, life got far worse. His former girlfriends Kathleen Bennett and Ashley Wright had spoken to the police about him, alleging past violent behavior.

That was only the beginning. Investigators soon discovered that he had lied to an officer about his whereabouts on the day of the murders. He claimed that his cousin David Nulf had driven him to Aquarium World in Lafayette that day. Police found a store receipt that showed the checkout time as 5:21 P.M. Logan had gone there alone. Police learned from Nulf that Logan had asked him to lie about the trip. These fabrications came at a time before the bodies were even discovered.

Logan might have been lying to cover up a probation violation. But it looked far more sinister to some of the investigators. FBI Special Agent Nikkole Robertson seemed particularly interested in Logan, but it was Sergeant Fred Rogers of the Pulaski County Sheriff's Office who was perhaps the investigator most devoted to Logan as a suspect. A big, muscular guy with a thick neck, Rogers seemed obsessed with the Logan lead at times.

In any case, Logan's probation violations were enough to justify incarcerating him. He was arrested and thrown in jail on February 27, 2017.

Amid his legal woes, Logan hired Logansport defense attorney Andrew Achey. Achey promptly released a statement declaring that his client was not a murderer.

Investigators searched Logan's house and property twice. They found no evidence linking him to the crime. And while his jaunt to Aquarium World was technically not an alibi, the documented trip would have left him precious little time to commit a double homicide. Logan was also an exceptionally tall man, something none of the witnesses who saw Bridge Guy had described. Some investigators were skeptical that he could be the killer. But that did not stop the leads, however shaky.

Perhaps sensing it might help them with their own cases, some incarcerated informants came forward with information about the case. A couple of prisoners claimed that Logan had confessed to them that he was responsible for the killings. James Haas, a killer who murdered a man his former girlfriend was set to remarry, told investigators that, while behind bars, Logan had a propensity to touch himself sexually while whispering the name of at least one of the dead girls.

It was an intriguing story; the only problem was that it was not true. Haas was a liar. Investigators descended on the jail and watched the surveillance footage. They discovered that the interactions between the two inmates were minimal; Logan was barely around Haas long enough to speak a few words, let alone force him to overhear an incriminating round of masturbation.

On January 9, 2018, Judge Kurtis Fouts granted Achey's motion to modify Logan's sentence. He was released from jail and ordered to serve the rest of his time at home by wearing an ankle monitor. Logan returned to his beloved acres a shattered man. He had to scramble to reorganize his finances, just to avoid losing his house. He loathed the police and the prosecutors for ruining his life. He hated how everyone in Delphi stared at him, wondering.

Unified Command moved on from Logan, infuriating some of the investigators who still believed in his guilt. Unsurprisingly, leaks about his culpability would continue to drip for years.

One person who kept his own counsel on the case was Carroll County Sheriff's Office Chief Deputy Mike Thomas. He was not an investigator in the Delphi murders case. His role at the sheriff's office was far more managerial in nature. Still, he cared deeply about the case. He knew Libby's family and wanted to solve the murders for them. For their part, Libby's family liked Thomas and found him to be compassionate and friendly.

Thomas felt he had been blocked from helping in the double homicide case. Liggett and Hammond were the detectives. They were assigned to the case.

When Thomas got a chance, he would head over to the old REMC building and get to work by going through files. Liggett or Hammond would notice him toiling away on the case. Sometimes they would let the sheriff know.

"What?" Leazenby was always baffled. "He's not even assigned to the case."

Thomas did not agree with how Unified Command was handling the investigation. As a deputy, he had undergone trainings, courses taught by retired law enforcement officials on homicide cases. Two or three times, Leazenby caught Thomas in the old REMC building himself. He would pull his chief deputy aside.

"Mike, what are you doing?"

"I'm working on this case," Thomas would say.

"No, you're not."

Carroll County Prosecutor Robert Ives grew weary. The burden of the Delphi murders weighed heavy on him. And he was no longer the young man who had first stepped into the prosecutor's office in 1987.

Since then, the citizens of Carroll County would elect him on and off. But on November 10, 2017, Ives chose to walk away.

Ives's natural successor was Jerry Bean, his longtime deputy. But when the Carroll County Republican Party caucused, an opponent came to the forefront. Nicholas McLeland, a local defense attorney, challenged Bean. Bean had experience and had previously been the prosecutor of Tippecanoe County. But he was set to retire soon himself.

McLeland was from Delphi, and graduated from the local high school in 1998. After a brief sojourn to the New York City area, he attended the University of Toledo's law school. He joined the National Guard, becoming part of the 38th Sustainment Brigade's Trial Defense Team. That gave him experience as a sort of public defender for soldiers in trouble. In civilian life, he also did defense work in Delphi and the surrounding area. But having kids made him rethink pursuing criminal defense. The prosecutor's position becoming open seemed to offer him a perfect opportunity to make that transition.

McLeland won.

He took office in January. The brand-new prosecutor inherited two major crimes: the Flora fire and the Delphi murders. Arson is a notoriously difficult type of crime to investigate and prosecute, with key evidence often burned or washed away. Meanwhile, the Delphi case was nearing its first anniversary with no arrest in sight. Still, McLeland was determined to make progress on both cases and find justice for those six girls. Toward the end of the month, he attended his first briefing with Unified Command. At the old REMC building, he sat at a large table. Holeman delivered a presentation on both cases, with other investigators chiming in occasionally. As he clicked through his slides, images of the crime scenes flickered on the screen. McLeland felt sick.

Throwing himself into the work, he found himself studying a variety of files from his predecessor. He encountered one concerning a man named Kegan Kline. It was a horrifying case. A predator had been caught with child sexual abuse materials—often abbreviated CSAM—the new term for the old crime once called child pornography. Investigators became interested in Kegan, of course, because of his possible connection to the murders in McLeland's county—but Kegan himself was a resident of Miami County. So McLeland reached out to Jeffrey Sinkovics, the county's seasoned prosecutor.

Passing along a summary of the case, McLeland asked his colleague if he was planning to prosecute Kegan. It was the first time Sinkovics had heard of it. When the FBI and the Indiana State Police had raided and searched the Kline home back in 2017, they certainly had not briefed him on what they had found. In the immediate days after the murders, there had been so much going on. McLeland's predecessor Ives and an Internet Crimes Against Children Task Force detective had apparently come to the belief that there was not enough to prosecute Kegan.

The precis of the case McLeland provided was far from enough to help Sinkovics determine whether he should file charges against Kegan Kline. So he contacted the ISP—who obviously knew far more about the whole thing than he did. He asked them, "Can you tell me more about this case? Are there prosecutable charges here?"

The answer that came back from an ICAC detective surprised him a little. "There's nothing prosecutable here."

Because Sinkovics respected ICAC and the ISP, he took that answer seriously, assuming they knew what they were doing. In any case, Sinkovics had plenty of crimes in Miami County to keep him busy. He concentrated on those and let the Kegan Kline case lie.

For McLeLand and law enforcement, working the Delphi murders case could be an intensely frustrating experience. Time and time again, the investigation would find what seemed to be a promising lead, start exploring it, become convinced that they were nearing the answer they had so long been searching for and then abruptly discover a piece of evidence that completely disproved the whole theory, leaving them back at square one. Some compared those dizzying highs followed by crushing lows to riding a roller coaster. Others like Liggett became devil's advocates, skeptical of all theories. To McLeland, the experience reminded him of a segment on *The Price Is Right* television show. A yodeler would be seen merrily traipsing up a mountain, only to all too often fall violently to the earth.

At times like this, some on the team would feel discouraged and begin to fear the case would never get solved. But that would not stop them from getting back on the mountain and trying once again. They knew they owed that to Abby and Libby.

Police were not the only ones investigating the murders. Almost from the very beginning, the crime generated an inordinate amount of online interest. In the days after the murders, Facebook groups devoted to the case began popping up. Some were dedicated to raising awareness about the case and supporting the victims' families and the wider Delphi community. Other armchair sleuths intensely scrutinized the Snapchat photos of Abby on the bridge, trying vainly to find any clues hidden in the backgrounds of the images. The picture of Bridge Guy also came in for study—and, after staring at the low-resolution image for hours, people jumped on various web forums to ask each other questions about it all. Could Bridge Guy be carrying a puppy? Was he wearing a fanny pack with an insulin pump? All sorts of bizarre and untrue rumors swirled about what the crime scene looked like; people claiming to have been members of the search party that found the girls announced they had seen dolls hanging from the trees near their bodies.

Perhaps the most damaging aspect of the heightened attention was how some people began to openly suspect and target the families. Becky, Anna, and even Kelsi found themselves at one time or another being accused of bearing some sort of responsibility for the murders.

But it would all get much, much worse.

The Pattys received some tips of their own, from an unlikely source. In the early days of the case, they found themselves facing a harbinger of the online chaos that was to follow: Julie Melvin. She worked as an obstetric nurse anesthetist in Indiana's Hamilton County. Her social media profiles espoused lofty Christian ideals. Middle-aged with a singsong voice, her large brown eyes were curiously empty. She had a remote connection to the Pattys, and she was ready to exploit it for all it was worth. Melvin's sister Diane was the birth mother of Cody Patty.

In the beginning, Melvin was a friendly presence. She would ring up Becky and urge her to search Libby's room for a diary. A clairvoyant told her it could contain an important clue. Still reeling, Becky would look. Eventually, she stopped. Diane mentioned her sister was blowing a fortune on psychics. One apparently told Melvin that if she drove to Fort Wayne and sat in her car at a particular stoplight at a specific time, she would glimpse the killer driving by in a red van.

Then whispers started to get back to the Pattys. Melvin was claiming to have close ties to Libby's relatives. But the Pattys heard she was also telling people that they had kept Cody from her family. Becky bristled. The Pattys had not only raised Cody, they also took in Diane and let her live with them. Melvin had never once expressed interest in Cody before. She did not seek to take him in or adopt him. She did not even go to his graduation ceremony. She was a distant figure until she could use her biological relation to seek attention in a murder case. The relationship between Melvin and the Pattys crumbled further when it came out that Diane—after a discussion with Melvin about possibly finding the killer in the crowd at the girls' memorial service—had taken pictures that showed the caskets and part of Libby's head. Melvin insisted that the intention was to help find justice for the girls.

For years, Melvin would remain at the center of a certain contingent of online sleuths. Documentarian Hannah Shakespeare even relied on her as an inside expert source in a scrapped Lifetime documentary. Melvin's ability to attract acolytes spoke to a truism: in the minds of many, any information was better than no information, and conspiracy theories blaming the Pattys always played with those who struggled to accept that terrible things could happen to good people.

CHAPTER TWELVE

Elvis Fields walked up to his little trailer. He paused for a moment in the cold air, turning to glance back at the parked car where Indiana State Police Detective Kevin Murphy waited. Murphy was there because of Fields's sister, Mary Jacobs. She swore her brother was the Delphi killer.

Jacobs had quite a story, and she was eager to tell whoever would listen. She said her brother tried to give her a blue jacket back on Valentine's Day 2017. Babbling, he tried to hand it over to her until she snapped and said she already had a coat. She claimed he said he was in a gang, that he had a brother, and that he had put leaves and sticks on the body of a girl called Abby. That he had fashioned an antler-like crown of twigs and placed them on her head because she was a little troublemaker.

Murphy was one of many troopers who had pitched in to help with the Delphi investigation, although he was not a part of Unified Command. That winter, he teamed up with Holeman to tackle the Jacobs interview. Holeman thought Murphy was highly effective, running down and clearing lead after lead.

But the Jacobs angle turned out to be different from the others. On February 1, 2018, Mary Jacobs sat for a polygraph test with Stephanie Thompson, a state police examiner. Jacobs passed, but the polygraph only focused on whether she believed her uncorroborated statements were true.

The investigators were skeptical. She seemed to harbor a lot of resentment for her brother. The only sticks near Abby's head were the ones lying beneath her on the ground.

On February 27, Holeman and Murphy headed down to Rushville, Indiana, where Fields grew up and remained living in a trailer park. Nestled along the Flatrock River, Rushville was to the southeast of Indianapolis, over two hours away from Delphi.

The investigators went to the city's police station to talk to Fields. Todd Click, the city's assistant police chief, ran the recording system for the interview. He was a man with a shaved head, a thick neck, and a pleasant demeanor. Click had grown up in Rushville too. Fields was a couple of years ahead of him in school. Fields had struggled with schooling and bullying.

In the interview, Murphy took the lead. Holeman hung back, asking a few questions here and there. Fields was a middle-aged man with narrow eyes and deep laugh lines that ran like canyons down to his jaw. He struck Holeman as relatively honest, a bit of a good old boy, just maybe a bit slower on the uptake than most.

Fields denied making incriminating statements to Jacobs. He also volunteered a DNA sample, allowing the investigators to swab the inside of his mouth. That saliva could help clear him in the case. When the interview was over, Murphy drove him home. Fields was almost at his trailer when he whirled around and hurried back to Murphy.

He had a question. If his spit was found on Libby or Abby, but he could explain its presence, would he still be in trouble?

At the time, Murphy felt more annoyed than anything else. He wondered if Fields was playing with him. After Fields departed once more, Murphy headed back to the police station. He had not recorded the interaction, so the bizarre question now existed only in his memory. He told Holeman all about it.

"I just think he was fucking with me," Murphy told Holeman.

No saliva had been found on either Libby or Abby. It was not a stretch to imagine someone saying something strange about spit a short time after donating a DNA sample. The two detectives departed Rushville.

But Murphy kept coming back.

On August 22, 2018, Murphy teamed up with his fellow FBI Task Force Officer Greg Ferency to interview another one of Fields's sisters, Joyce Moffitt. Her brow was furrowed and her cheeks were swollen, but she had narrow dark eyes that resembled those of her brother. She posted borderline incoherent comments on her own Facebook profile picture threatening suicide and accusing unnamed others of bad-mouthing her. This was the third interview police had conducted with her. In all her previous discussions with detectives, she had denied that her brother had made any incriminating statements to her.

Now, suddenly, Moffitt was spouting a story about a confrontation she had in her kitchen with Fields in October 2017. She claimed that Fields said he was on the trails and the High Bridge on the day of the murders, that two men had killed the girls, and that he had spit on one of them.

But there were problems with the sisters and their stories. Murphy saw bottles of pills prescribed for psychiatric issues in one of their homes. But neither one of their stories had much by way of corroborating evidence. Murphy wondered if the women were simply unwell and making up tales. After one interview Murphy did alongside Indiana State Police Detective Roland Purdy, the two troopers called up Holeman and told him they thought the family was "crazy."

By the end of the series of interviews, one of the sisters seemed to be under the impression that their brother was a serial killer. Not only had he participated in the Delphi murders, but also he had murdered yet another sister and buried her in a barn. Police checked out the spot in question and found nothing.

Many detectives might have looked at the Fields lead and dismissed it as a bizarre bit of family drama. Strange statements aside, the concrete evidence seemed to point away from Fields's involvement. But Murphy and Ferency kept at it. As a result, both detectives spent quite a lot of time at the station in Rushville. They got to know Click. Walking into Click's office, Murphy shared the question Fields had asked about spit. He was beginning to second-guess his first impression. Could Fields have guilty knowledge of the crime?

One of the only things the two investigators had in common was they were both flung into the Delphi case. Murphy was a tall, thin man, completely bald, with an almost gaunt face. A detective with a strong reputation and a nervous energy, he was often asked to play the part of a crazed hostage-taker in SWAT rescue scenarios. He was sworn in as a trooper in 1995.

Click had never had much time for state police. He told others the organization as a whole tended to shove its way into cases and take over, crowding out smaller local agencies. His view was not uncommon. In years past, new police officers at the Indiana Law Enforcement Academy would even complain about the standoffishness of their trooper counterparts.

But Murphy and Click were able to work together closely. Joining them was Murphy's colleague Ferency. Bald with a gingery beard and a fondness for baseball caps, Ferency was popular among his colleagues for his friendliness. He made people feel as though they mattered. Ferency was tough and well-read, and he even edited *SWAT Digest*, a publication catering to the tactical community. He was an officer with the Terre Haute Police Department.

Murphy and Ferency let Click in on their Delphi work. They were well aware of Brad Holder and his friend Patrick Westfall. They were particularly interested in that lead.

Other investigators no longer viewed Holder as a suspect. Purdy had even interviewed him as an informational witness to learn more about Norse paganism. That was back when investigators were considering the possibility of some ritualistic or religious significance to the sticks at the crime scene.

Buckley had gone and found a Purdue University professor, Jeffrey Turco, who was an expert in ancient Norse mythology and history. Turco had told detectives that the formation and shapes of the sticks meant nothing. They were not runes. That meant they indicated nothing either way.

Another aspect that troubled investigators like Buckley was the victimology. White supremacists with Norse pagan beliefs had a history of assassinating political enemies and murdering minorities—not sacrificing white children in a ritual. After talking with Turco, Buckley told Unified Command that the angle was not going to lead to a suspect. He had come to a dead end.

But Murphy and Ferency seemed less certain. They wanted to know if there was a Rushville connection. They asked Click for help.

Click began searching Rushville's records. He could not find anything on Holder or Westfall. He turned to Facebook. Holder's profile was open to the public. Click scrolled through picture after picture, until he came to the image of a group of men standing before a privacy fence. Each wore a Vinlanders shirt. Click saw the face of a local white nationalist, Johnny Messer. He had found a connection, albeit a very thin one. Messer's uncle had once roomed with Fields. Click shared the news with Ferency and Murphy.

From then on out, the trio operated like a team. The task force officers went out and did more field work. After all, Click still had responsibilities in Rushville. But they kept him apprised, and together, they developed a theory. Holder and Westfall were considered the ringleaders, based up north, with Holder in Logansport and Westfall in Delphi. Messer and Rod Abrams, Fields's roommate, were situated down in Rushville. Fields was the link between both groups.

The group interviewed him. But Fields denied knowing anything about the murders. He said he did not know Libby and Abby. He had never been to the trails at Delphi. He had never killed anybody. He did not even drive a car.

"What am I going to do?" Fields asked. "Hop on a turtle? Ride on a turtle's back up there?"

Fields had a tendency of saying odd and unsettling things. But the truth was they had no evidence against him. There was barely even a link between Fields and Holder and Westfall. And Fields's phone records backed up his assertions. They showed that his device remained on and in the same spot in Rushville from 10:30 A.M. to 7:30 P.M. on the day of the murders. The investigators reasoned that the man must have left his phone back in Rushville while he was off in the woods of Delphi.

The three investigators dug into the theory of Odinist involvement in the murders, delving deeper into the underworld of pagan white supremacist gangs. Ferency uncovered a twenty-five-minute Facebook video that stuck with him. Shot by Holder, the footage showed men pouring water on a tree in Fort Wayne as part of some ceremony. Westfall said a prayer for a Native American tribe. Then he strode into sight. He appeared to mark something on the tree. Ferency wondered if the killer had done the same thing at the crime scene with Libby's blood.

Police investigators are human beings. Sometimes, emotional investment in an outcome can outweigh logic or facts. A strong feeling can become like a thick haze that obscures everything else.

In May 2018, the families of the girls headed south to Nashville to attend CrimeCon. Only in its second year, the convention was dedicated to all things true crime. They were there to raise awareness about what happened to Abby and Libby. The case was big news in Indiana. But not everyone was aware of the story. The families thought if they could put the case in front of the right person, that might spark recognition or a fleeting memory. They did not travel to Tennessee alone. Superintendent Doug Carter was originally supposed to go. Then when he was detained, Sergeant Kim Riley was slated to accompany them. But that ended up not working out either. So state police sent Holeman down instead.

Anna, Becky, and Mike sat on a panel to discuss the case, along with Holeman. Later, YouTubers would take footage of the state police sergeant's nervous fidgeting and claim that he was flashing Masonic hand symbols.

The Pattys found the experience tough, but rewarding in its own way. They were able to connect with other families of the murdered and missing. Some of those cases were still unsolved after decades. To the Pattys, it was like all those grieving loved ones were walking the same path. They could take guidance from those further along on the journey.

Events like CrimeCon became a part of the lives of the families. They spoke at festivals. They sat for media interviews. They raised awareness about the girls wherever they could.

They also got involved with the burgeoning social media community that formed around the crime. Becky and Tara joined the many Facebook groups that popped up focusing on the case. They answered questions from posters, thrilled that so many people from around the world wanted to help. Only later did they realize that some were not there to help at all. Some wanted to slake their own morbid curiosity. Many others wanted to find someone to blame.

There was a cost to public advocacy. The more the families put themselves out there, the more support they received. But a small and vocal group grew to hate the relatives of the girls. They would post conspiracy theories blaming the girls' relatives for the murders on social media. One of the favorite internet parlor games was picking apart minor misstatements by Libby's family in media appearances. Other times, they would just spread outright lies.

Early on, Becky would try to reason with people. The truth was on her side. She thought that would sway the case obsessives who had unilaterally decided her family was hiding something.

In one instance, online sleuths claimed that in her December 2017 appearance on the *Dr. Phil* show, Becky had said something like, "They've got our girls." That was supposed to indicate the family's awareness of a shadowy "they"—perhaps cartel leaders or other drug kingpins. Becky denied saying anything like that. The case obsessives derided her as a liar. When no one could find clips of Becky saying those words, then the narrative switched. The *Dr. Phil* show must have taken down the relevant clips. One poster came forward, noting that they were unable to find the quote, despite recording the entire episode when it first aired. Even when confronted with irrefutable proof, the truculent sleuths would not back down. If the quote did not appear on *Dr. Phil*, then she must have said it somewhere else. Becky realized that many case followers were so entrenched in their views that they did not care to receive any information that conflicted with their beliefs. They would dismiss it, or claim that it was proof of an even grander conspiracy.

When the online contingent blasted her for getting a time wrong or not realizing that Libby had grabbed her swimming sweatshirt to wear out that day, Becky explained that many of her initial statements to police had been made in the chaos of the early search. Instead of empathizing with those at the heart of the case, many online sleuths suggested that the members of Libby's own family had murdered the girls. They speculated one or both of the girls was pregnant, or the victim of abuse from family members. None of those things were true. But that never stopped people from saying them.

When a case goes unsolved, family members of a murder victim often come under increased scrutiny. In certain instances, the circumstances of the crime point to familial involvement. That was not the case in Delphi. But in the eyes of some members of the public, mustering sympathy for the girls' relatives became impossible as time went on. The families of Abby and Libby could not be decent, ordinary people who suffered an unimaginable tragedy. They had to be culpable somehow. There had to be a twist.

Mike Patty sometimes felt Becky was too sucked into the online nonsense, that the constant barrage of hate was toxic. Becky felt it was a small price. She distanced herself from the bad faith commentators. But she did not retreat. Along with the other relatives, she kept telling the story of the girls.

On a mild day in autumn 2018, Click and Ferency went to Delphi together. They wanted to walk where the girls had walked. They wanted to take in the scene and imagine what might have happened.

Ferency hated heights and declined to accompany Click onto the bridge itself. Crossing felt like an eternal march. Rotting boards sagged beneath Click with each step. Sometimes he found himself hopping over gaps big enough for a man to fall through. Every so often, he would stare down at the landscape far below—rugged and hilly for Indiana. He wondered why no one had heard the girls scream. On the other side, Click jogged down a steep decline. He stood by the edge of Deer Creek, then decided against wading across.

The two investigators had a theory. Abby was dating Holder's son Logan. Or, at least, they had met a time or two. Perhaps Westfall's son and Logan Holder had arranged to meet the girls to celebrate the Feast of Váli, a holiday commemorating the slaying of Odin's blind son, Höðr, by his half-brother, Váli. After the girls stepped onto the bridge to follow their dates, Brad Holder followed behind them to prevent their escape. Libby began to feel uneasy. She filmed Holder. Click and Ferency developed a theory for the audio on her phone. They thought the speakers of "guys" and "down the hill" were two separate people. Holder gave the directional orders, and a different person, possibly Fields, referred to the girls as "guys."

Click and Ferency reasoned that the girls began making cracks about the ritual. Westfall became enraged. He forced the girls to strip, to humiliate them. But the girls were not cowed, so they kept up the teasing. Westfall killed Libby first, brutally slicing her throat. He then turned on Abby to prevent her from sharing what she had seen. Or else Holder did. The detectives were not entirely sure. Abby received one stab to the carotid artery, and then, once she stopped bleeding, she was re-dressed in Libby's clothing. Little twigs were placed near her head. In Norse myth, Odin's daughter Hela was often depicted with antlers. They wondered if that was a sign of remorse. Then Holder, a man obsessed with carving runes out of sticks and photographing runes he came across in nature, fashioned the stick symbols as an afterthought.

The theory had problems. There was no real evidence for any of it. Why would Holder need to corral invited guests on the bridge? Why did the girls not greet him, address him by name, or reference either Logan or Westfall's son in the footage from Libby's phone? Why did Libby instead comment on the man's gun? Why did the video not capture anyone else? Were Abby and Libby really the type of young women to poke fun of sincerely held religious beliefs, especially in the presence of their dates? Would two frightened teenage girls really keep mouthing off to a group of grown men who had just forced them to strip nude? How did a large group of men murder the girls without leaving forensic evidence or attracting the attention of searchers? What about Holder's gym alibi? Were the sticks near Abby's head truly representative of Hela? Would Holder and the others have left behind a couple of lopsided branches and an ambiguous bloodstain, or would the signatures have been more obvious? Was Fields even a pagan? Why did none of the phones picked up in the woods that day belong to Holder, Westfall, Fields, or their alleged coconspirators?

Still, the investigators kept at it. Again and again, McLeland and those with Unified Command told them to find probable cause on their suspects. That never happened. Instead, the trio became an island within the investigation. They began to give off the impression that they thought they were alone in their fight to solve the case.

CHAPTER THIRTEEN

In public, the relationship between the families and law enforcement was strong. Privately, things could be fraught at times.

The families had faith in the dedication of the investigators, but there were still tensions. For one thing, detectives would not publicly clear the relatives of the victims. Investigators had ruled out family involvement early on, as well as any possible connection to Derrick's drug abuse. But they reasoned that if they had to clear one person, they might find themselves facing an unending chorus of similar requests from all the hundreds of people who came into contact with the case.

As for the prosecutor, not everyone felt too sure about McLeland. Becky thought him overconfident. Rumors spread online that McLeland was related to Libby. The truth was Libby's grandfather Brad German's wife had once been married to one of McLeland's uncles. That was the extent of the family tie. McLeland's father and some of his uncles went to school with Mike Patty. When he was eighteen, he played on a community softball team with Brad German. But most of Becky's concerns came out of whether or not McLeland would be ready for such a high profile trial. He had only tried one other murder case.

In one of the prosecutor's early non-murder trials, Mike Patty sat on the jury. McLeland lost. Afterwards, he sought out the jurors to ask them how they came to their verdict.

"You didn't prove your case," Mike told him.

That interaction haunted the Pattys. They hoped that McLeland would do better for Abby and Libby.

One of the investigators did have a tiny inkling of what the families of the girls were going through. In 2013, Liggett's younger son Cole was eighteen. His personality was always on the less serious side, but he surprised everyone when he announced his intent to attend college to study drafting. That summer, he had gone out to a concert with friends. They crowded into a Chevrolet Blazer. There were not enough seatbelts for everyone, so Cole went without. When the Blazer's tire blew out, the car crashed and rolled over. Everyone was bumped around. Everyone except Cole. He was thrown from the vehicle. He died of his injuries. Liggett had been out on the road working when he got the call from the hospital.

Liggett knew that was not the same. Murder was a uniquely vicious way to lose a child, especially ones as young as Libby and Abby. But he had gone through the loss—the maddening sense of disorder that follows a child dying before their parents or grandparents, the hollow, lingering absence at birthday parties and holidays and family dinners, the void that seems to swallow everything up.

Everything came crashing down during a phone call. Lieutenant Colonel Larry Turner rang Holeman.

"We've got something to tell you," he said.

He had Stacy Bozinovski on speaker. She was an experienced examiner. She had seen all manner of disturbing things throughout her career.

But now Bozinovski had terrible news to share. Before she could say it, she started crying. Through tears, she told the startled Holeman that they had no offender DNA. The male DNA they had found had come from a CSI who had helped at the autopsy.

"What?" Holeman was shocked. "What are you talking about?" There were supposed to be safeguards in place. Namely, laboratory personnel were required to have their DNA profiles logged into the system to prevent such issues.

Bozinovski explained that the CSI was so new at his job, his DNA had not yet been entered into the system when she checked.

"It's okay," Holeman told her. "It's not your fault."

She kept crying though. And Holeman knew how she felt. All that time, investigators had been operating under the belief that they had the offender's DNA. The sample was small, but testing was always improving. What they had could ultimately allow for an identification down the road. They had collected samples from so many locals, so many persons of interest. Leazenby and Becky had already talked up the prospect of DNA evidence in the news media.

Now, they had nothing.

Everyone wanted to be a hero. Investigators would march into a meeting with Unified Command and declare how they would be the ones to solve the Delphi murders. They would allude to likely mistakes made by the Delphi team, then share how they would fix those errors. They would predict future awards and honors, detective of the year, commendations.

Those newcomers inevitably lasted a week or two. Then the parting recriminations would begin. "Ah, you guys fucked this up. You're never going to solve it. I can't solve it. Nobody's going to solve it."

Like doomed figures from a myth, these newcomers each attacked the case and lost. Holeman watched them all fall away. He felt nothing but disdain. The case devoured the ones who did not flee. Holeman knew that from experience.

"All right, well, take your ass back to your fucking post and fuck shit up there," Holeman felt like saying. "Because we don't fucking need you."

Too many officers seemed to take the view that a single sleuth could crack open a case on sheer brilliance. That story might play well in popular culture, but Holeman had a far more practical view. Solid police investigations featured standard operating procedures, strong communication within a team, and meticulous documentation.

Other police officers were not the only ones who took note of the Delphi murders. Some true crime celebrities stepped in too. Famed genetic genealogist CeCe Moore quietly helped the state police process cigarette butts through DNA phenotyping firm Parabon NanoLabs. The DNA on the cigarettes all came back to searchers. Podcaster and author Paul Holes, an investigator who worked to identify Joseph James DeAngelo as the Golden State Killer, even offered to work with detectives.

Holeman appreciated the sentiment. He knew many people wanted to help. But as the months went on, he eventually grew wary of the offers of investigative assistance. In his view, the original sin of the case was the chaos of the early days. There had been far too many helpers. Information had not flowed easily. Holeman could be confrontational, and his detractors found him territorial. He knew they all called him an asshole behind his back. Holeman saw himself as doing what needed to be done to guard the case.

Still, the murders remained unsolved. Something was not working, and Holeman could scarcely bolt the door from all outsiders. So when superiors told him to invite in officers from the Georgia Bureau of Investigation and homicide detectives from the Indianapolis Metropolitan Police Department, he did so.

The visiting investigators took in all the information about the case. They audited the work of the Delphi team. Holeman felt they rarely had many substantive notes. Their reports confirmed his feelings: that the Delphi investigators seemed to be doing all they possibly could. Roy West, a seasoned IMPD homicide detective, did point out that police ought to canvass the surveillance footage at every McDonald's on the roads around the High Bridge. Holeman reminded him that Delphi was rural. There was one McDonald's near the courthouse, and few other fast-food joints in town. The FBI's ERT had already canvassed the few stores in the area.

Holeman had always been skeptical about forensic sketches. Most of the investigators were. Sketches were simply artistic interpretations of a witness's fleeting memory. They could be helpful in some cases. In the Delphi case, the one they had released seemed only to cause chaos, spurring behind-the-scenes arguments between detectives and prompting internet sleuths to post side-by-side comparisons of the sketch and their own random "persons of interest."

And now the investigators were preparing to unleash yet another one.

The first sketch—the only one released to the public so far—had come about from Sarah Carbaugh's description. Drawn up by FBI Special Agent Thomas Plantz on June 19, 2017, it showed a middle-aged man. Bags sagged beneath his drooping eyes. Scruff surrounded his weak chin. His hair was messy, sticking out this way and that from underneath his strange cap. His mean-looking mug had been out for years, with no results.

But there was another sketch in the case. It came from the description of Betsy Blair.

Holeman thought the sketches looked pretty similar when it came to the man's basic features. Carbaugh was younger, and she thought she saw an older man. Blair was older, and she thought she saw a younger man. Take those perspectives away, and both sketches showed a white man with a wide mouth, thin lips, narrow eyes, and eyebrows with a similar curve to them. The poofy hair could be a weird cap registered wrong in the brain, or vice versa. Even the noses resembled one another in shape, although the older man's appeared more bulbous.

Within Unified Command, some of the investigators thought it might be time to mix things up. Like Carbaugh, Blair had only a fleeting view of Bridge Guy. Carbaugh was closer to him, as she drove her car along

300 North. But Blair had seen him full on, out in the open, not through the glass of a car window. She also came forward right away, unlike Carbaugh, whose extreme anxiety and fear had prompted her to withhold her sighting from the police until months later. Perhaps Blair's description was more accurate. Maybe now was the time to find out.

The case was in a lull by the spring of 2019. The members of Unified Command were still working it hard, taking calls about the Delphi murders every day, filing away leads. McLeland even brought on Mullin as his investigator that year. The former police chief would continue working the case for the prosecutor's office. But no truly major developments were underway. The investigators wanted to ensure they were doing everything they could.

Perhaps as a sign of growing desperation, Holeman even sought outside help. He looked to the Sherry Black Foundation, an organization dedicated to supporting agencies in solving homicides. He brought in Patrick Zirpoli, a former Pennsylvania state trooper who worked as the organization's senior investigator, and retired psychologist Richard Walter .

The two consultants told Holeman and the others that they believed the killer was power assertive. The profilers from the FBI had not provided much guesswork about the Delphi killer. But the ideas from Zirpoli and Walter matched the profile from the United States Marshals Service's Behavioral Analysis Unit (BAU). The profilers believed the man who killed Libby and Abby was likely a predator obsessed with control. Kidnapping the girls, humiliating them by forcing them to strip, killing them so brutally—it was all a pathetic attempt to wield power.

Zirpoli and Walter said the killer would remain in hiding unless challenged. Somebody needed to address him publicly, to push him into making a mistake. The only question was who?

The members of Unified Command did not have much trouble with their decision. Carter was the natural pick. Articulate and authentic, with a penchant for emotional, off-the-cuff speeches, the superintendent could elicit a reaction. As the leader of the state police, he also represented a level of authority that might compel a response from a controlling killer. That was the true purpose of the conference: speaking to the murderer directly.

The investigators scheduled a press conference to give Carter a prominent platform for his words.

In preparation, Holeman met with Zirpoli. Walter called in via video conference. They organized a few strategic planning meetings. Carter pitched in. He came up with a few challenges himself. He planned to accuse the killer of hiding in plain sight. The superintendent also thought it might be a good idea to add to the sense of confrontation by saying the killer might even be in the crowd at the press conference. The police needed to bring the fight *to* the murderer, to tell him they were coming for him.

Despite all the tough talk, the press conference felt somewhat like a last resort for the investigators. They were all tiring of the annual press conferences and the scrutiny, criticism, and speculation they inevitably sparked. All that outreach had never yielded any tips that moved the case forward. Still, their options were dwindling. At least by addressing the public, and perhaps the killer, the investigators of Unified Command felt they would be doing something.

As the plans for the press conference came together, Unified Command welcomed a new face. A trooper at the Lafayette post was now working the case full-time as a detective. The superintendent had ordered the new addition himself. Concerned that Harper's retirement might be imminent, Carter wanted another full-time investigator on the Delphi case.

There were no detectives to spare. Holeman called Buckley and asked what trooper they should pull off the road.

Buckley did not hesitate. "Dave Vido."

Vido had never forgotten the Delphi case. He wanted to fulfill the promise he made to the relatives of the girls back in 2017. He accepted the temporary duty assignment. Most lasted ninety days. His would stretch on for years. The week of the press conference was his first one working with Unified Command. He found himself joining the team just as everything changed.

CHAPTER FOURTEEN

The meeting in the kitchen boiled over into a fight just a few minutes before the press conference was due to start. Facing off, Carter and Leazenby were locked in a heated debate. The flare-up came amid months of tension between the Indiana State Police and the Carroll County Sheriff's Office. Outside, representatives of the national and local news media waited. They had gathered in the Wabash and Erie Canal Interpretive Center to hear about a major update in the Delphi case.

The day was April 22, 2019. Carter was scheduled to unveil new clues in the Delphi case. The state police would show the video of Bridge Guy walking along the planks. Now the public could observe the man's gait along the uneven railroad ties, or at least a few frames of it. Police would add another scrap of audio to the mix. Instead of just "down the hill," reporters would soon hear: "Guys, down the hill." Carter would also introduce a brand-new suspect sketch. That was what the conference was about, at least on the surface.

The disagreement between Carter and Leazenby came about over one piece of advice from the consultants. They stressed that only one person should stand up behind the podium to address the killer.

Leazenby balked when Carter told him he would do the press conference on his own.

"I want to be up there."

As far as Leazenby was concerned, he was the sheriff. Carter could take the lead and do all the talking. But this was a county case. The sheriff needed to be out there. Leazenby recognized the possibility that his desire might be prideful or political, but he did not care. He did not want to relinquish what he saw as his responsibility. So Leazenby kept pushing Carter.

The argument between the superintendent and the sheriff went back and forth. Both men grew red in the face.

Finally, Carter snapped. "You're going to stand there and look like a fucking idiot."

Leazenby was stoic. "Then I'll stand there and look like an idiot."

The sheriff got his way. At the conference, he hovered over Carter's right shoulder, a mute, solemn presence, his arms held behind his back, his mouth drooped into a frown.

Taking the podium, Carter spoke off-the-cuff, often pausing and choking up. His emotive style mesmerized some viewers. He spoke more like a hometown sheriff than a cold-eyed bureaucrat. But most of what he said had been carefully vetted by the team.

"Directly to the killer, who may be in this room: We believe you were hiding in plain sight," Carter said, voice trembling. "For more than two years, you never thought we would shift gears to a different investigative strategy. But we have. We likely have interviewed you or someone close to you. We know this is about power to you, and you want to know what we know. And one day, you will."

It was a press conference for one. Detectives would have no way of knowing if the message had even reached their intended audience. For online sleuths, though, the speculation was too tempting to resist. On social media, they picked apart Carter's speech, as if every word might contain a hidden code to the killer's true identity.

A few times, Carter veered off script. He often did when he spoke from the heart. The murders of the girls genuinely affected him. He had met with the families. He saw their pain. He saw the pain of his officers, men he cared about, like Holeman.

"I recently watched a movie called *The Shack*," Carter said. "And there's also a book that talks so well about evil, about death and about eternity. To the murderer: I believe you have just a little bit of a conscience left. And I can assure you that how you left them in that woods is not, is not, what they are experiencing today."

Afterward, Holeman headed over to Carter. "What the fuck's *The Shack*?" That had not been brought up in any of the strategic planning meetings.

"Oh, you need to read the book or watch the movie," Carter told him.

The detective watched the film. Based on the novel by William P. Young, the story follows a father grappling with his Christian faith after a serial killer abducts and murders his daughter.

Holeman believed in God, although he had fallen away from organized religion. Clearly Carter was just trying to appeal to the remote possibility that the killer or his loved ones might have a shred of remorse, or else a twinge of fear of facing eternal damnation in the next life. Holeman was not so convinced. He imagined that the killer's religiosity or lack thereof would not be much of a factor either way. Faithful or faithless, some men seemed hungry to slaughter the innocent. Oftentimes their family stuck by them, enabled them, covered up for their transgressions until their sickness and violence exploded into public.

And sometimes even afterward too.

The families of Abby and Libby learned about the new direction fifteen minutes before the rest of the world.

Becky's first thought was that she had wasted two years of her life. All that time, the families and their supporters had plastered the sketch of the older man across neighboring counties, police departments and festivals across the United States, and social media. The rise of the new, younger sketch made all that effort seem futile.

But in the aftermath of the new direction press conference, the families did what they always did. They moved on. Dealing with the police could be frustrating. When the relatives were ushered into the room with Unified Command and told the news about the pivot, the mood became tense. But ultimately, the prevailing feeling amongst the families was one of resignation. They realized that the law enforcement officers were still working hard on the case. The families had gotten to know them over time. They knew Carter took their case personally, often welling up when he discussed the girls. They knew Leazenby and Holeman would always make time to take their calls and hear their concerns. They knew Liggett would not divulge much information to them because he was meticulous about protecting the case's integrity. They knew Vido and the others would do everything they could to get answers.

If the detectives felt they needed to start over, the families of Abby and Libby could accept that unwelcome news. Despite their anger and weariness, they did not surrender their faith in the investigators.

The news sounded great at first. Murphy had the impression that Holeman's Pennsylvania experts had recommended that the state police divert all their attention to the Rushville lead. Elated, he shared that with Click.

For the trio of investigators, that brief moment was one of validation and relief. They each believed in the Odinism angle. Now it seemed like those in Unified Command finally agreed.

The moment was fleeting. Murphy had misunderstood. Again and again, Holeman and McLeland had encouraged anyone working on an angle in the case to find probable cause for an arrest. But the three investigators had not been able to do that.

Murphy did not say he had been feeling pressure from his colleagues on the FBI task force to resume his usual duties. He did not say anyone in Unified Command or the prosecutor's office was responsible for this unwelcome news. He did not say that the monthslong investigation he had poured so much of himself into had elicited no probable cause against Holder, Westfall, Fields, Messer, or anyone else. He did not say that many of the facts of the case conflicted against their Rushville-centric theory of the crime. He simply drifted away from the case.

Ferency and Click kept on it. They never got the evidence they so desperately wanted. Once again, the road led away from Rushville.

Vido stared at the files. The predator lurking in Libby's phone had escaped justice. When he was assigned the case, the other investigators had mentioned Kegan Kline. Vido worked on a few other leads before Holeman asked him to focus exclusively on Kegan. He read about the interactions between Libby and the @anthony_shots account, how she had been messaging the predator on the morning of her death, before heading to the trails. He saw that investigators busted Kegan and his trove of CSAM in a raid just about a week after the murders. But somehow, Kegan was never charged. Something had gone very wrong.

Vido put in a request for a new digital forensic examination. Software had improved and there was always the possibility that new clues might emerge. Sergeant Christopher Cecil got to work on Kegan's heap of electronics: the iPod Touch, the iPhone 4, the iPhone 3, the Galaxy S5, the Galaxy S4, and the Nextbook Tablet. Cecil was the commander of two Internet Crimes Against Children groups. One was the ISP's unit, the other was the Indiana-wide task force. He was an expert at uncovering materials carefully hidden on the devices of child predators.

The advent of technology expanded the investigative capabilities of officers like Cecil. But it also unleashed a rogue wave as far as evidence to analyze. Cecil and his small team at ICAC were extraordinarily busy. In a typical year, they handled around twenty-five hundred cases. Under normal circumstances, the influx of new cases was so constant that Cecil could rely on spending no more than a week or so with a suspect's phone before it was time to start the process over with a new suspect and a new device. But, of course, 2020 was not a typical year. It was the first year of the COVID-19 pandemic. The deadly virus did not discriminate, spreading during court appearances and interrogations and arrests. Law enforcement and the courts were strongly urged to slow things down, to take things easy, to get as many cases continued as possible.

This lull meant Cecil would get something quite unusual when it came to the Kegan Kline case. He would get *time*. Thanks to the pandemic slowdown, Cecil got to spend about three months concentrating entirely on Kegan's devices.

He found terrible things.

CHAPTER FIFTEEN

Predators stalk where prey gathers. The advent of the internet and social media applications lured in a generation of children eager to connect and explore online. But wherever children are, sexual offenders are lurking. In the modern age, predators looking for a victim to abuse need not drive down a street in a van with offers of candy or puppies. Nor must they wheedle their way into a target's life through sports or religion or education or any number of other ruses. They need only send a friend request, or like a post, or leave a comment. The tiny screen of a phone provides them enough of a window to steal through. In rare instances, sexual predators rape, kidnap, or kill victims after a lengthy online grooming. Most of the time, they coax, coerce, and confuse children until they capitulate and provide sexual images on demand.

In other instances, CSAM consists of images and videos of adults sexually abusing children. Dead-eyed toddlers with grown men. Little ones raised to be pimped out. The worst of the worst.

Cecil found all of that on Kegan's phones and devices. The suspect was deep into a world of horrors. He not only had a collection of disgusting images and videos created by other predators, but he was also a producer of CSAM himself. He had tricked young girls into sending him all manner of sexual images. As he dug into Kegan's devices, Cecil kept in constant contact with Vido. They had plenty of meetings and calls to discuss the Kegan Kline case. On June 12, 2020, Cecil turned the report over to Vido.

Moments of vile exploitation eternally frozen in time. That is all CSAM really is. Working such cases can have a significant toll on investigators. Vido had to look at what was on Kegan's phones. That was his job. But the experience was devastating. He could never forget the evil he witnessed. He had been a practicing Catholic. Seeing what he saw in the Kegan Kline case, and the murders of Abby and Libby, made him lose faith.

But the revelation of what Kegan was doing to children made Vido all the more determined to work the case as hard as he could. As far as he figured, somebody had to.

So Vido did not look away. He and the other investigators agreed early on that even if Kegan had nothing whatsoever to do with the Delphi murders, even if his communications with Libby were nothing more than an awful coincidence, he was still a man who needed to spend a very long time in prison.

Summer was starting to heat up as Vido got to work. He picked up the case where it had been dropped three years before. And he soon got some help.

Brian Harshman wanted in on the case. He frequently conveyed that to Holeman. A master trooper with the Indiana State Police, Harshman wore his white hair and beard trimmed short. His eyes often looked sad even when he was smiling. Holeman kept turning him down. He would tell Harshman that the case was a nightmare. Nobody should want to get involved. Holeman felt he was doing him a favor. But Harshman was persistent. He wanted to help. Holeman relented. Harshman joined the case in the summer of 2020.

Around that same time, another newcomer joined the team. The United States Marshals Service obtained information about the @anthony_shots profile. Deputy US Marshal Jeremy Clinton and other marshals came to work on the case. Harshman and Clinton would work closely with Vido on the Kegan Kline lead, and came to be a part of Unified Command.

Together, they resolved to work the two cases jointly, on parallel tracks. They had the Delphi angle, the possibility that Kegan might have had something to do with the murders. And they had the crimes around his cache of CSAM. The first track was a Carroll County case. The second happened in a different jurisdiction entirely. Kegan lived in Peru, which meant his CSAM crimes were committed in Miami County. The Lafayette post would need to bring in the prosecutor's office in Miami County.

On June 18, 2020, Vido, Clinton, Harshman, and Holeman met with the team of attorneys. Prosecuting attorney Jeff Sinkovics brought his chief deputy, Peter Diedrichs, and deputy prosecutor, Courtney Alwine. McLeland was there, too. They all sat down together.

Sinkovics had concerns. In fact, he was baffled and frustrated. Back in 2017, the state police had told him there was nothing prosecutable about the Kegan Kline case. The state police assured him they would take the blame for the oversight. So many tips and agencies and investigators had been involved in the beginning, which led to lost information and nonexistent follow-through at times. The meeting was uncomfortable, but necessary. In the end, the Miami County team was willing to forge ahead with the investigators.

Now the police were asking Sinkovics to charge Kegan. After reviewing the evidence, the trio of prosecutors immediately agreed to take the case. But it still was not a quick process. The lawyers had to go through all the CSAM themselves to figure out precisely what Kegan Kline would be charged with. Then those charges had to be written up. Sinkovics and Diedrichs both gave up part of their Father's Day to work on the case.

On August 19, 2020, investigators finally caught up with Kegan. Vido, Harshman, Clinton, and a few others gathered near Kegan's girlfriend's apartment in Kokomo. When they were ready, they stormed the place with guns drawn. Moving quickly and yelling that they were police, the officers searched for Kegan. The apartment was filthy. They discovered their quarry sitting amid the squalor, completely nude. They handcuffed him and led him away. Later on, Kegan would tell people he had a gun in the apartment that day. He said he ought to have refused to surrender and tried shooting at Vido and the others instead. He would soon be charged with multiple counts related to CSAM possession.

Kegan was taken to the small interview room at the Peru post of the Indiana State Police. Sitting there, freed of the handcuffs, he stared at Vido and Clinton, his moon face utterly inscrutable.

Vido sat across from Kegan. For months, the detective had waited to get Kegan in a room. Orderly and determined to learn the truth, Vido had prepared extensively for the interview. So had Clinton, who opted for a chair in the corner. The two men worked well together. Vido knew that Clinton spent many off-duty hours delving into the data. The case meant a lot to them both, and they became close working on it together.

They wanted an accounting of Kegan's crimes against children, but they also wanted to know whether the man had anything to do with the murders of Libby and Abby. Hours of planning, reviewing phone data, and reading over notes went into the meeting.

"How did you meet Liberty German?" asked the detective. Vido already knew the answer, of course. Kegan had done what he always did. He approached one girl with his @anthony_shots persona. Like a virus, he spread across adolescent friend groups, connecting with a litany of girls on Instagram and Snapchat.

Kegan protested that he barely remembered talking to the murdered girl. "I didn't even know who she really was until after I saw that on the news and I was like, 'Oh, wow, that name.' Like I remembered that name."

"When would you say you realized that . . . that it was Liberty German, the girl that you were talking to, was killed?"

"I don't know. Probably, I mean, a little bit after probably happening. I mean, probably after it happened and I saw, like, her face and saw her name. Then." Kegan did not seem to think the fact that he had spoken to Libby on the day she was killed had much significance. "I mean, a lot of people get killed and then people talked to [them], what do you mean? That doesn't mean that I killed them."

"I didn't say that." Vido decided to move on, to a conversation Kegan had had with a girl online the day the bodies of the girls were discovered. "She said, 'Did you hear about Liberty?' You respond on Anthony Shots, 'O.M.G. what happened?' That's talking to someone about the two girls that were missing and then wound up dead . . . [The] same person, or the girl that you were talking to, says that Anthony Shots was meeting up with Liberty German."

"That's a total lie," Kegan said. "That's a total lie. That's a total fucking lie."

"How do you know?"

"Because I didn't fucking murder someone, yeah, so yeah I know—"

"Listen to me," insisted Vido. "I can honestly sit here and I'm telling you I do not believe that you killed Liberty or Abby."

"Okay. Thank you."

"[It] make[s] sense for us to question," Clinton said "question you about looking that up when you're one of the last people to ever spoke to her before she wound up dead. Or excuse me, Anthony Shots was one of the last, the Anthony Shots account is one of the last people to speak to her before she winds up dead."

"Right," Vido said. "And then you said that it could be because a friend of a friend says, 'Well, hey, I talked to such and such and their friends' but you're searching about . . . 'Can law enforcement trace I.P. addresses from social media?'"

Kegan acted as if he did not understand why the police would find that search the least bit incriminating. "Well, yeah," he said. "Why wouldn't I look that up? If I'm looking at stuff on the internet?" Kline refused to budge from his insistence that he had no information about the murders of Abby and Libby. "I literally have no clue, like I don't know anyone. I don't know anything about that whole case."

"Yes, you do, man," Clinton said.

"I just," Vido started, "I can't wrap my head around why you're willing to put all of this on you. Why are you protecting somebody else?" This was a reference to the investigator's theory that someone besides Kegan Kline had also accessed the @anthony_shots account—or at least been given access to information from the account. That person, according to the police, could very well have been the one responsible for the murders. They suspected that person could be Kegan's father, Tony Kline.

Something seemed to finally dawn on Kegan. "You think I know who killed them?"

"Absolutely."

"Well," said Kegan. "You're obviously terrible at your job. If you really honestly think that, you're absolutely terrible at your job, sir. I'm sorry to say that but—"

Vido ignored the jibe. "Do you know who killed those girls?"

"No." Kegan Kline, in fact, would maintain for years that he knew nothing about the murders—up until the point he realized that seeming to have information about the killings could benefit him.

The search for evidence against Kegan Kline precipitated a rift in the investigation. The FBI had maintained a presence in the case since early on. Holeman and Carter credited the Bureau with helping to tame the organizational chaos that occurred in the earliest days of the investigation. ORION had been a godsend. Agents like Peasley and Davies fit in well with the other investigators and worked the case doggedly. But Peasley was ultimately transferred. Davies retired, although he later came back and signed on as a special deputy to keep working with Unified Command. Others had departed over time, such as Robertson, when the Logan lead went nowhere. By 2021, the FBI's role in the case was a reduced one. They did not have many agents involved, and they were not doing much work at that point. The personnel shake-ups were not the only issue.

The FBI kept its own records. In the minds of Unified Command, particularly the state police, it would be more accurate to say the Bureau jealously guarded its own records. Prying away pertinent information was challenging and frustrating. A natural rivalry already existed between federal and state law enforcement, but the widespread feeling that the Bureau was gatekeeping did not improve camaraderie. Even McLeland, the elected prosecutor, struggled with access issues as he attempted to assemble and organize all the Delphi files.

Things came to a head in August 2021. Investigators were digging into the Kegan Kline lead. They knew from phone extracts that Kegan had done a search on the Marathon gas station in Delphi on the day of the girls' murders. If they could secure footage of him shuffling around the station just before the girls were killed, that would be a huge step toward probable cause. Back in 2017, the FBI's ERT had been responsible for canvassing and gathering footage from area shops.

But they had a problem. Three agents from the FBI's ERT had indeed gone to the Marathon. They walked in and tried to extract data. There was a glitch, and they hauled out the equipment to work on it remotely. But the agents later returned the equipment to the gas station without having extracted anything. For reasons unknown, they had not bothered to get the relevant footage off the system. Now it was gone forever. They had no way to see if Kegan had been at the Marathon that day.

When state police confronted the Bureau on this mishap, the FBI turned around and blamed the issue on Sergeant Josh Rozzi of the Peru post. The state police knew Josh Rozzi was not to blame. The partnership between the FBI and the state police frayed. Those in Unified Command realized that perhaps it was time to streamline. Individual FBI special agents were still a boon to their team, and in fact continued to assist with the investigation. But struggling with dual, walled-off caches of records made no sense. Pointing out that there was no federal nexus, Carter told the FBI it was time for them to step back.

In some ways, being behind bars was not as much of an adjustment for Kegan as some might have expected. Even while he was a free man, the parts of his life that meant the most to him were spent online. And being incarcerated placed surprisingly few limitations on his digital existence.

Inmates at Miami County Jail were given a tablet-like device that allowed them to send and receive "chirps," which were essentially text messages. For Kegan, getting that access was much like receiving the keys to the kingdom.

He immediately began doing all he could to feed his obsessions. He got phone numbers of women by any means possible—from his own memory, by tricking other inmates, and even by manipulating his own mother. When she expressed fear that he might want the numbers for unseemly purposes, he chided her for even thinking such things and insisted he was only trying to keep in contact with people.

Once he had the crucial contact information, Kegan would—of course—reach out to the women. The initial messages were rather benign, but he would soon get up to his old tricks, alternately trying to wow his audience by telling lies about his wealth and attempting to elicit sympathy by sharing manipulative untruths about his health. Then things would progress toward the sexual; Kegan would ask explicit questions about their genitals, inquire about how often they masturbated, and go into detail about what precisely he would like to do to them sexually. To keep the women interested, he would often make promises about what he could do for them financially, but he would get vague if asked for details about when they could expect their windfalls. ("My mom has cancer bad," he chirped to one woman, "so Im not sure what day she would be feeling well enough to bring u the $.")

It was, in many ways, a comfortable existence for Kegan. But then, in early December 2021, he got word that things would soon change. The Indiana State Police were about to make things very, very public.

CHAPTER SIXTEEN

The ISP generally made it difficult to miss updates in the Delphi case. The "new direction" press conference, for instance, was announced days in advance so the public—and the media—would have time to make plans to attend. But in retrospect, to investigators like Holeman, that strategy had backfired, eliciting rampant speculation and few decent tips.

So late in the evening on December 6, 2021, the ISP quietly posted a new release on their YouTube channel.

The video—rather simply titled "Indiana State Police Delphi News"—featured a lanky and boyish trooper dressed in full uniform, including his hat, standing before a shield-studded cloth background. He identified himself as Sergeant Jeremy Piers—the public information officer of District 14 of the Indiana State Police. And then he delivered a carefully worded bombshell.

"While investigating the murders of Abigail Williams and Liberty German, detectives with the Carroll County Sheriff's Office and the Indiana State Police have uncovered an online profile named @anthony_shots."

Piers informed viewers that the profile was active from 2016 on Snapchat, Instagram, and possibly other social media sites. Pictures of fancy cars and a handsome, shirtless young man appeared on the screen. The man in the photographs was not really Anthony. He was a model. A predator had stolen his photographs to set up the account, the goal of which was to entice young girls into sharing nude pictures and their home addresses.

"Investigators would like any individual who communicated, met, or attempted to meet with the @anthony_shots profile to contact law enforcement," Piers said.

At that point, the police were running out of leads on Kegan. They had gone through his devices. They had talked to many of his victims, as well as plenty of witnesses. Interviews with Kegan tended to go nowhere. He was a difficult subject. He lied constantly, and then brushed off any irrefutable proof that he was lying. Judging from jail calls and chirps, he had a particular dislike of Vido. But the investigators generally found it impossible to build up any rapport. Kegan was too mercurial for that. One moment he wanted to talk and share and wheedle. The next, he would grow angry and profane.

But there was more work to be done. Vido and the others knew the scope of Kegan's crimes was far beyond what they had found so far. Plenty of the child victims had used phony names themselves when communicating with @anthony_shots. It was time to let them know it was safe to come forward about Kegan.

Piers gave the tip line number and email address that had specifically been created to take information related to the Delphi case. The new direction press conference had been an attempt to speak directly to the killer. This new outreach was focused instead on victims of a predator. The short video concluded by again showing pictures of Abby and Libby.

It took less than a day for WISH-TV reporter Demie Johnson to reveal that the user of the @anthony_shots profile was Kegan Kline. Suddenly everyone knew who Kegan was.

One unexpected effect of Kegan's newfound notoriety was that it immeasurably improved his sex life. Before, he had to scrounge around for phone numbers of women to chirp; now women started reaching out to him on their own. These women had a mission: By and large, they believed Kegan had information about the Delphi murders, and they were convinced they could somehow succeed where the police had not and get Kegan to reveal all to them. What they did not seem to realize was that Kegan had a mission as well; he was determined to exploit others for his sexual pleasure. This became a recipe for some bizarre and downright disturbing chirps back and forth between Kegan and his new correspondents.

He would hint that he would give up a detail or two in exchange for sexual content of some kind. Chirps would contain talk of the murdered girls amid discussion of fetishes and anal sex. In some fashion, this gave both parties exactly what they wanted—but it made unsettling reading for all the law enforcement and prosecutors who were keeping an eye on Kegan's communications. And, while Kegan almost certainly got sexual gratification from his end of the exchanges, nothing he gave the women served to move the actual investigation forward.

But the online community tried very hard to act as if it had. Details from the women's communications began "leaking," such as a letter Kegan sent to one woman that was featured in a YouTube video. At one point in his missive, Kegan made a comment that could plausibly be interpreted as suggesting he might have a foot fetish. This was seen as a highly damaging admission since, as everyone knew, one of Libby's socks was allegedly taken from the crime scene.

To investigators, of course, things like that meant almost nothing. They also did not believe they needed whatever help the women sexting Kegan believed they were providing. In fact, at this point, law enforcement seemed to be getting pretty far on their own.

In the late summer of 2022, Kegan finally broke and told them the story of the murders.

To be strictly accurate, Kegan did not tell just one story about the murders; he provided several accounts. In the first version, his father was drunk or high on something one night and had let slip the fact that he had killed three people in his life. The first was a guy named Dougie. He said the Dougie in question died in a car accident after someone swerved their vehicle into his lane, running him off the road. Investigators followed up on that, but the records in question no longer existed.

The other two people he claimed to have killed were Libby and Abby. But he did not go into detail, and Kegan did not know much about it. Vido kept pressing him though. Investigators did not have all of his communications with Libby, but they had seen enough to become convinced he was actively grooming and manipulating her to achieve some end. Perhaps the ultimate goal was to lure her out to the bridge that February afternoon.

And Kegan was not the only Kline under scrutiny. His father Tony was well-known in Peru, Indiana. Squat and stout with a big grin and an unexpectedly feminine voice, he was widely regarded as both a fun guy and a violent domestic abuser. For years, it was an open secret that he beat his former wife, Kegan's mother, as well as her son and daughter from a previous relationship. Tony once slammed his stepson's head into the bowl of a toilet hard enough that he left the child bloody and so scared he took off into the rainy night. Kegan was the one person in the household who emerged unscathed from Tony's physical abuse, although he grew up witnessing the violence.

But Tony's disturbing behavior was not reserved for those in his immediate family. He had a history of non-contact sexual offenses. He would call women, strangers and acquaintances. From his heavy breathing and groans, he appeared to be masturbating on those calls. He once got in trouble for stalking a former girlfriend's young daughter. And years before, his youthful nighttime exploits were infamous. Girls back then told each other to watch out for Tony. They said he stalked women and looked in windows at night.

Kegan started making noises about wanting to be put into witness protection. Investigators told him he just had not given them enough information to justify that. So Kegan conferred with his attorney, Andrew

Achey, then came back and told them what he said was the actual, true, 100 percent factual account of the murders.

On August 17, 2022, Kline met investigators in a room at the Grissom Air Reserve Base, a United States Air Force base spanning between the counties of Cass and Miami. The whole operation was carefully organized. All of Unified Command was there, including McLeLand. Vido and a US Marshal led the interview. The whole story spilled out of Kegan. He said he and his dad had driven over to Delphi that day in a red Jeep. Tony Kline was supposed to meet someone. They parked, and Kegan waited patiently in the vehicle while his dad went off for his rendezvous. Eventually his dad returned, his clothes bloody, and the Kline men began their drive back home to Peru. As they crossed a bridge over the Wabash River, they slowed down. Kegan chucked his phone off the bridge. He then watched as his father threw the murder weapon, a knife, into the greenish water.

This, of course, was the sort of story investigators loved to hear—mainly because it was full of details, just the sort of thing that could be used to confirm or debunk the account. There was, for instance, the red Jeep. The Klines had indeed owned such a vehicle.

By the time Kegan told his story, over five years had passed since the day his father—his clothes allegedly sodden with the blood of the children he murdered—had sat in that car. But despite that passage of time—and despite how hard and vigorously the Klines may have tried to wash the vehicle—it seemed entirely possible that some small traces of the girls' blood remained in the Jeep. So investigators got their hands on the Jeep and subjected it to a minute examination.

They found nothing.

A red Jeep is also a relatively conspicuous vehicle. After getting Kegan to tell them the route they took that day, investigators reviewed the Hoosier Harvestore video. A red Jeep never appeared.

Police knew they needed to keep trying. After all, they were asking Kegan to recall a route driven years earlier. Perhaps he was just mistaken.

They could not risk throwing the whole lead out. So one day, Holeman picked Kegan up and asked him to provide directions. Together, the detective and the detainee were going to drive to Delphi—the same route Kegan had supposedly taken with his father all those years before.

Kegan was sullen. He was not one for small talk. Occasionally, he would tell Holeman where to turn.

Glancing in the rearview mirror, Holeman could see Harshman following behind in a trail vehicle.

Finally, the detective and the suspect arrived in Delphi. Kegan's suggested route would have taken the red Jeep right past the Hoosier Harvestore. Clearly, he was lying.

Holeman felt in his gut that Kegan was leading them in circles. But they could not just give up; they could not leave any avenue unexplored. They had searched the Jeep and the traffic footage. The only place left was the river.

As summer turned to fall in 2022, the ISP dive team spent weeks searching the Wabash River. Clad in bucket hats and gloves and shorts, the divers waded through knee-deep water. The August heat beat down on their bodies as they hunched over, digging through the riverbed for a knife or a phone.

They found a lot of guns. They sent those to Oberg in plastic bags filled with river water, like strange fish won at a carnival. Oberg was able to test a few of the firearms, but she could not link any of them to the cartridge. The other guns were so rusted, they fell apart when she tried to examine them.

But divers never found the evidence they were looking for. They did not locate Kegan's phone, nor did they find a knife they could link to the crime.

It seemed as if, at long last, the Kegan Kline lead had been completely exhausted.

PART THREE

THE SUSPECT

"That's Bridge Guy"

CHAPTER SEVENTEEN

The Delphi murders investigation always remained a Carroll County case. State police were highly involved, but the sheriff's office was the lead agency. And as the search for the killer moved into its fifth year, the calendar dictated that there would soon be a leadership shake-up within Carroll County.

Leazenby's term of office was coming to an end. State law forbade him from running for the job again. Though no one could have predicted it, the race to replace him would become one of the most contentious contests in the history of the county.

Indiana holds a primary election in the late spring in which the Republican and Democratic parties select their candidates. Then those winners, at least in theory, square off against each other in the November general election. But the Democratic party is not especially strong in rural Indiana communities such as Carroll County. Their candidates do not tend to do well in the general elections, and often the party does not even bother to slate candidates. The real race—the election that matters—is the Republican primary. The actual general election sometimes will seem more like a formality than anything else.

In places like Carroll County, in just about every sphere of government, there is a smaller pool of qualified prospects for leadership roles. And in agencies like the sheriff's office, there is limited upward mobility. One is either a deputy, a detective, the solitary night sergeant, the chief deputy, or the sheriff. So it is typical for longtime deputies to begin eying the sheriff's star after a time.

It was long assumed that Detective Kevin Hammond might run. Hammond had lost to Leazenby in 2014. Perhaps now was his time.

But Hammond had at least one challenger. As far as Thomas was concerned, it would finally be his turn. He was immensely loyal to Leazenby, but some in the office felt Thomas was not cut out for the top job. He was not involved in the Delphi case but appeared to feel he was the only one capable of solving it. Another law enforcement officer—one living many counties away—reported attending a training with Thomas, only to have him share all kinds of thoughts on the case.

The other Carroll County deputies had worked with Thomas for years. They knew him well. They did not want him as their sheriff. As a group, they approached the man they felt would be a far better choice. They went to Tony Liggett. Only he had no intention of running for sheriff that year. The deputies asked him to reconsider.

Liggett thought about the request. He had a few ideas. He liked figuring out details. He thought he might be able to implement those and make the office more efficient. He might try to run it like a business. The more Liggett thought about the idea, the more he was intrigued. He told the other deputies he would run in the Republican primary. He brought the idea to Leazenby.

Liggett and Thomas were not close as it was. But they had the race between Leazenby and Hammond to look at as precedent. The tensions were real, but ultimately those campaign rivals had been able to set aside the election and continue working together for years.

In early January, Thomas and Liggett began filling out the paperwork necessary to become candidates in the Republican primary. So did Lee Hoard, who had previously served as sheriff from 1989 to 1998 and was also the former mayor of Delphi. Hammond ended up deciding to retire.

Leazenby met with each candidate in his little office. Propped up on the wall was a wooden panel, a gift from the airport police in Indianapolis in the aftermath of the Delphi murders. Below that was a row of cloth-lined plastic chairs.

Liggett sat down in one of those and explained his ideas. He wanted Leazenby's advice. Leazenby liked the detective. He was sharp and dedicated. He had the loyalty of the rank-and-file deputies. He gave Liggett his endorsement, and a word of warning.

"Get ready to go through the wildest roller coaster ride—emotionally and psychologically—you've ever gone through in your life," he said.

Liggett seemed skeptical. "Yeah, right." He seemed to think Leazenby was overexaggerating. He did ask the sheriff to stay on as his chief deputy.

Leazenby also met with his former boss. He had served under Hoard in the nineties. Leazenby respected him, but he was perplexed by his determination to take back the sheriff's office after so many years out of the game. The rank-and-file also wondered about Hoard's motivations. Some said the man was looking to earn a sheriff's salary once more.

Thomas was a different story. Leazenby told him as respectfully as he could that he was uncertain his chief deputy was ready for the job. Leazenby did not know how Thomas could effectively lead the office if those serving under him did not want him in the role.

Thomas began to suggest the lack of support from his peers had something to do with the Delphi murders—or, more specifically, how law enforcement responded to them. His campaign took on the feel of someone looking to take over the double homicide case rather than run the sheriff's office. The literature he distributed spotlighted how, while working as a deputy, he had found time to take a number of training courses ranging from "Solving Homicides" to "Indiana State Honor Guard." Thomas bragged about receiving "homicide training" from Brian Harris—a retired Houston homicide detective. On March 18, 2022, Harris ran a "one-day intensive death investigation course . . . designed for personnel with little or no experience investigating death cases." Having made a favorable impression on the man paid to instruct him, Thomas touted an endorsement from Harris himself.

"Over the last few years I have been briefed on a high profile case and without question Mike Thomas, if elected, would be able to follow his instincts and make progress on a case that has been a stain on Carroll County," Harris wrote.

In other words, Thomas and his supporters were bringing the deaths of Abby and Libby into the campaign, insinuating he would be able to get results in the ongoing investigation.

Despite his success getting plaudits from out-of-towners like Harris, Thomas found it more challenging to garner support closer to home. In fact, not one of his fellow deputies gave him the nod. Deputies took to Liggett's Facebook page, leaving comments of support in his campaign-related posts. It did not, then, come as much of a surprise when Liggett ended up winning the Republican primary by a healthy margin.

In most years, that would have been the end of the story. Instead, it was just the beginning.

The unsolved Delphi murders served as a dark beacon of sorts, drawing in the unwell and the lonely. Of course most case followers were regular people interested in news about the crime and the investigation. They were able to share their thoughts on the case without resorting to spreading misinformation or engaging in antisocial behavior. A tiny but loud minority took a far more extreme approach. With all of its twists and turns, and the guessing games encouraged by the capture of the suspect's visage and voice, the case gave overly online true crime obsessives a chance to work through their anger and paranoia on the unsuspecting locals.

Time and time again, outsiders—people who were not from Delphi, Carroll County, or even Indiana—inserted themselves into the case based on misapprehensions. That is how Angela Michos Sadlowski and Sue

Wright came to be involved. Neither woman had ties to the case. Neither resided in the state of Indiana.

Sadlowski was a licensed social worker associate from Greensboro, North Carolina. In her spare time, she also moderated a Facebook group for a Canadian conspiracy theorist who became obsessed with the case and falsely claimed to be a private detective. Wright apparently lived in a small town in Michigan. Her actual identity and residence were unclear, as the address she publicly listed led to a law office in a strip mall. Her online friends knew her to be an elderly woman who complained of a bad heart. Some said she had once worked as a nurse.

The two women apparently bonded over their shared interest in the Delphi case and what seemed to be their common belief that some vague, shadowy, and undefined corruption in Carroll County was to blame for the case being unsolved.

One thing that appeared to spur them on was their support of Mike Thomas. And in fairness to Sadlowski and Wright, that was one true connection they had forged with Carroll County. Reeling from the contention within the sheriff's office, Thomas had turned to a different group for support. He set up an account on the messaging platform Discord and joined a server called "The Knot." The server had been set up as a place to discuss the Delphi case, and it boasted a few big names. Barbara MacDonald was on there. She was a journalist at HLN and the host of a popular podcast on the case. MacDonald had worked to gain the trust of Libby's family. She dined with them, checked in on them, and hugged them in front of the crowds at CrimeCon.

She did not say much on The Knot. On a previous Discord server she belonged to, she got to be far more candid there than she could be at her job at HLN. On one occasion, she explained she believed Logan was the guilty man. Thomas rarely posted, but he did lurk.

MacDonald was a journalist for a national broadcaster. Thomas was a high-ranking sheriff's deputy. The pair's presence bolstered the confidence of those on the Discord. The members began to feel as though they had an inside scoop on the case. Many became fully enamored of MacDonald's theory. After all, she was an excellent source. And Thomas was so honest, so committed to transparency, he was willing to join the ranks of Discord. Among a certain segment of online fanatics, the prevailing sentiment was that Thomas must become sheriff. Only he could root out corruption and solve the case.

Meanwhile, Liggett—who enjoyed almost unprecedented support from his colleagues—was cast as the villain. When Liggett prevailed in the primary, it was a major blow to the Discord theorists. So Sadlowski and Wright decided to step up on Thomas's behalf. They believed his opponent had only been able to win because he and his supporters had violated federal law.

Sadlowski and Wright put these allegations in a lawsuit—a case that on its first page announced it had been filed against Carroll County itself. The pair went on to call for an "investigation of the Carroll County Board of Elections, Carroll County Sheriff's Office, Sheriff Tobe Leazenby, sheriff candidate Tony Liggett, the Flora Fire Department, Financial Builders Federal Credit Union, and municipal employees of Carroll County." They accused some of the defendants of violating the Hatch Act, a 1939 federal law regulating the political activities of federal government employees. They alleged that others had failed to prosecute Hatch Act violations, including the Carroll County Board of Elections.

No legal authority agreed with them. Not even the United States Office of Special Counsel, a federal agency responsible for enforcing the Hatch Act.

So, in short, two internet sleuths sued several agencies over a law that did not apply to said agencies, and they sued an additional agency for failing to enforce a law it had no power to enforce.

The lawsuit was thrown out, and Sadlowski and Wright were ordered to pay court costs. But the damage had already been done. For those who did not read beyond headlines or carefully follow a news story through to its conclusion, an impression had been created that something dirty was going on in Carroll County. And in that climate, one man saw an opportunity.

Mark Pinkard, a forty-nine-year-old detective with the Lafayette Police Department in neighboring Tippecanoe County, decided to run in the general election as an independent candidate, filing the required paperwork about a month after Thomas lost in the primary. Liggett knew him, and had seen him at some of the primary debates. Pinkard had worked on the Delphi case in the early days.

Pinkard was soon endorsed by former candidates Hoard and Thomas. On June 22, 2022, a civilian posted on Facebook endorsing Liggett, thanking him for rushing over on his day off to answer an urgent call in the middle of the night. In the comments, Hoard posted a campaign photograph of a smiley Pinkard and taunted, "He's coming for you!"

Pinkard would also enjoy considerable support from outside the state—primarily from the internet subset that shared Sadlowski and Wright's unsupported belief that the Carroll County Sheriff's Office was corrupt and could only be cleaned up by someone other than Tony Liggett. These strident voices seemed to dominate online discourse on the election. As one example of many, Sadlowski's Canadian friend posted his feelings about the race on the "Carroll County Conspiracy" Facebook group, writing, "Vote Mark Pinkard for Sheriff. Put an end to the tyrannical system that these criminals have built."

No one, it should be stressed, ever explained precisely what it was about the legal process in Delphi that was tyrannical. Nor was it explained what Liggett had done to warrant such extreme concerns about his character, beyond his being one of the leading figures on an investigation that had not produced the results some people wanted.

Sadlowski even took more direct action in her war against Carroll County. She later claimed online to have hired someone to follow McLeland. It was unclear what exactly she hoped that that person would find. The only fruits of that surveillance that were shared publicly was a blurry image of McLeland watching a school basketball game. After the photo appeared online, some of Sadlowski's acolytes offered the utterly absurd speculation that McLeland's attendance at a school function might mean he was a secret pedophile.

Back in the sheriff's office, Leazenby reminded Liggett that he had told him so. Campaigning was indeed a roller coaster—perhaps in this case, more like a roller coaster careening off the tracks.

"You were right," Liggett said, watching the tide of hatred rolling in online. People accused him of swinging, of owning a sketchy massage parlor, of running a dogfighting ring, of covering up for child killers, and of being a child killer himself. They said Liggett was a drunk who threw key parties. Liggett felt confused. His father was an alcoholic, so he rarely drank. He loved fishing. Sometimes, at the end of the year, he would throw a fish fry for colleagues in law enforcement. Thomas had even gone to a few of those. Those parties centered around eating delicious fish, not spouse-swapping. The only time keys came up were when somebody had too much to drink, and their car keys were taken until a designated driver was procured.

Liggett shook his head. Most sheriff's elections did not become so fraught. The people stirring up the anger online did not know him. Most did not even seem to be from Indiana.

Leazenby was getting attacked too. But he was the kind of person who did not dwell on such things. Happy-go-lucky in his own way, Leazenby had the remarkable ability to decide not to care about the hate.

"Stick to a higher level," Leazenby told Liggett. "Do not stoop."

Liggett tried to keep that in mind. Most of the extreme fury came from outsiders, but it was fueled by those closer to home.

CHAPTER EIGHTEEN

Richard Allen had no idea what was coming for him. In the five and a half years since the murders, his life went on much as it had before. He was still married to his high school sweetheart, Kathy Allen, still worked at the local CVS, and still enjoyed the occasional night out playing pool. A pudgy-faced man with a white-streaked beard, large, pale eyes, and a potbelly, Allen was only five feet five.

At work, Allen was a shift manager. A longtime retail veteran with management experience at Walmart and CVS, he had a few issues with other employees. Some bore the brunt of Allen's controlling side. They felt he was a micromanager who fixated on their work and made their jobs harder. But to the rest, he was quiet, unobtrusive, and relatively well-liked by his team. Most of the CVS workers did not know him too well. He did not talk much about himself, although he would sometimes surprise everybody with his sense of humor. Back in his Walmart tenure, he displayed a darker side. Some who worked under him found him to be a leering creep, oozing desperation.

At JC's Bar and Grill on Wabash Street, Allen kept those flashes of personality under wraps. He was known as standoffish, a stark contrast with his wife's bubbly attitude. But he did not cause any problems, never had to be bodily removed from the bar. Kathy Allen was a receptionist for Horizon Veterinary Service. She struck people as a smiling, cheerful woman, so unlike her husband.

The Allens lived in a house built from sand-colored bricks on Whiteman Drive. They both came from Miami County. Allen was raised in the tiny community of Mexico, while Kathy Allen hailed from the county seat, Peru. But the Allens had lived and worked in Delphi for many years. They raised their daughter, Brittany, there, but she had since moved away. Between work and the bars and home, Allen lived a quiet, small-town life with his wife and small tan dog. Sometimes he would hang out in his garage or sit on a chair out in his driveway, drinking beer, just watching twilight fall.

Some of his tastes tended toward the macabre and strange. On computers linked to his "foojack" Gmail account, he had searched for morbid, disturbing films—the "darkest shit" and "most fucked up things" on Netflix. He wanted to watch movies about teenagers taking men prisoner and the best "kidnapping and hostage movies" ever made. He looked at strange pornography featuring elderly women defecating. Allen had searched for updates on the Delphi murders, unsurprisingly given the strong local interest. He asked existential, possibly suicidal questions: "Should I die now?"

Allen was not an especially emotionally strong man. From time to time in his career, he earned a promotion to a higher managerial position. But the new role never lasted long. The stress would overwhelm him. Every time he had to make a decision, he found himself obsessing over how people might react to it. Would they be disappointed in him? Often he would come home after work and curl up, defeated, in a fetal position on the floor. When things got that bad, he relied on the women in his life to put him back together again. Either Kathy Allen or his mother, Janis, would find the words to build him back up, to reassure him, to make him feel strong enough to face the world again.

The essential fragility of the man was sometimes replaced by sudden unpredictable outbursts of anger and violence. At least once, matters escalated to the point of Kathy Allen calling the police after her husband jammed a gun in his mouth and threatened to kill himself. But the couple stayed together, sharing an almost abnormally strong bond that outsiders sometimes found difficult to understand.

As the summer wind started to turn cold, neither of the Allens suspected the forces in motion—forces that would tear apart their life together.

September 21 was Bill Shank's birthday. He and his wife, Kathy, had had a wonderful life together, marrying on Valentine's Day in 1977 and then living in Delphi in a home not far from the courthouse. Over the years, Kathy Shank would spend a great deal of time inside that grand limestone building. As a social worker, she had seen terrible things, all manner of neglected and abused children. But she tried her best not to let any of those horrors bleed into the life she shared with Bill. He supported her throughout her career, all the times she had to head out on a case late at night, helping her do whatever she needed to do to support the county's troubled children.

Together, the couple raised a daughter. They also carefully grew flowers in their garden. But then everything changed. Bill got cancer. On October 16, 2013, he died in the home he shared with Kathy. He was seventy-three.

After that, Kathy Shank sold the house. She left Delphi, settling down about ten miles away in her hometown, Flora. She sometimes traveled out of state to visit her daughter's young family. But most of all, she volunteered, spending hours almost every week doing whatever she could to help with the investigation into the Delphi murders.

Initially, Kathy Shank acted as a sort of receptionist, greeting people when they came in, getting an idea of what information they had, and then steering them toward the officer most appropriate to receive it. As time passed and as fewer and fewer people dropped in, Kathy's role gradually morphed and she took on additional responsibilities. By the fall of 2022, she was working primarily to organize the files.

She had plenty to do. Unified Command had moved several times over the years. At that time, they occupied their own building. Folders were scattered everywhere. The information badly needed to be arranged in some semblance of order. This was the sort of work Kathy Shank was especially good at. Working in child protective services, she knew paperwork. Back in the day, law enforcement dreaded seeing Kathy Shank on the job. Her presence meant plenty of reports, a prerequisite in cases involving kids. Back when Mullin was a deputy, he had a joke for whenever she walked into the sheriff's office. He would cross two fingers in the shape of an X and hold them up at her, as if to ward off the additional reports. But all that experience meant Kathy Shank was the perfect person to tame the jumbled mess of files in the Delphi case. She felt ready for the enormous task. She liked to stack and label and categorize and then carefully sort everything into filing cabinets.

The prospect of that familiar work seemed especially welcoming when she drove to Unified Command headquarters on September 21, 2022—which, of course, was Bill's birthday. Being busy would help her take her mind off the day.

As she flipped through the folders that day, she came upon a particular tip sheet. What she read on it left her confused. Toward the end of the day, she brought it over to Liggett. He was at his desk. He was the only investigator there.

Kathy Shank handed Liggett the lead she had never heard of. "Did you know this?"

Liggett took a look. "Yes, we know that."

Kathy Shank went back to organizing. She found yet another tip sheet. It said a Department of Natural Resources officer named Dan Dulin, mere days after the murders, interviewed a male Delphi resident identified as Richard Allen Whiteman. He reported that he was on the trails on February 13, 2017, from 1:30 P.M. to 3:30 P.M. As Kathy Shank well knew, that meant the man was placing himself in the vicinity of the murders at roughly the time the killings had occurred. Not only that, but the man had recalled seeing three girls on the trail that day, specifically describing one of them as having dark hair.

The tip was labelled as "cleared."

None of this sounded right. Kathy Shank had volunteered for Unified Command for years. She knew the timeline. She had memorized the names of all the witnesses. Like the others in Unified Command, she had studied the all-important flowchart that illustrated the details of the day in February, laying out the movements of each person who had been on the trails that day. No one named Whiteman was on that chart. Or Allen. Or anyone who might conceivably be this mysterious new guy. Kathy—who had gone through hundreds of case-related files and folders—knew she had never seen those names before. She also realized that Richard Allen Whiteman was likely not the man's real name. As a former resident of Delphi, Kathy Shank knew full well that *Whiteman* was the name of a road.

What made this especially interesting to Kathy Shank was the girl with dark hair Richard Allen Whiteman had reported seeing on the trails. She was real. Her name was Railly Voorhies, and she had been walking the trails that day with her friends Breann Wilber and Anna Spath. They had all seen Bridge Guy. He had even scowled at Voorhies when she offered him a chipper greeting.

How on earth could Richard Allen Whiteman have described Railly Voorhies and her group that soon after the murders unless he had been there and seen her? And if he *had* been there and seen her, didn't that mean he was Bridge Guy—the man they had been looking for all these years?

Minutes later, Kathy Shank went back to Liggett with Dulin's lead sheet. He read it. He was about to tell her that Unified Command knew all about that one too, but he stopped himself. The man reported seeing a group of girls—the same girls who had seen Bridge Guy. Intricate timelines hung on the walls, listing all the witnesses on the trails. Those were each etched into Liggett's memory. He could wake up in the middle of the night and recite those names. But this man was not up there. Liggett froze. So did Kathy. They remained that way for some time.

When they snapped out of it, Liggett logged into ORION and got the tip narrative on Allen. He also called Mullin. "Hey, what are you doing? I think we found Bridge Guy. You ought to come back here."

CHAPTER NINETEEN

Nicholas McLeland was sitting in his office when Liggett called him. Beneath the row of cabinets behind him sat an image of his hand alongside those of his two daughters. They had each placed their palms on a computer scanner and hit the button. He listened as Liggett described what Kathy Shank found.

"There was no follow-up done on him," Liggett said. "We've got to talk to him."

McLeland had to admit that Allen certainly sounded like Bridge Guy. But he did not want to allow himself to get too excited. He could not afford to jump to conclusions. The investigators would need to find probable cause against him before they could move forward.

Dulin was busy with some administrative work when his office phone rang. The caller was Mullin. The prosecutor's investigator wanted to know if the name *Allen* meant anything to Dulin. It did not.

Mullin requested any information Dulin had on Richard Allen of Delphi. Dulin pulled out a thick Department of Natural Resources binder and flipped through it. He also checked the DNR's point-of-sale system for fishing and hunting licenses. He discovered fishing licenses for Richard and Kathy Allen, which also included their addresses, phone numbers, heights, and weights. The credit card and IP address for the purchases came back to Allen.

But something was strange about the entries. Before April 1, 2017, Allen listed his height as five feet four. After that date, he grew two inches to five feet six. He also claimed to have dropped fifteen pounds. Weight loss was within the realm of possibility, but adults did not usually shoot up two inches.

Mullin explained that Shank had uncovered a lead sheet. The detail about a man who walked the trails while staring at a stock ticker sparked a memory. Dulin found himself dragged back to that long-forgotten conversation in the Save A Lot parking lot.

By this time, it was twilight. Holeman was out of the office, burning brush on the other side of the ditch that lined his land. When Liggett's call came, he was sitting on his tractor, watching the fire.

Liggett started off the conversation with an odd question. "Hey, do you know Richard Allen or Richard Allen Whiteman?"

"No," Holeman said. "Doesn't ring a bell. Why?"

"That's Bridge Guy."

Holeman leaned back on the tractor. "The fuck?"

"That's Bridge Guy, Jerry." Liggett was speaking faster than he usually did. "I'm telling you, this is Bridge Guy. I know it's Bridge Guy." He quickly ran through the tale of what Kathy Shank had rediscovered.

Smoke hung in the darkening sky. Liggett—the eternally blunt devil's advocate who kicked down every theory that came up in the case—actually sounded hopeful that an answer had come at long last. Holeman did not know whether he found that encouraging or alarming. "Okay, Tony—well, calm down."

"You know I don't get excited about this. And people thought it was this guy and this guy, and I was always like, 'Nah.' But I'm telling you, it's this guy."

Holeman absorbed what Liggett was telling him. "What do we need to do? What do you want?"

"Let's run him through the Fusion Center." That was the intelligence branch of the Indiana State Police. "I want to find out . . . vehicles, where he worked, where he lived, who he's been married to, does he have any kids?"

"Okay, full meal deal. I got you. I'll send it up."

Holeman immediately called the Fusion Center. He spoke with an ISP intelligence analyst who had access to a trove of records—social media data, vehicles, phone numbers, residences, and more. She sent back everything she found.

Word spread quickly. Over the next day or so, Holeman called Buckley to deliver the news and then drove over to Vido's house. The detective—who had since been promoted—had taken some time off work. For years he had toiled on the horrific Kegan Kline case and the Delphi murders simultaneously, which had meant viewing all manner of horrors. Investigating the possibility of a link between Kline and Delphi had not resulted in answers. Most investigators worked multiple cases, mitigating the sense of failure when progress slows in one. Vido had played a key role in putting Kline away, but he felt he had struck out on Delphi. It had taken a toll. Vido felt he had not been spending enough time with his family. He was on a break from work. Holeman found the detective in his front yard, laying down sod.

Kneeling in the dirt, Vido felt a wave of shock come over him as Holeman explained the new lead. Allen certainly sounded like Bridge Guy. Vido wanted to know everything. He wanted to hit the shower and then hurry back to the Unified Command center. But first he needed to plant all the sod before it rotted on the pallet.

Holeman got to work helping him. His knees would not let him do much, so he broke out a tractor instead and started tilling the ground. As they planted the green squares together, Vido decided to drop the rest of his time off. He needed to get back to work.

The full group met up at Unified Command and reviewed what they had learned from the analyst. The man's actual name was Richard Allen, and he lived on Whiteman Drive. Somehow those details got written down wrong. Dulin's attempt to correct the mistake had not stuck. The disaster was compounded when somebody marked the tip as cleared. Those two clerical errors were enough to bury the lead for years, beneath all the useless suggestions about genetic genealogy and Sasquatches and deadbeat fathers. The road to hell had not been paved with good intentions so much as flooded with them, resulting in an impassable mire that had taken years to fight through. Kathy Shank had blasted through all of that in a single afternoon.

But the tip took some explaining. Liggett ended up in an unusual position. The devil's advocate found himself on trial, arguing for an angle he actually believed in. The other investigators took a little joy in trying to kick down the facts. One by one, though, the other members of Unified Command found themselves swayed.

On paper, nothing about Allen contradicted any commonly held beliefs about Bridge Guy. He was a middle-aged Caucasian male. He was local to Delphi, holding down a job at the town's CVS. Other than Voorhies and her group, he said he saw nobody on his walk to the High Bridge. He was too busy staring at the stock ticker on his phone.

That detail about his phone was odd because his phone never turned up in the tower data, which detailed the presence of phones in the area. All those years ago, Dulin had taken special care to jot down Allen's mobile equipment identifier (MEID). The investigators pulled the Bureau of Motor Vehicles records for Allen's car. In 2017, he drove a black 2016 Ford Focus Special Edition, a fuel-efficient midrange option. Taking the obvious next step, Mullin pulled up the Hoosier Harvestore video, which depicted the traffic in the vicinity of the crime scene on the day of the murder.

At 1:27 P.M., a black Ford Focus zoomed across the screen. If that was indeed Allen's vehicle, it would put him in the area of the trails at exactly the same time he had told Dulin he was there. But could they be certain it was Allen's car? Over and over, the men watched the image of the car speeding by, hoping to find some sort of identifying feature—something unique to confirm the vehicle was his or rule that possibility out.

They found something.

The tire rims on the car in the video were unusual. Light streamed through them. That was not a standard feature for the Ford Focus. So—what sort of rims were on Richard Allen's car?

To find out, Liggett drove over to the CVS parking lot, which was just a short distance away from the front door of the sheriff's office. Liggett was confident his plain black Ford truck would not attract any notice. He circled through the mostly empty lot. When he found Allen's Ford Focus, he pulled out his phone and took pictures. Sunlight shone through the rims.

Holeman and the others looked at the photos. They had to agree with Liggett. Things were starting to stack. They called McLeland. The prosecutor listened as the investigators of Unified Command rattled off the latest developments. McLeland agreed; the news was promising. But it was not probable cause. For the case to go forward, somebody needed to interview Allen. They needed fresh information that could be put into an affidavit and used to justify a search of Allen's property.

During all those years after he first approached Dulin outside the Save A Lot, Allen had never had to answer difficult questions about that winter's day. That would soon change.

CHAPTER TWENTY

Exactly five years and eight months—or 2,008 days—after he shuffled down the trails of Delphi, Richard Allen was headed to talk to investigators. He visited the Delphi investigation center on Thursday, October 13, 2022.

By then, the Unified Command team had spent weeks studying what little public information they could find about Allen. Unlike other persons of interest, he did not have any criminal record. No history of violence. No known links to the girls or their families.

Allen had already provided valuable intelligence to investigators. Speaking to Dulin years ago, he claimed to have parked at a Farm Bureau building. Investigators imagined he was referring to the abandoned Child Protective Services building, alongside which witnesses had spotted a mysterious vehicle parked during the afternoon of the murders.

But Unified Command needed much more.

McLeland informed them that the information Dulin gathered years ago was stale from a legal standpoint. If the investigators could not reconfirm Allen's statements about his whereabouts, garments, and movements that day, they would have nothing fresh enough for a search warrant. And if Allen declined the interview, they would lose their only chance to surprise him. He could easily slip away once more.

The members of Unified Command devised a plan. The whole operation was far-flung and intricately choreographed. Everyone had their roles. Liggett and Mullin would take on Allen.

Together, they drove up to his house and knocked on his door. The two investigators had both watched so many promising leads burn out. They approached Allen with a detached coolness. They were there to get information. Once they had that, they could either clear Allen, or pursue him.

Allen opened the door. The investigators explained they were there about the Delphi case. They were following up on some early leads. Allen looked a bit surprised, but he recovered well enough. He told them he only needed a moment to get ready. He permitted the investigators to step inside his home. Liggett noticed some taxidermied fish hanging on the wall. Allen explained that he had caught them in Deer Creek.

While the investigators stood around waiting, Allen disappeared to use the restroom or find his shoes or change his clothes. Then he ushered them to his garage, where he lit a cigarette. He needed a smoke before he headed out. They all left to go to Unified Command's headquarters together. Allen readily got into Mullin's unmarked 2014 Buick, knowing he could leave at any time.

When they arrived at headquarters, Mullin and Liggett even showed him around the place so he could get out on his own if he decided to leave.

Investigators would sell him on the idea that it was just a routine check-in on a forgotten witness, with mild-mannered Mullin taking the lead. Taciturn and wearing a brown sheriff's office polo, Liggett would interject only when necessary. He did not mind. He thought Mullin was the best interviewer he ever sat in a room with. Kind and nonthreatening, the prosecutor's investigator had a way of building rapport with subjects. That might not last, though. Depending on Allen's answers, the questions might get tougher as the interview went on.

The investigators and their new person of interest filed into the drab interview room. They settled down in chairs around a narrow white table. Allen sat on one side, facing the investigators. He was clad in jeans and a black long-sleeved shirt. He wore a mustache, white streaked with brown, and his whitish beard trickled down from his chin.

Clearly relaxed, Allen listened to the friendly prosecutor's investigator read him his Miranda rights. That was just a "formality," Mullin assured him.

"I want to make sure you understand you're not under arrest or anything like that, okay?" Mullin held up his palms, in a placating gesture. "And the door here is open. You can leave at any time you want. Would be glad to give you a ride back or whatever."

Allen made a move to bolt toward the door. He and Mullin shared a brief laugh. Then Mullin placed a Miranda waiver before him.

"Okay." Allen signed the piece of paper.

Nearby, in a sparse back room, Holeman watched Allen on a little closed-circuit television. He was not alone. Vido, Harshman, Davies, and Buckley were there too, along with other detectives from the Lafayette post like A.J. Smith and Josh Edwards. They all wanted to observe Allen, to hear him speak. They wanted to see if he was anything like Bridge Guy. When Allen did open his mouth, Holeman was struck by the voice coming through the TV speakers. The tone ranged from gravelly to unexpectedly high. But he sounded familiar.

"That's the Bridge Guy audio," Vido said.

And, considering his stout but short frame, none of the detectives had any problem imagining him staggering across the bridge and muttering his orders to the girls. "Down the hill." The investigators had listened to the audio hundreds of times.

Back in the interview room, Liggett told Allen, "We're just going back to the beginning of the case and we know you had talked to Lieutenant Dulin. We just want to figure out what you saw when you were out there."

But first, they needed some basic information from Allen. Leaning on the table with his arms crossed, he told the detectives he was fifty years-old.

"I'm in the fifty-year-old club this year, too," Liggett said.

"I'm beyond that, actually," Mullin said.

Allen looked up from the form he was filling out. His voice filled with mock surprise. "No!" He was comfortable enough to kid around with the investigators.

Allen chatted breezily about his five decades on earth. He talked about his phone, his marriage, his twenty-eight-year-old daughter, Brittany, and her Canadian husband, Paulo. He and the investigators shared a bit of a laugh when Allen mentioned he was from Mexico—the Indiana town, not the country.

A quiet man who claimed to care deeply about what others thought about him, Allen had grown up in Miami County, running track and playing football in school. As an adult, he served in the National Guard and attended courses at Ivy Tech. He was not a religious man. When he was growing up, his parents were not churchgoers.

He had faced his share of troubles. He talked about his high blood pressure and cholesterol, as well as his depression and anxiety. In 2010, he suffered a heart attack that required a few stents. He shared his work disappointments. In 2013, he ditched Walmart after a decade-long tenure that saw him rise to a leadership role and flame out. Then he went to work at CVS. The same thing happened twice. First, he served as a manager at the location in Peru. Later he moved to the one in Delphi, the city's only pharmacy. Allen said the retail management jobs "just didn't work out" the way he had hoped because they forced him to fixate on bureaucracy and spreadsheets. One job left him so exhausted that he crashed his car after falling asleep at the wheel.

Allen also provided a few basic facts about his online life. He had an Android phone back in 2017. He had email accounts with Google, Yahoo, and Frontier. His cellular provider was Ting Mobile.

The investigators soon guided their quarry to the morning of the killings. Allen had that day off. He said he spent time with his mother, Janis. She was recovering from hip surgery. His half-sister Jamie showed up, and the Allens were all set to go eat lunch together. For reasons he did not make clear, Allen chose not to join them.

"I wasn't about that," he said.

Instead, he departed around 11:00 A.M. and headed back to Delphi alone.

Unbeknownst to him, as he chattered away, investigators were running down all the people closest to him. There was a good possibility that once his family members realized Allen was on law enforcement's radar, they would refuse to talk. If so, the only chance investigators might get to speak with them would be now, while Allen was distracted.

Harper and a United States Marshal went out to interview Kathy Allen. Brooks Johnson, a first sergeant at the post in Bremen, headed to Nappanee, a city in northern Indiana where Allen's daughter, Brittany, lived. Throughout Mullin and Liggett's interview, Holeman kept checking his phone for updates. But he looked up when he heard Allen lie.

In 2017, Allen told Dulin he had been at the trails around 1:30 P.M. But now he abruptly switched up the timeline, claiming to have arrived around noon, after grabbing a jacket at home. The day he went out to the trails was "warmer than normal." He saw a group of girls. He said nothing to them. He saw no one else. But then again, he said he was a bit distracted, watching his stocks on Datek, an online brokerage service. Later, when he got to the Monon High Bridge, he clambered onto the first platform and gazed down at the fish swimming in the creek. Before leaving the trails, he rested on a bench for a few minutes. He said he was gone by around one o'clock.

Allen was now telling them he had left before the girls had even arrived. The investigators wanted to lock him into that little black car zooming across the footage from the Hoosier Harvestore. So they pushed back a bit.

"Which way do you think you would have traveled to get to this building that particular day?" Mullin asked.

Allen pondered the question. He said he went to the trails regularly, though as little as once a month or as often as twice a week. Typically, Allen would drive "through town." Mullin knew exactly what that meant. That route would not lead past the Hoosier Harvestore. He kept prodding. Allen said he did not recall which way he drove on the day of the murders. He conceded that while he typically took the town route, he had accidentally come the other way before. That other route, the "country" route, would have taken him straight past the Hoosier Harvestore. So it was possible he had gone a different route. One telling detail was that Allen claimed to have seen the parking lot near the trails had cars in it, and that he drove onward to find a different place to park. In order to see that, he would have had to be on the route that would take him right past the Hoosier Harvestore.

As far as vehicle choice, Allen indicated he normally took his other car on shorter drives. For a trip to Peru, though, the Ford Focus was the more reliable vehicle. Later, he tried to back off of that and declared that he could not remember which car he drove.

Sitting across from the investigators, Allen presented a gregarious front. But as he recounted the day, a restlessness seeped into his affect. And a certain defensiveness. Of course, he said, he had not kept his presence on the trails a secret. He had told his wife. After news of the murders hit, she pushed him to act. Kathy Allen told him that authorities were looking for people who had walked the trails that day, people who might have seen something. That was why he had called into the tip line. But he only vaguely remembered talking to Dulin.

"What were you wearing that day?" Liggett asked him.

Allen described Bridge Guy's outfit. Blue jeans. A hoodie sweatshirt. A dark blue or black jacket, either Carhartt or a similar knockoff. Older tennis shoes or combat boots. A skullcap. Allen noted that he always kept one in his jacket.

Mullin wanted Allen's phone. An extraction would allow them to check for possible connections between Allen and the victims, or between Allen and the Klines. They could scan for CSAM or suspicious searches. Mullin asked Allen if he was okay with them extracting his phone. It was a standard question.

Allen balked—as if he only then realized the seriousness of his situation. "I'm not going to be somebody's fall guy," he said. But his affability was only cracked, not shattered. He promised the investigators he was not questioning their integrity.

"We're talking to everyone that was out there that day," Liggett told him. The questioning was nothing personal.

But Allen's cheeriness took yet another hit when Liggett and Mullin asked permission to search his house. First, Allen politely suggested that he would allow a search if they obtained a warrant. He then asked to talk over the decision with his wife. Nervously, he told the investigators that he and his wife were regular viewers of *Dateline*, a popular crime series. This meant he knew how the process worked.

The idea of police getting ahold of his phones bothered him. "Am I an angel of a person? No." He held up his hands and smiled, bitterly. "I mean, I'm like everybody else. And I guess I don't want you . . . maybe I don't want you looking at every website I've visited. And so I think I'll talk to my wife and if she's cool with it then we'll do it."

He also assured them he was not an idiot. While he understood the police were after closure for the families of the girls, there were things he wanted to remain concealed. The investigators argued that they were only doing their jobs.

Allen asserted that he understood that, but he had nothing to do with such a "horrible thing."

"My wife doesn't even know I'm here talking to people," he said.

Even as the tension ramped up, Allen maintained a relatively calm, matter-of-fact demeanor. Again and again, he deferred to Kathy Allen in his conversation with police. "I'm going to talk to my wife before I do anything. This affects her as much as it affects me."

At one point, Mullin's phone rang. He knew McLeland was calling. The prosecutor had told his investigator to keep him updated. He was not watching the interview live, but he wanted hourly check-ins. Mullin let the call go unanswered.

After that back-and-forth, Liggett and Mullin stepped out for a moment. Shifting in his seat, with one arm draped over the chair next to him, Allen stared at his phone. Then he set it down and sat very still. His pudgy face took on a pinched quality. In the back room, Holeman kept checking for updates from the team conducting the family interviews. One by one, they rolled in.

Brittany was quiet. She did not say much to Johnson. But Allen's wife had plenty of things to share.

Kathy Allen told Harper and the marshal that her husband had a history of anxiety and depression. He had engaged in disturbing suicidal behavior. Once, in front of his wife and daughter, he had put a gun in his mouth and threatened to pull the trigger.

Just after the murders happened, he confided in his wife that he had been out on the trails that day. But he denied ever going on the bridge. She had to convince him to take that information to the police. He had been so reluctant to call in the tip. Before that, he had also dissuaded her from helping with the searches for the girls. She also confirmed that Allen owned a gun, along with a collection of knives and a Carhartt jacket that was still in the closet.

Holeman relayed all of that to Liggett and Mullin before they returned to the interview room, carrying pictures. Mullin pulled his chair up so he was sitting on the side of the table, much closer to Allen. The investigators first showed Allen a printout from the Hoosier Harvestore video. He denied recognizing his car. Then the investigators revealed something that seemed to shock Allen. They explained that they had talked to his wife and daughter. There was a lot to clear up.

"We've heard that you have some issues," Mullin said.

They knew about the suicide threat. All of Allen's mental health struggles. And they had gotten all of that information by going around his back and talking to his family.

The next picture they pulled out was of Bridge Guy. Allen laughed. Behind him, light filtered into the room through the single window's thin, diamond-patterned curtains. "I've never met these girls," he said. "If [the photo] was taken with the girl's phone, it wasn't me."

Liggett pointed out that the Bridge Guy dressed identically to the way Allen had described his own clothes.

Still marveling over the fact that police had talked to his wife, Allen argued that nobody who really knew him would say he was a murderer. "If you want to arrest me, that's fine," Allen said.

A few times, he declared that he was done with the talk, that he felt the interview had shifted into an outright interrogation. He repeated himself, noting that investigators had gone behind his back to talk to his family members. Darkly, he told them they had lost his trust.

"This seems to have taken a turn, you know?" he asked.

Still, Allen never made a move to get up.

Liggett touched the picture of Bridge Guy. "We just need to know what happened."

"It's not me," Allen said. "You're not going to make me believe it's me. You're not going to find anything that ties me to those murders, so I'm not really that concerned."

Keeping his voice low and soothing, Mullin told Allen, "I believe you're a nice guy."

Allen chuckled. "Oh, okay."

Things only got more heated from there. The investigators and the person of interest started talking over one another.

Allen's tone became sneering and petulant as he sat frozen in his seat.

He was furious that the investigators had talked to his wife. He was angry that they seemed to be implying that he could be involved in the murders. And still, Mullin asserted that he believed Allen was "not a mean fellow." He was giving Allen an opening to confess. But Allen was adamant. He was not Bridge Guy. Liggett left the room. It was all down to Mullin and Allen.

"Is that person you?" Mullin tapped the picture of Bridge Guy. "That's the question we have to answer. If that person is you, we know this person followed the girls all the way to the other side of the bridge and then told them to go down the hill."

But Allen kept denying that he could have anything to do with the murders. Finally, he put a stop to the questioning.

"You've lost my trust. I'm not going to talk to you anymore. This is stupid. Now you've pissed me off."

"Well I'm sorry about that," Mullin said, meekly.

"Are you arresting me?"

Mullin told him that he just wanted to get things worked out.

"Am I free to leave or not?"

Quietly, Mullin told him, "You've always been free to leave."

"Thank you." Allen stood up. Then he paused and glared at Mullin. "You're an asshole." With that, Allen stomped out of the room. Mullin followed him.

Rushing out of the back room, Vido hurried after the suspect. He caught up with Allen as he stormed out of the Unified Command center. Vido asked him to come back, to at least talk to him. But Allen was furious and on the defensive. He raised his voice at Vido, saying he cared deeply about what others thought of him.

"If you care about what people think of you, come in and talk to me," Vido told him. "I've talked to hundreds of people for this case. A majority of them are willing to do everything that they can to clear their name from this investigation."

But Allen refused to help. He knew the police thought he was a killer. He was done.

After the interview, Liggett, Mullin, and Holeman agreed that they had probable cause for a search. They had gotten exactly what they needed; Allen had refreshed and confirmed all the old, stale information. He admitted to walking the trails that day, specifically on the bridge. He said he was dressed identically to Bridge Guy. He said he passed by the girls who reported seeing Bridge Guy.

The investigators' opinions ultimately did not matter; what counted was the view of Nicholas McLeland, Carroll County prosecutor.

McLeland was not the kind of prosecutor to get pushed around. He had made that clear over the course of the Delphi investigation. Even when investigators were leaning toward other suspects, he never got overly excited. Some within Unified Command, including Holeman, wanted him to consider filing charges on Kline. There were a few meetings where those investigators would practically back McLeland into a corner, telling him that the time had come to file. But the prosecutor held firm, adamant that he needed evidence tying a suspect to the crime scene. In the end, that had been the right call.

If the investigators were going to compel McLeland to file warrants on Allen, they would have a lot of convincing to do.

McLeland needed enough to file a strong probable cause affidavit. Something that would withstand attack. Something that would not get suppressed.

Holeman, Liggett, and Mullin went over the whole case again. And again. They wrung as much probable cause as they could from the facts. Finally, they convinced McLeland. The four men put the search warrant together.

Written over several hours, amid debate and anxiety about the newly unfolding lead, the affidavit was an imperfect document. Rife with grammatical errors, it also included factual mistakes, such as incorrectly locating the crucial phone beneath Libby's body instead of Abby's. Jumbling together all kinds of information about the witness sightings of Bridge Guy and various automobiles, the affidavit was less a persuasive essay arguing for the existence of probable cause and more of a somewhat indecipherable litany of facts. Nobody was completely happy with it, but now that they had an actual lead to chase, there seemed little point in waiting around. Allen now knew he was a suspect. The affidavit did not need to be perfect. It just had to be good enough.

Liggett offered to be the affiant.

"Tony, are you sure you want to do this?" Holeman asked. He was concerned that with the sheriff election, Liggett was taking on too much. "If you want, I'll have Jay Harper do it."

The murders were a county case. Liggett replied that he could do it.

From there, McLeland called Judge Benjamin Diener. Then he and Liggett headed off to Allen's house to present the warrant. McLeland made sure to call the judge ahead of time, to ensure they were not interrupting anything. Holeman went straight to Whiteman Drive. Around five o'clock in the afternoon, police descended on the little ranch home.

The investigators marched down the Allens' neat cement walkway, past the patch of ivy where a stone cat lurked near a statuette that resembled Hebe—the goddess of youth—baring one breast and clutching a plate and cup. A metal disc emblazoned with a silhouette of the sun stared out at the detectives as they knocked on the door.

Vido ran the search. He got to work straightaway. First, he secured the scene. Then he talked to Kathy Allen. Next, Vido went and interviewed the neighbors. He did not get much information from them. They did not know the Allens well. They felt the family kept to themselves. All they really knew about Allen was that he hung out in his garage quite a lot. Vido headed back to the house. He ran into Allen again, but the man was still not interested in further conversations.

As the supervisor on the scene, Holeman also approached the Allens. He needed to explain a few practical matters to them. He found the couple sitting in a van, watching the parade of uniformed troops invading their home. The Allens emerged to listen to Holeman explain that the police had a search warrant, and that Holeman wanted to do a walkthrough to take photographs of the house. That way, if anything got damaged, the Allens could document it and get compensated. Kathy Allen clambered back into the van. Allen followed Holeman over toward the house.

"If there's anything already broke, let me know," Holeman said. "If we break something, there's a process that you can start and get reimbursed for it."

Allen turned his pale gaze to Holeman. "It doesn't matter. It's over."

Holeman paused. In a perfect world, he would have gotten Allen's bizarre comment on tape. But he had not planned on interviewing Allen, had not imagined the man would say anything worth preserving. Holeman did not even have a digital recorder on him. He was only there as a supervisor, explaining the process.

On search and seizure operations, "old guys"—higher ups—are barely tolerated. They are widely considered a distraction at best and an outright nuisance at worst. As such, they are often banished to lesser assignments like watching the back door. So, after his exchange with Allen, Holeman decided to stay out of the way and hang out in his car.

Troopers flooded into the home and began searching the place. They hurried past the little tiled fireplace, the master queen bed, and the greenish blue kitchen cabinets. They were looking for clothing. Knives. Allen's firearm. Anything that could connect him to the murders. In the back, they found a bonfire area, heaped with ashes.

In the house, Vido directed the others. The Allen residence was relatively clean and tidy. Cats scampered away from the searchers. Troopers hauled away a closetful of Allen's clothing, including dirty boots, a blue Carhartt coat, skullcaps from Adidas and the Indianapolis Colts, ten pairs of gloves, and one lonely spare.

Vido walked around with Trooper Mathew Clemens, who snapped photographs. They went through the garage, the kitchen, the laundry room, the office, and the spare bedroom. In the garage, they found the Ford Focus with light shining through its wheels, along with box cutters and knives. In the kitchen, a little basket on the countertop held keys, Allen's name tag, and more knives and box cutters, all the items he carried with him on a daily basis. In the spare bedroom, a photo album dating back to 2008 held pictures of the Allen family on the trails of Delphi. A photograph dated February 2016 showed "Ricky" posing by a tree. Another picture from a month later showed a fishing trip to Deer Creek, down off the Monon trail. Allen had spent quite a bit of time on the trails by the High Bridge. Vido ended up taking some pictures of the albums too. Those seemed quite important. Allen was no stranger to the trails.

Investigators also dug through a plastic bag piled high with Allen's old technology. They seized seventeen phones, but one phone was conspicuous in its absence. The phone that Allen used in 2017 was not there. Dulin had written down its MEID number. It was nowhere to be found. There were plenty of laptops, chargers, and pagers though.

Allen owned a trove of knives too. Seventeen were found throughout the garage and the master bedroom. Vido and Harper sorted through the weapons: silver-bladed knives, rusty knives, filet knives, folding knives, knives with handles of wood and ivory, knives with gold guards, knives from brands like Gerber, Old Timer, Ozark Trail, Rapala, Sabre, Sharp, and Best Defense. There were four multi-tools—devices containing different metallic implements, including knife blades—in red, blue, black, and green and gold. They even found a small katana with a bright red tassel.

Investigators took a custom vehicle operations motorcycle cover bag, along with a motorcycle cover. Working with Clemens, Harper also sealed up an envelope containing a cutting from the carpeted area beneath the spare tire of Allen's Ford Focus. That was marked for a lab exam. Technicians swabbed the driver's lap and shoulder belts from the Ford Focus, as well as the passenger side of the carpeted floorboards.

The most crucial find was carried out of the Allen residence in a sealed cardboard box. Contained within was a loaded black SIG Sauer P226 pistol that Liggett found in Allen's nightstand. Police noted garments from the man's CVS uniform peeled off nearby, designating his side of the bed. There was a gun case in the master closet. The handgun used .40 S&W rounds. The unspent cartridge found between the bodies was a .40 S&W cartridge. There was plenty of Blaser ammunition in the house. Troopers confiscated a trigger lock, an empty white Winchester Supreme Elite ammo box, and a sealed plastic bag with two magazines.

Night fell, and the air grew cold. Through his windshield, Holeman watched troopers move in and out of the house carrying boxes. Nearby, a cigarette tip glowed orange in the darkness. Allen had departed his own vehicle to smoke a few cigarettes. Blowing smoke out of his mouth, he strolled over to where Holeman was parked.

"Hey, can I sit in your car?" he asked. "My wife has to use the bathroom." Barred from her home, Kathy Allen had left her husband alone as she drove off to use the restroom at the veterinary office where she worked.

"All right, no problem," Holeman said. "Yeah, you can sit in here."

Allen climbed into the back of his car. They sat in silence for some time.

"Can I get out to smoke a cigarette?" Allen eventually asked.

"Yeah." Holeman watched Allen smoke. He then went back to what he had been doing before: using his phone to scroll through sales listings for pedal tractors.

Sliding into the back seat, Allen hovered behind him for a moment. "Oh, you like pedal tractors?"

"Yeah. I collect them." Holeman told Allen he owned five or six. Exactly how many, he could not quite remember.

"Oh, that's cool." As the troopers went through his house and seized his property, Allen spoke with Holeman about pedal tractors. Then he abruptly changed the subject. "Did you guys detain my wife?"

"What?"

Allen repeated the question.

"No. For what?" Holeman asked.

"I don't know. She's been gone an awful long time."

"Well, I know where she works. I can take you out there if you want."

"No, no. It's over anyway. It doesn't matter. It's over."

A vehicle soon rumbled up to the house. Kathy Allen had returned. She emerged from the car with a friend. They were both crying. Allen left Holeman to go speak with her.

Inside, Vido watched a United States Marshal pick his way through Allen's nightstand. There, the marshal discovered a wooden keepsake box. He and Vido searched through it. Within, Allen had stored pictures from his National Guard days, employment documents, a letter from his mother, photographs of his daughter, Brittany, and a variety of patches, pens, and coins. Something brassy glinted among Allen's little personal treasures. Vido felt like he had just been punched in the gut. He was staring at a single Smith & Wesson Winchester .40-caliber cartridge: the same type of cartridge discovered at the crime scene.

As the troopers finished up, Holeman sought out Allen once more. He wanted to do another walkthrough so Allen could see the lack of damage for himself.

Moving through the home, Holeman told Allen he would soon send him a list of all the items they had seized.

"It might be a day or two, but paperwork takes us a while," Holeman said. "We didn't bust any holes. We didn't put things back in the proper place, probably. We took clothes out—we probably didn't refold them, we just stuffed them back in. But we didn't damage anything."

Throughout Holeman's routine speech, Allen kept replying the same thing again and again. "It doesn't matter, it's over."

As the search ended, Vido, Liggett, and a marshal spoke about some of the evidence collected from the home: knives, boots, the carpet cutting from the Ford Focus, and the SIG Sauer.

Vido brought up the cartridge in the keepsake box. The rest of the ammunition in the house seemed to be Blaser—all except that one, left nestled in with Allen's prized possessions.

Only time—and the forensics examiners—would tell if the cartridge at the scene even matched Allen's SIG Sauer. But the cartridge from the keepsake box haunted the investigators that night. What would make a round worth treasuring alongside precious memories?

CHAPTER TWENTY-ONE

All the evidence seized from the Allen home was hand-delivered to the forensic examiners at the Indianapolis lab.

Once again, the task of testing those items fell to Oberg and Bozinovski. The case thus far had not proved forensically rich. Oberg had a few inconclusive and negative results. Bozinovski could not find any offender DNA.

Bozinovski got the first crack at the S&W cartridge. She swabbed the brass for DNA but did not discover any. Next, it was Oberg's turn. She accepted the cartridge ensconced in a sealed envelope that was itself concealed in a paper bag. She also examined and classified Allen's SIG Sauer, measuring the gun from every angle. She ejected several cartridges from the firearm. They did not leave particularly strong marks. A lot of that depended on the force of the racking. Oberg fired the gun, then ejected the fired round. That provided more clarity. She set out to compare the two cartridges, the one from the crime scene and the one from Allen's firearm.

Oberg stared through the lens of her microscope at the canyons and cliffs. Then she took a step back. She called Harper. He did not pick up. She called again. She needed to talk to him. It was urgent.

In the days since the search, the initial burst of activity had faded. Investigators were now waiting to hear from the lab. If the cartridge at the scene came from Allen's SIG Sauer, or better yet, if they found blood from the victims on any of his possessions, they had a case. If not, the whole thing might unravel.

Back in Lafayette, Holeman received an alarming call from one of his superiors, Lieutenant Colonel Kevin Hobson. He sounded displeased. "I don't know what kind of operation you're running. I don't know how you get your troopers to lie for you, but I just talked to Dave Vido and Harshman. I don't know what you told them, but they're scared to death of you."

Holeman was baffled. "What're you talking about? Nobody's scared of me. I treat everybody nice. Why would they be scared of me?"

"They wouldn't tell me if the gun came back to that round."

"What're you talking about? I haven't got anything back from the lab."

That was not what Hobson had heard though. Major Sid Newton had just called him with news. "He says Melissa Oberg just came down and said the gun matched a round that you guys found on the scene."

"Are you fucking with me? Because this ain't funny."

"No, no. I'm dead serious."

"I got to go." Holeman hung up on the lieutenant colonel and rang Oberg. "Melissa, why didn't you call us?"

She had tried, she said. The forensic examiner had been ringing Harper all day, eager to share the news that she identified the round recovered from the crime scene as having been cycled through Allen's gun. Unbeknownst to her, Harper was busy qualifying on the range.

Holeman got off the call and proceeded to ring Harper himself. He tried to get ahold of everyone he could. Then he thought better of it and rang back Oberg. He wanted to make sure she was confident in her results. Oberg said she was sure. She was not the only examiner who came to that determination either. Her supervisor, Mark Keisler, had checked and verified her work without even knowing her findings. He ran the lab's Forensic Firearms Identification Unit and had previously served as president of the Association of Firearm and Tool Mark Examiners.

Holeman called McLeland. He called Liggett. He called everyone he could and told them the bullet was a match. Holeman even arranged for Oberg to come in and meet with Unified Command.

She explained to the group that in her expert opinion, the minute striations and impressions punched into the cartridge corresponded to the components of the firearm. There was sufficient agreement to conclude that the cartridge found lying between the girls had been ejected from the gun Allen had owned since 2001.

Oberg went over all the guns she had tested. Some of them she had excluded. Others were inconclusive. If the investigators could wrangle any of the guns back into the lab, she could probably rule them out now that she had a positive result.

Excited, Holeman called Bozinovski. He wanted to know if there was any other good news on the forensics front.

"Nope," Bozinovski replied. "I haven't found anything, but we're still working on it."

The investigators waited. They debated. The cartridge was good evidence. But hypothetically, Allen could argue that somebody had borrowed his gun, or that he frequently shot targets out there. They needed to rule out any other possibilities. They needed to see if he could explain himself.

But Liggett had trouble imagining how Allen could wave away so many coincidences.

"That's him on the video," he said. "I'm telling you. That is him. It looks like him. Sounds like him. That is him. We got his car on video. We got these girls describing him, and now we got this round. He put himself there." Liggett kept going back to that. "He said he was there."

One topic that never came up in their discussion was the fact that the sheriff's election—in which, of course, Liggett was a candidate—was fast approaching. It did not occur to any of them that the election should factor into their decision-making. They had aggressively followed the evidence they received when it came to their attention; nothing had been delayed so that an arrest would more closely coincide with the time for voters to visit the polls. Perhaps someone concerned with optics might have suggested waiting until after the election to move on Allen—but that would have meant allowing a possible killer who knew he was the target of a murder investigation to remain free for weeks, giving him the chance to harm others or himself.

That was the crucial point for the detectives. As far as they were concerned, a murderer was wandering around Delphi. They were eager to arrest him.

"Slow down, slow down," McLeland told the investigators. They were close, but he did not think they were there just yet.

There was no way around it. They would need to interview Allen again.

Mullin did not want another go-round. His polite manner had clearly ticked off Allen.

"Well," Mullin recalled, "he called me a donkey butt." Since Mullin did not swear, "asshole" somehow became "donkey butt" in his retelling.

Liggett felt he, too, had failed to build up much of a connection with Allen.

That left Holeman. He did not want to do it. He had once considered himself an excellent interviewer. As a detective, he had locked suspects into phony alibis and gotten confessions in drug investigations. But that was years ago, before he started "riding the desk" as a supervisor. In Holeman's view, some of the other investigators were acting as though he had built up a whole relationship with Allen. During the search, he had only had a few brief—and frankly odd—interactions with the man.

But others in the group insisted. Feeling he had drawn the short straw, Holeman finally agreed. With that point settled, another problem for the investigators to grapple with remained: How on earth would they get Allen to agree to a second interview?

There was no guarantee he would not just hire a lawyer and refuse to talk further. The investigators still had one card to play though. They had the Ford Focus, which they had seized during the search. If Allen wanted his car back, he would need to deal with them.

Mullin had Allen's number. He called and set up a time for Allen to pick up his car at the Lafayette post. That day came and went. Allen never appeared.

The investigators were despondent.

"What the fuck?" Holeman said. "Why wouldn't he show up? Did somebody leak something out?"

The investigators challenged each other. Word about the cartridge could have gotten out and spooked Allen. Could news about a new person of interest have leaked? Together, they decided that was not the case. If explosive news about Delphi had spread, they would have all heard about it by then.

So Mullin tried again. He scheduled another pickup time on October 26, 2022, a Wednesday. The designated time passed once more. Holeman figured that was it. Their person of interest was just jerking everyone around.

But then, as Holeman was walking around the post, he heard something out front. The Allens entered the lobby. Allen took off his dark Carhartt jacket and gave it to his wife. Beneath the jacket, he was clad in dark sweatpants with white stripes down the side and a T-shirt that clung to his potbelly. Allen dug his hands into his pockets and scooped out everything—loose change, his wallet. He handed it all to his wife.

"Why did he empty his pockets out?" Holeman whispered to Harper. "It's weird. What the fuck?" For some reason, Allen had shown up jail-ready, as if he expected to get arrested. Holeman had never seen that kind of behavior before from a suspect. Beckoning the Allens, he ushered the couple deeper within the post.

Unknown to the Allens, McLeland and Liggett were also at the post. The men, along with Harshman, Vido and Clinton, were huddled in a tiny room, not much larger than a closet, preparing to watch the interview on closed circuit television.

The interview room was small and drab. Next door was all the recording equipment. Holeman glanced over it. Everything seemed in order. He and Allen went into the small space together. Holeman reminded Allen that he had been read his Miranda rights days ago. That was sufficient, legally speaking. Then Vido knocked on the door.

"Come on out here," Vido said to Holeman.

When Holeman emerged, Vido told him the recording was not working. The investigators had worked out a plan to communicate over email during the interview. But Holeman had not yet checked his email to see Vido's message telling him to stop the interview.

"You've got to be kidding me," Holeman said.

Vido fixed the problem by resetting the system.

Holeman returned to the interview room, and a text from Vido appeared on his phone: "We think it's recording." Holeman went back to talking to Allen. He gave him some information on the items the police had seized during the search.

To build up the rapport everybody seemed to think he had with Allen, Holeman adopted a genial tone. Over the years he had completed training in a number of different interview methods. One method, the Reid Technique—named after former Chicago police officer and polygraph expert John E. Reid—was often criticized for its strong emphasis on verbal confrontation. But Holeman felt a good interviewer was flexible. His goal was to apply whatever technique got the job done. Compassion, righteous anger, and deception were all on the little table separating interviewer and subject. The key was finding out what specific alchemy would fit an interviewer's personality and prompt the subject to open up.

Dressed in a blue shirt, a tie, and dark jeans, Holeman looked less like a detective and more like a regular guy Allen might run into at the local bar or in the aisles of CVS. Holeman was a friendly person. His wife liked to tease him that he was a social butterfly, so very different from the shy teenager she once knew. So—in his talk with Allen—Holeman led with affability. He used personal examples about himself swapping clothes with his son, letting a friend borrow a truck, and selling a gun to his son-in-law. But Allen did not respond much to Holeman. He remained flat. If he sounded calm in the first interview, he sounded apathetic now.

Holeman liked Allen as a suspect. But perhaps a cartridge from the man's gun had ended up at the crime scene for good reason. Or maybe Allen was covering for somebody who had borrowed his SIG Sauer. Kathy Allen had been a neighbor of Tony Kline's for years, so perhaps there was a connection to him. Either way, Holeman wanted the truth. But one by one, Allen tossed away lifelines. No, he had never loaned his gun to anyone. Yes, he gathered mushrooms. No, he had never hunted for them on Ron Logan's property. No, he had never been out there at all, come to think of it.

For McLeland, this was a crucial moment. If no one other than Allen had access to the weapon that had left a cartridge at the crime scene, then he had to be the guy.

Allen did not even seem particularly interested in the questions. So Holeman decided to hit him with the bad news. He pulled out Oberg's report, which showed the forensic examiner's opinion that a cartridge ejected from Allen's SIG Sauer showed sufficient agreement with one that ended up at a crime scene.

"Okay," Allen said, placid as ever.

Holeman offered to let him read the report.

"I don't need to read it," Allen said.

Holeman said he was on Allen's side. The prosecutor and the other investigators were pushing to lock him up forever.

Allen chuckled. "This is ridiculous."

Holeman said Allen was making it hard with all those cryptic statements during the search about it all being over.

"You made comments like that to me that really concerned me," Holeman said.

Blankly, Allen clarified: "What I mean by 'it's over' is that you've already started something here that there's no backing out of. The damage is done, I guess, is what I'm saying." His life was over because his neighbors had seen a search going on at his house. His reputation would be ruined forever.

Holeman pushed more. He echoed Allen's statement from the first interview. "Listen to me, Rick. I don't believe you should be the fall guy." But, the detective added, there was a big problem. Experts had concluded that Allen was the man on the video. They were certain it was his voice.

That was not entirely true. The investigators on the case—the detectives who had stared at the footage on a daily basis for years—were convinced that Allen was Bridge Guy. His voice—at times scratchy and low, then higher-pitched at others—was a strong fit. But no independent experts could confirm that opinion. The video was too blurry. Bridge Guy had been too succinct with his, "Guys, down the hill" line. Credible experts needed far more words to put together a legitimate comparison. Holeman was exaggerating to see how Allen would react.

Allen was adamant. He was not the murderer. He reminded Holeman that he had already admitted to being on the bridge because he was trying to help with the investigation. But he had no explanation for the cartridge evidence. "I don't even know how my bullet would have gotten out there. If that's even my bullet." Holeman warned Allen about what lay ahead of him. When the media got hold of this case, Allen would come across as a monster. By coming clean, he could get out in front of the whole thing. Perhaps he really was just a man with limited involvement—a witness who could give up the real mastermind, the true killer.

"Tell me how this round got next to one of our girls—in between both girls," Holeman said.

"I don't know."

"You do know. And if you don't tell me, you're going down for this."

Allen shrugged and laughed at that.

"I'm serious," Holeman said. "This isn't a joking matter."

"I'm not joking. Do you realize what you've done to me? This is like . . . you've talked to the people I work with. You've talked to my neighbors." That was agony for a man with Allen's anxiety. But the news was not yet out about a new lead in the case. Allen told Holeman that he assumed he would be arrested. "The damage is done. Go ahead and do what you're going to do." Holeman said that he had a warrant for a buccal swab—not Allen's arrest. But even as he goaded Holeman to make an arrest, Allen would not budge on his story.

"Anybody that knows me knows that I could never—even if I wanted do something like that—that's not who I am." Allen said he would not confess to a murder he did not commit. He claimed he never met the girls. He said that the cartridge could not have come from his gun. He was an innocent man whose life had been ruined because of some tragic error.

"I've dealt with not wanting to live for seven, eight years now. It's been a long fucking battle. And with what you guys have done to me? Kill me. I don't give a fuck. You'll make my wife rich."

Holeman got up to leave. Shaking his head, Allen waited. He leaned over to glance at Holeman's picture of the cartridge. He rolled his neck and let out a deep sigh.

When Holeman came back, he brought along Vido. Holeman pulled a chair so he could sit close to Allen. He slipped on a pair of reading glasses. Vido slid on a pair of medical gloves and instructed Allen to open his mouth. The suspect complied. Vido stuck a swab in Allen's mouth, swirling it around inside his cheek. Then he sealed the sample and headed out again.

"Ball's in your court, Rick," Holeman said tersely.

"You just took my DNA." Allen laughed.

"So what you were telling me out there—it's over, huh?"

Allen let out another derisive laugh. "The damage is done."

"I'm sorry that you think this is funny. You keep laughing. Maybe it's just a nervous laugh—I don't know but I'm trying to help you. Why is all this evidence clearly indicating that you're involved?"

Allen fell back on his denials. He acknowledged that others might have seen him on the trails, perhaps even people he had not seen himself. But he maintained the police would never be able to prove that he had committed the crime. Holeman pushed him. He encouraged Allen to consider what everyone would think of him.

"The media's mild compared to social media," Holeman warned him. "It's going to portray you as this monster. Are you a monster?"

"They're already going to do that."

Allen became agitated, rolling his eyes at Holeman. He began to tell the detective to arrest him.

Holeman departed once more. Allen was not in custody. He was free to leave. Still, he stayed, hunched over, alone in the interview room. He shook his head and said, "Fuck." When Holeman came back, he gave Allen a quick forensics lesson about the extraction and ejection marks.

"I'm not going to sit here and tell you something that's not true just so you can feel better about this," Allen said.

"I already feel good about this," Holeman told him. "I feel good about what the experts are telling me. I feel good about the scientific evidence. I feel good about the witness statements. I feel good about everything." Holeman said the only thing he did not feel good about was the possibility that Allen could truly be covering for someone else.

"Maybe I'm wrong. Maybe you did do this all by yourself."

Allen snickered at that.

Over the course of the interview, Holeman encouraged Allen to take breaks. He got him a bottle of water. He allowed him to go and smoke a cigarette outside.

Holeman did not tell Allen that detectives were talking to more of his relatives. Bob Burgess, a first sergeant at the Peru post, drove a few miles away to Mexico to interview Janis and Marvin, Allen's mother and stepfather.

Janis remembered a strange interaction with her son a few days after the murders. He called her up, sounding nervous. "They're going to pin this on me," he told his mother. He explained he had been out there on the trails and had smoked a cigarette. He imagined they would find the butt and tie it to him forensically. Janis found the conversation odd.

But Holeman did bring up another one of the suspect's loved ones. He offered to bring in Allen's wife, but not before making sure to mention a few of the things she was telling detectives.

Kathy Allen said her husband had discouraged her from helping out with the searches when the girls first came up missing. She alluded to Allen's anger issues. She said Allen's depression had gotten worse for the past seven or so years.

"I could see why, if I killed two girls, I'd have depression too," Holeman said.

That day, Kathy Allen was learning everything that the police had on her husband. Holeman brought that up to Allen. "I don't think you're a bad person, neither does she," Holeman told Allen.

But the suspect lowered his head and smiled. "What kind of good person kills two people?"

All kinds of things could spark a monstrous decision from an otherwise decent human being, Holeman said. Some kind of inciting incident. A bad reaction to drugs or alcohol. Then he asked Allen to prove he was sincere by submitting to a polygraph examination.

"I ain't fucking taking a polygraph," Allen replied.

"See, you're not cooperating. We asked you to give us your DNA, we asked you to look through your phone. Now I'm giving you the opportunity to prove your innocence by taking a polygraph."

A polygraph would only measure Allen's stress reactions to specific questions. It would also not likely be admitted as evidence in court. For investigators, though, it could offer another chance to lock a suspect into a story. Another opportunity for Allen to be honest. Another moment for Holeman to confront him, to chip away at his excuses.

But Allen was adamant. "Nope. I have issues, but I take meds."

Holeman explained that the examiner would get a baseline of his heart rate and reactions.

"Nope. I'm not doing anything for you guys."

Holeman departed.

Dressed in a white jacket and ripped jeans, Kathy Allen entered the interview room. Allen embraced her, resting his head on her shoulder and patting her on the back.

"It's going to be all right," he told his wife in his calm, almost breezy manner. "They're trying to tell me that you actually believe that I did it. And I just can't believe that."

Kathy Allen was quiet for a moment. She appeared to be in shock. "I'm trying to figure out why there's a bullet out there, dear—"

Allen cut her off. "I know. You think I'm not? And that's what I told him. I can't explain something I don't understand."

Allen pushed forward.

"You know me." His voice barely changed as he spoke to his wife. With Holeman, he was flat and deadpan. With her, he was still flat but more assertive. "You know this isn't something I could do. And I know that you know that. You don't have to tell me that."

Allen sat there, legs crossed, fingers interlocked, and dictated to his wife what she must think. He did not offer explanations, or even speculation. He told his wife he knew she could never believe he would do such a thing.

Despite those clear instructions, Kathy Allen had questions. "How did a bullet from your gun get out there?" Then she began to whimper. She said that police told her he kept a matching cartridge in his keepsake box next to the bed they shared.

"I can't explain it," Allen said.

"I can't either and they keep asking me and I don't know how to answer that," she cried. "There's no way for me to know."

"I don't know how to explain something that isn't possible," Allen said. Then he added, "I know that no bullet from my gun was connected with a murder in any way shape or form. And there's no way a bullet from my gun would have been near Abby and Libby's murder or anything else because I never even seen those girls. Period! And I didn't even have my gun that day."

Her voice nearly at a whisper, Kathy Allen told her husband that she had thought he had not walked on the bridge that day. That was what he had told her, at least.

"I went out to that first trestle," he said.

"Oh. Okay. I don't remember you telling me that."

Frenzied, the Allens went back and forth about the issue of the trestle. Finally, Kathy Allen said, "I didn't know you were on it. I'm sorry."

"Well, don't worry about it."

"You told me you weren't."

"Huh?"

"You told me you weren't so I just—"

"No, I told you that I walked—" Allen tilted his head in apparent exasperation.

"Okay."

Allen looked intently at his wife. "I love you, baby."

"I love you, too."

"I don't know what they're trying to do but I know that that's not what I told you. I love you." He reached for his wife and leaned in for a fleeting kiss. "They're not going to get away with this. This is exactly what I would never want for you and there's nothing I can do about it."

For a moment, Allen shifted the conversation from talk of his actions on the trails to the behavior of Holeman and the rest of law enforcement. "They're not going to get away with this. Not going to say I did something I didn't do. I know you know me, and I know you know I couldn't do this."

Allen said he was sorry they both had to go through such an ordeal. After all, he was a man who cared deeply about perceptions. Speaking in a monotone, he talked about how half the time, his fears about other people thinking poorly of him were not even rooted in reality. Still, he was always moping about the subject. He even brought up caring especially about what Jori Epler, his boss at CVS, thought of him.

All throughout the monologue, Kathy Allen barely responded. In the end, Allen finally turned his attention back to his wife. "Just tell them that you want an attorney and they'll have to let you leave. Don't worry about me."

Holeman was struck by the Allens. Kathy Allen seemed standoffish, like she wanted to bolt out of there. Allen's self-deprecating routine was equally bizarre. Holeman thought that a typical person, if wrongfully accused of a heinous crime, would be demanding top-shelf legal assistance at any cost. From the sweatpants to his persistent demands to be arrested, Allen did not act like any other suspect Holeman had ever encountered. He stepped back inside. He asked Kathy to tell her husband to take a polygraph.

Allen started yelling. Holeman shouted back. Kathy Allen sat placidly, silent.

"You're going to drag your fucking wife and your daughter through this because you're too fucking bullheaded to get out in front of this and admit you made a mistake," Holeman said, knocking on the table with his fist. Holeman was a drug enforcement guy. In interviews with dealers, investigators often tried to establish dominance. That could require confrontation, yelling, and even swearing. The goal was to show Allen who was in control.

Allen leaned forward. "So tell you I did something. I did something that I didn't do?"

"Tell me the truth," Holeman fired back. "The truth, Rick—"

"I told you the truth and you don't want to hear it."

"The evidence tells me otherwise. The evidence clearly indicates you're involved in this."

"No, it doesn't."

"It fucking does."

But Allen remained unmoved. He insisted the cartridge was not his. Holeman took issue with the insinuation that police had planted evidence. "I'm telling you that we had this fucking round on February 14, 2017, it's been secured in a fucking laboratory and we've tested other guns," Holeman said.

Allen was unmoved.

"You think we went and stole your fucking round and threw it down by a fucking dead girl's foot? This ain't fucking TV. This is realistic."

Allen asked Holeman to let his wife leave the room.

"Absolutely." The investigator sprung up to let Kathy Allen out.

"Can I kiss her?" Allen asked Holeman.

"Yeah, kiss her," Holeman said, sounding exasperated. Allen hugged his wife and kissed her grimacing face.

"Do the right thing, Kathy." Holeman turned toward Allen's wife. "Tell him to do the right thing."

Kathy Allen said nothing. She did not tell her husband to do the right thing. She just left.

Holeman looked back at Allen. "You're going to put your family through this for no reason." Then he walked Kathy Allen out.

"Motherfuckers," Allen muttered.

When Holeman returned, Allen glared at him.

"What?" Holeman asked.

"You're going to pay for what you've done to my wife," Allen said. "You want to fuck with me, fuck with me. But you leave my wife out of this." He paused. "Fuck, leave me out of it."

"No, you're involved in this. Your fucking round's there, Rick."

"No, it's not."

"I can see you're getting fucking pissed off, I understand—"

Allen raised his voice. "I am pissed off. Did you not see my wife?"

"Did you see these fucking two dead girls dead?" Holeman held up the sheets of paper on the desk.

Allen yelled his response. "No!"

Rapport-building and mild confrontation had not yielded much additional information, so it was time for one last strategy. "That's what happened. You got fucking pissed off at them." Holeman was yelling by then. His voice was so loud that the sound came out warped on the recorder. He pounded on the table with his fist to emphasize each point. Looking slightly amused and taken aback, Allen raised his eyebrows and jerked back his head. "You fucking dragged them down a fucking hill—and you fucking killed them."

"I didn't—"

"Don't fucking tell me you didn't."

Defiant, Allen's eyes widened. "I didn't kill anyone."

The suspect was done.

"I'm done talking. Arrest me." Allen balled his hands into fists and held them out in front of him, as if he was offering his wrists for handcuffing.

Holeman smacked the papers down on the table.

"Happy to. Be fucking happy to. Because I tried to fucking help you and you wouldn't fucking do it."

"Oh, you're helping me," Allen said, sarcastically.

Allen would not back down. And he would not take a polygraph.

"You're guilty and I know it and I'm going to prove it," Holeman said.

Allen had a slight smile frozen on his face. "Okay."

"And I'm not paying for any of this shit. You're paying." Holeman pointed at Allen. "This is on you. This ain't on me. It's fucking on you, Rick."

Holeman stepped out. This time, he consulted with the rest of Unified Command. They all agreed. It was time to arrest Allen.

Alone inside the interview room, Allen fumed. "Fuck. Fucking police."

Holeman came back in, unclipping the standard-issue handcuffs from his belt. His tone now perfectly even and quiet, he informed Allen he was being detained. He put the handcuffs on Allen. Then he checked the cuffs to make sure they were double-locked, and not too tight around the detainee's wrists. He did not want Allen to be uncomfortable.

The arrest gave Holeman no relief. He knew that preparing for a trial would be the real work. The misfiled tip sheet would look bad. The technical issues with the recorder would come off as incompetent. Trial preparation would make everything the investigators had gone through—scrounging through the mess of leads, interviewing every dirtbag for miles, and coming up empty again and again—look like nothing.

Still, he knew McLeland was confident in the case. So were the other investigators. Holeman himself became totally convinced of Allen's guilt as he sat across the table from the man. In that small room, Holeman watched the suspect fold his arms, obstruct, double down, and manipulate his wife with his sulky little excuses.

Holeman led Allen out of the post and into his car. The drive to Delphi was a quiet one. Sitting in the back seat, Allen asked no questions. Driving past the lavish new home of the family behind a local farming enterprise, the detective and the suspect commented briefly on the lucrative nature of the sweet corn business. Well into the journey, a strange expression came over Allen's face. Holeman figured it was because of the odd route he was driving. He called it the "back way." He asked Allen if he was familiar with the route.

"Nope. I've never been this way."

Holeman possessed unique expertise on how to get to Delphi fast. For five years, he had often sped that way in darkness, in snow, and in rain. "It's quicker."

CHAPTER TWENTY-TWO

The Richard Allen case forced McLeland to make a controversial decision just as things were officially beginning. A probable cause affidavit (PCA) essentially outlined to judges all of the evidence law enforcement believed justified the arrest. Typically, a PCA would become immediately available to the public. But this situation posed a problem.

There was a possibility Allen had not acted alone, that perhaps the Klines or even someone else had taken part in the killings in some fashion. Tony Kline and Richard Allen were around the same age. Peru and Mexico were right next to each other. At the time Allen was dating his future wife Kathy, she lived in a house right near the Klines. Peruvians came forward, saying they thought the men might have known each other. Ultimately, Vido, Harshman, and Clinton found coincidences that could be ascribed to small town living, certainly nothing more concrete linking the Allens and the Klines. In the end, activity from the phones of both Klines showed them as being in their home on the day of the murders. Nothing tied father or son to the crime scene.

But McLeland had no way of knowing the outcome of that side of the investigation. If another theoretical killer got an idea about what the police had, including potentially identifying information about eyewitnesses—then that person could tamper with evidence linking him to the crime or even threaten or intimidate witnesses who could place him there. Some of the witnesses had been juveniles at the time of the crime. There was also the matter of social media to contend with. Self-proclaimed internet sleuths were sure to hound anyone connected to the case.

The prudent and responsible thing to do was to seal the PCA—and McLeland chose to do so, even though he knew full well that doing so put him in an uncomfortable position. He would have to stand before an expectant press to announce the long-awaited arrest in the case without being able to explain what had led to that arrest or why law enforcement felt confident they had the right man.

Under Indiana law, the PCA would remain sealed for thirty days. McLeland would then have to make his case to Judge Benjamin Diener, who would determine whether to keep it sealed permanently. The prosecutor felt that if he could seal it just long enough to redact the witness names from the document, he could avoid flinging more people connected with the case into the whirlwind.

Hope could be a painful, scarring thing in the Delphi case. That was one reason the investigators were often slow to alert the families of Libby and Abby about case developments. But with Allen's detainment, the time had gone to gather the relatives in the Command Center. There McLeland and the investigators announced that they had a suspect named Richard Allen in custody.

After the initial shock ebbed, Becky had a question. She and the other family members had spent years advocating for their girls. "What do we do now?"

McLeland's answer was simple. "Nothing. We got it. You just step back."

Becky looked across the gathered investigators. She had another question, directed at the whole group. "If this was your daughter, would you just step back and do nothing?"

The nothingness of watching and waiting was perhaps more daunting than the years of constant motion and turmoil and heartache. The investigators fell quiet.

McLeLand was sympathetic. He knew it would be hard for the families to stay silent. But he could not have guessed how hard.

On October 28, 2022, representing the State of Indiana, McLeland formally charged Allen with murdering Abby and Libby. He filed a sealed copy of the probable cause affidavit for Allen's arrest.

Clad in protective gear and guided by sheriff's deputies, Allen stood before Judge Benjamin Diener and listened as his bond was set at $20 million. In response to Benjamin Diener's questions about legal representation, Allen said he intended to hire his own attorneys. The judge told him he had twenty days to do so, in order to comply with the deadlines for filing certain motions.

The scramble for legal representation largely fell to Kathy Allen. She kept her husband updated about her progress during their regular phone calls.

Allen told her not to worry about him. He told her to move on. She told him she had gotten a lawyer, but the retaining fee would be thousands of dollars.

Allen waved her away and told her not to waste her money.

After news of the arrest broke, Delphi found itself under siege—not by enemy soldiers but rather an army of reporters. Outlets from Indianapolis, Lafayette, and beyond—men and women driving colorful, logo-emblazoned vans and brandishing microphones—descended on the city once more, just as they had when the girls first disappeared.

But there was little information to be had. The PCA was sealed. Employees at the jail and courthouse were reticent when asked about the arrest.

Journalists took turns knocking on the door of the silent Allen residence on Whiteman Drive. Red-and-white wires snaked out of the wall next to the door where the bell had been torn out. There was very little to be done in terms of doorstepping at other spots along Whiteman Drive. A note on a nearby day care begged journalists to keep away. Residents in one home called 911 on employees of the ABC affiliates. Someone burned yard waste nearby, and the air blurred with smoke.

Reporters also showed up to the modest home of Janis and Marvin Allen in nearby Mexico, Indiana. Though no one in the press knew it at the time, this was the very place Allen acknowledged leaving before heading to the trails on the day of the murders. Journalists found Marvin—a tan, thin old man, glasses covering his often-bewildered eyes—exiting his garage. When asked if he had a comment on his stepson's arrest, Marvin said nothing. He merely drifted inside his house, keeping his movements fluid. All the way down the driveway, he stared straight ahead, as if he had not heard a word about what had happened.

As McLeland expected, he faced criticism for sealing the PCA. While some questioned his motives and suggested there might be some vague, undefined but definitely sinister reason he wanted the document to remain sealed, others simply began to doubt his legal acumen. Perhaps, some suggested, the prosecutor just was not up to the challenge presented by such a difficult case. McLeland even looked young. He was scruffy—sometimes sporting a full-fledged mustache. He liked to wear his hair longish and slicked back.

This was not the first time McLeland had faced such negativity. Often when lawyers from larger communities like Indianapolis or Fort Wayne came to try a case in Delphi they would dismiss the prosecutor as a small-town bumpkin who would be easy to defeat in court. There was a part of McLeland that actually relished being the underdog. When people underestimated him, he felt it only made them more vulnerable. When people doubted his abilities, it energized him, making him determined to prove them wrong.

Everyone hoped more information would come out at the press conference McLeland and the investigators held a few days later to officially announce the arrest. When Julie Melvin showed up, Becky asked Holeman to convey that Libby's family did not want her around. He did so. Later, Melvin would tell other online sleuths that as she began to depart, Carter himself allowed her back in. Melvin lived close to Carter, and had struck up an acquaintance with him. The state police superintendent had no idea that his neighbor was also a prominent internet crank obsessed with the Delphi case.

Melvin told the other sleuths that she stuck around the press conference because she felt leaving would be allowing the devil and his demons to win. She would tell others that Becky exuded selfishness and hatred, that she had demons in her mind, body, and soul. She prayed that Satan would one day release Becky from his stranglehold.

Meanwhile, members of Unified Command stood onstage at the Delphi United Methodist Church to address the public.

"I am proud to report to you that today—actually last Friday—was 'the' day," Carter said.

Then the superintendent said something that caught everyone's attention.

"We are going to continue a very methodical and committed approach to ensure that if any other person had any involvement in these murders in any way, that person or persons will be held accountable."

The arrest was an earth-shifting development. Still, the press conference made one thing clear: The public would remain in the dark about many of the details of the case.

Leazenby faced a rather immediate problem. By statute, it was his responsibility to house Allen in the Carroll County jail. But the jail was small. Built in 1983 and commanded by Sergeant Lori Sustarsic, the lock-up had only thirty-four beds, concealed behind large, colorful doors. Overcrowding was common, leaving some inmates occasionally bedding down in the library. To avoid that, the sheriff's office had a line item in its budget to send prisoners out to other county jails. The size of the jail was not the only problem, though.

Leazenby had limited staff. The sheriff's office was a thirteen-person crew. He worried he did not have the manpower or resources to guarantee the safety of a man charged with the brutal murder of two children—especially with the flood of overwrought coverage the arrest was attracting on both social media and the mainstream press. As a result, Leazenby had already moved Allen over to the jail in nearby White County, but that hardly seemed a long-term solution.

Fortunately, the state had a provision in place to deal with this sort of situation. If a sheriff felt that having a particular inmate in the county jail created a risk to the inmate or the others, he or she could ask the court to transfer that individual to the Indiana Department of Correction, which had substantially more resources than a small county. Leazenby filed the request on November 3, 2022, and Judge Benjamin Diener quickly approved it. Allen was moved to a secure cell in Indiana's Westville Correctional Facility.

While this transfer later attracted much scrutiny, most people at the time focused not on the judge's decision to authorize a transfer but rather on the way he did it. What should have been a routine legal document of only a few lines instead became a bizarre two-page rant in which Benjamin Diener railed against the public's "blood lust" for information about the case. He also claimed YouTubers had already posted information about his family, and—for good measure—complained that most public servants were "woefully underpaid."

Later on this same very busy day, Benjamin Diener abruptly announced he was recusing himself from the case.

The Indiana Supreme Court responded quickly, appointing Allen County Superior Court Judge Frances Gull to hear the case.

Gull had spent decades as part of the legal community in Fort Wayne, Allen County's largest city. She joined the prosecutor's office in the mid-eighties and became a judge in the mid-nineties. Her most significant work on the bench might arguably have been her long tenure overseeing the community's Drug Court. Through a combination of compassion and sternness, she shepherded addicts along the rocky road to recovery. By 2020, the program had close to a thousand graduates.

But the Indiana Supreme Court may have been more impressed by the fact that Gull had presided over one of the Richmond Hill cases, in which several people blew up a home in an Indianapolis subdivision in an effort to collect insurance money. The explosion ended up killing two people and seriously damaging thirty-three homes. The resulting trials attracted a great deal of attention and publicity, and the general consensus was that Gull had handled the one she ran quite well. She seemed, then, as if she could be a perfect fit for the Allen case.

At this point, one rather serious problem remained: Allen himself did not have an attorney.

PART FOUR

THE WAIT

"Just don't talk anymore"

CHAPTER TWENTY-THREE

At Allen's first hearing on October 28, 2022, he had told the court he did not need to have a public defender appointed. He would find an attorney for himself. It took him only a very short time to change his mind. "I am begging to be provide with legal assistance in a Public Defender," he wrote the court a few days later in an ungrammatical letter. "I had no clue how expensive it would be just to talk to someone."

While it was clear that Allen would indeed need a public defender, finding attorneys to take that role proved difficult. At least one prominent defense attorney was contacted and let it be known she was not interested in being on the case. Others in the legal community could not help but speculate about who might ultimately get the position. The nod eventually went to Brad Rozzi, an attorney in Logansport. He wanted it badly, and he occasionally practiced in Carroll County. When Benjamin Diener was still on the case, Rozzi had shown up and told the judge he wanted to take the case. McLeland was aware of him too. The two men had actually attended a year of high school together in Logansport. McLeland had lived there for a year after his parents divorced. But Rozzi was older, and they had not moved in the same circles.

The Rozzis were widely considered a law enforcement family. Rozzi's brother Josh was a sergeant at the Peru post. His father, Randy, had served as the chief of police for Logansport and later as the Cass County coroner. In Logansport and the surrounding region, Rozzi worked on criminal law and divorces. Slight and tanned with sharp features, Rozzi always dressed the part of a hard-charging attorney, favoring meticulous, tailored suits. He was known to be somewhat abrasive in the courtroom. Supporters might call his style swaggering, while critics might dismiss it as condescending arrogance. He was also a generous employer who volunteered his time to Freedom Hunt, a charity devoted to creating opportunities for children with special needs to learn to hunt animals like deer and wild turkey.

At the time he took on the case, Rozzi was involved in a murder case with multiple defendants. One of the other defendants was represented by Stacy Uliana, a well-regarded defense attorney. Uliana was perhaps best known for securing an acquittal for David Camm, a former Indiana State Police trooper who had twice been convicted of murdering his family. Rozzi naturally thought to ask her to come in and be his cocounsel on the Allen case.

Uliana said no. But she did have a suggestion. Rozzi ought to reach out to attorney Andrew Baldwin of Franklin, Indiana.

Everyone in the Johnson County legal community had an Andy Baldwin story. Baldwin, a rare attorney who focused entirely on criminal law, was known to be a bit of a sloppy dresser. He also once owned a car that was in such poor condition, he needed to stick his foot out the front door and use it to get the vehicle moving. People who saw that spectacle said it reminded them of something out of a *Flintstones* cartoon. But he was also a fierce and relentless advocate for his clients, an attorney well-known for getting acquittals—or making favorable deals—in cases other lawyers regarded as unwinnable. Like a good actor, Baldwin was a chameleon who had the ability to put everything into each performance. With his graying beard, big frame, and unfussy outfits he could appear charmingly relatable to clients and jurors. His voice could boom in anger, or falter under the weight of his emotions. His blue eyes were always ready to well with tears.

For Baldwin, crime was a profession and not a hobby; he did not follow stories about murder and violence in the news or in documentaries. In fact, prior to his own involvement in the case, he did not know much about the killings at Delphi. Mitch Westerman, a friend and former colleague of Baldwin's who had worked at the law firm in an administrative capacity after failing the bar exam, remembered that the attorney was unaware of the key case details. While Westerman and his Air Force buddy obsessed over the case and other true crime stories, Baldwin came into things a total novice. Even a couple of weeks into Baldwin's representation of Allen, the attorney still did not recognize the significance of the phrase "down the hill" to the case.

Unbeknownst to the attorneys, Allen had already started down a path that would make their lives increasingly challenging.

Kathy Allen got a call on November 14, 2022.

A prerecorded message let the inmates introduce themselves by name. In that little sound bite, Allen called himself "Ricky." His voice sounded ragged, and identical to that of Bridge Guy. The message went on to identify him as an inmate at the Westville Correctional Facility.

Kathy Allen picked up the phone. Her husband's arrest was still so raw. "I don't want to upset you anymore." Allen's voice was thick with tears. "All I want to do is to be able to help you."

He had an idea.

"I'm not saying anything, but if it gets to a point that it's too much, you just need to call the investigators and tell them to come and get me and bring me to you and I'll tell them whatever they want me to tell them . . . 'cause whatever things they want me to say, I'll just say it."

Kathy Allen's voice was gently chiding. "No, no, no."

Allen became hard to understand. He was crying. He knew those who loved him were hurting. He felt like he might be talking to his wife for the last time. That was how he felt anytime he talked to her, now that he was in prison. Kathy Allen told him she wished she could hug him once more.

"I can't explain what's been going on. I don't want you to worry about me. I am a man and I will take care of myself..." Allen's weepy assurance may have been news to his wife, given his pattern of collapsing under the strain of his responsibilities. "I'm worried about you. And that's all I do, is worry about you."

Her voice became flat. "You need to hang in there, honey, okay?"

Then Allen began crying harder. "Nobody loves me anymore."

"Stop, that's not true."

Breathing heavily, Allen repeated his offer to "tell them whatever they want me to say." Kathy Allen tried to soothe him. But Allen would not have it.

"Okay. I don't need you to try to be strong for me, okay? You need to be weak. You need to be held. You need to take care of yourself, okay?"

Beginning to cry, Kathy Allen responded, "Okay, dear, okay."

Sniffling, he asked if she was going back to work. Kathy Allen said her employer at the vet office did not want her coming in.

"They don't?"

"They're afraid for me."

Allen calmed down. "Oh, okay." A robotic voice interrupted the conversation, alerting the couple that they had one minute left to speak. "I'm sorry, baby. Just one more thing I fucked up for you."

Allen welled up again saying goodbye. "You don't know what I'd give to see you just one more time," he said. "You just know if anything happens, I'll see you in the next lifetime."

In a way, the Allens were never alone on a call. Police investigators received all the recordings of their conversations. It fell to Harshman in particular to listen to Allen's calls.

To the investigators who heard the recording of Allen's offer, the implication was clear. He was admitting his guilt and offering to confess whenever his wife said the word. But the offer of telling detectives what they wanted to hear was ambiguous. Especially compared with what followed.

The Carroll County election was held on November 8, 2022. Despite the weeks of sniping, Liggett easily prevailed over Pinkard. The sheriff-elect carried 55 percent of the votes, or 3,402 voters. Pinkard received 2,790 votes, or 45.06 percent.

In other counties and amid other circumstances, Liggett's win might have been considered a comfortable victory. For Carroll County, the results spoke to the intensity of the election cycle. Still, the 10 percent margin was a strong lead, representing Liggett's widespread institutional and public support.

When Rozzi and Baldwin first visited Allen at Westville, Baldwin felt as if they had the red carpet laid out for them. The pair was warmly greeted by Warden John Galipeau, who allowed them to bypass some of the normal security measures and offered to do whatever he could to help them.

The collegial feelings continued at the next pretrial hearing, which was largely devoted to McLeland's ultimately doomed attempt to keep the PCA sealed. But there was another matter to consider; on the day of the hearing, McLeland filed a request for Gull to prohibit the attorneys and potential witnesses from speaking about the case with the media. He explained that a gag order was necessary because he did not want Allen's right to a fair trial to be jeopardized due to the excessive media coverage and publicity the case was already generating.

The attorneys made their cases for and against sealing the PCA in open court—Gull would soon decide to make it public—but their discussions about McLeland's proposed gag order were confined to a private meeting in Gull's chambers. In a professional back-and-forth, Rozzi and Baldwin argued that the gag order just was not needed since the two of them had absolutely no intention of trying the case in the public sphere.

"***PRESS RELEASE***," read the top of a multipage document the defense team emailed to reporters on December 1, 2022.

"We do not want to try this case in the media," it said—but then, in the paragraphs to follow, went on to do just that. The lawyers stressed that Allen—whom they referred to as "Rick"—was a fifty-year-old man with no criminal record. They claimed Allen was "confused" as to why he had been arrested.

Baldwin and Rozzi went on to discuss how the arrest had occurred shortly before the sheriff's election. The clear implication was that the arrest had been motivated less by evidence and more by some vague improprieties on the part of the sheriff's office.

They then discussed the round that linked their client to the murder scene. Derisively referring to it as a "magic bullet," the attorneys claimed "the discipline of tool mark identification (ballistics) is anything but a science" and promised to challenge it in court.

Rozzi and Baldwin added that "Rick has nothing to hide" and spoke in a pleased way about being "inundated" with tips from the public.

To wrap up, the pair noted that "we have received very limited information about this case . . . To the extent we continue to discover information that points to Rick's innocence, we will offer up this information to the public."

Rozzi's and Baldwin's "***PRESS RELEASE***" forever changed their relationships not only with McLeland but also with Gull. Over and above whatever concerns the prosecutor and the judge may have had with the content, the very existence of the document came as a surprise to each. Just a few days earlier, the defense had sat in the judge's chambers and assured all that they would not be trying the case in the court of public opinion. Now they very clearly were. McLeland felt they had lied to him. The incident convinced him that the defense attorneys intended to play dirty. Perhaps worst of all, the end of the defense team's document seemed to promise more of the same in the future.

But they would never get the chance. Less than a day after the press release was sprung on her, Gull issued an order: "Counsel for the State of Indiana and the Defendant, as well as their professional staff and other personnel, Law Enforcement Officials, Court Personnel, Coroner and all family members are prohibited from commenting on this case to the public and to the media, directly or indirectly, by themselves or through any intermediary, in any form, including any social media platforms."

If the defense wanted to continue making their case to the public, they would need to find another way to do it.

CHAPTER TWENTY-FOUR

Pilgrims flocked to the Monon High Bridge. Men and women from all over the world followed the case, and many of them wanted to walk where Libby and Abby walked, to see what they had seen. Dr. Monica Wala was just one of the many who made that journey.

Social media had drawn her into the case. She had a long commute to work each day and liked to fill it by listening to true crime podcasts. The murders at Delphi had long been a favorite topic for such outlets. Hosts loved to speculate over possible hidden meanings in the public words of investigators, scrutinize stills from Libby's video for hidden clues, and accuse one person after another of somehow being involved in the murders.

Just like the others who made the trip to the trails, Wala soon went back to her own life, her interest in the case even stronger than before. But there was a difference. Unlike most of the others, the pale young woman with magenta hair was a part of the system. She worked as a psychologist at Westville Correctional Facility.

Wala did her best there; she tried to speak with every prisoner in the unit at least twice a week on rounds. But these were not the leisurely sessions therapists in private practice might enjoy with their patients, idly talking about life issues as everyone sat in comfortable chairs.

In Westville, visits on rounds took place at the front door of a prisoner's cell—and these were metal doors. Wala could not really see her patients at all, except glimpses of them she sometimes caught through a small opening usually used to deliver food. And her chats with them were not meandering discussions about their childhoods; she was only tasked with getting the most basic, actionable information from them.

How are you?

Are you thinking of harming yourself?

When Dr. Wala learned that Allen would be added to her list of patients, she made a point to notify her supervisors of her pre-existing interest in the case. They all agreed it would not be a problem. Wala's role would be to try to help Allen, not to make any efforts to elicit information about his case. There should not be any conflict.

After the PCA was released, Todd Click gave it a very unsympathetic review. To him, the only thing the PCA proved was Allen's presence on the trail that day—and only because Allen readily admitted it. Nothing else in the document made much of an impression on him. He remained convinced that the circumstantial evidence he, Murphy, and Ferency had gathered was far more impressive than anything the state had against Allen.

This put Click in an uncomfortable situation. It seemed a realistic possibility that he and his two colleagues had uncovered facts and evidence that had somehow eluded the investigators at Unified Command. Perhaps they had arrested the wrong man?

Click was alone now. Murphy had moved on. Ferency was dead. On July 7, 2021, a former federal correctional officer and mayoral candidate named Shane Meehan had driven his truck up to the brick FBI building in Terre Haute. He hurled a flaming Molotov cocktail at the building just as Ferency happened to walk outside. Then Meehan shot at him. Wounded, Ferency tried to return fire. Meehan walked up to him and shot him in the head, killing him. Questions about Meehan's mental competence were dragging out the whole legal process. Keeping the Odinist theory alive would fall to Click.

Wala worried about Richard Allen. Adjusting to life in Westville was not easy. In a matter of weeks, he had gone from living in a home with his devoted wife to living alone in a secure cell, listening to other inmates scream that he was a child murderer who should kill himself.

She did whatever she could to help him—which admittedly was not much. She advocated for him to get a visit from his wife, Kathy, and she worked to ensure he would have a working tablet so he could communicate with his family. The small window in his cell was so badly scratched and damaged it was difficult to see through; she worked through channels to get it replaced so he could at least glimpse the outside world.

At one of their one-on-one therapy sessions, during which Allen would be kept in a triangular three-by-three cell, she gave him handouts on depression and anxiety. She gave him crossword puzzles and colored pencils. She also provided him with *Man's Search for Meaning*, a book by Viktor Frankl about his time as a prisoner in a Nazi concentration camp. She also sometimes let Allen know about what she was seeing on social media. Some people were saying the case against him did not seem strong, that they supported him. She thought if Allen heard that, he might feel less alone.

A few months into his retirement, James Luttrull was enjoying life after a career spent immersed in tragedy.

Since his days as a young prosecutor in Indianapolis, he had worked on many brutal criminal cases. Luttrull had not originally planned to work as a prosecutor forever. But he saw the devastation wrought by acts of violence, and the necessity of competent, fair prosecution. In one instance, he watched an elderly robbery victim identify her stolen wedding ring on the stand, the one her late husband had slipped on her finger as he promised to love her forever. Shaking, the woman slid it back onto her own finger, and as she left the courtroom, wore it with the evidence tag still dangling. Things like that forced him to stay. He worked nearly thirty-six years with the prosecutor's office in Grant County prosecuting attacks, rapes, and vicious murders. He came to put a lot of focus on crimes against children in particular, attending special trainings to better hone his ability to assemble and try such cases.

An easygoing, thoughtful man with a deep love of the arts and eyes that often squinted intently through his glasses, he long thought that he had become numb to the work. Overtime, he realized he was really relying on his wife Debbie, their children, his faith in God, and things of beauty—a wonderful book, or music by Miles Davis, Van Morrison, or Johann Sebastian Bach—to keep fighting.

After he lost his reelection bid in a heated 2018 race, he went to work for the Indiana Department of Child Services and then the Godly Response to Abuse in the Christian Environment (GRACE), a nonprofit dedicated to confronting abuse in Christian organizations. His entire career was spent dealing with the fallout from evil acts.

Retirement was going to be different. The Luttrulls spent time traveling to North Dakota and Australia to visit family. He took classes on Flannery O'Connor and Malcolm Guite and contemplated taking up writing. The Luttrulls were also considering visiting the great cathedrals of Europe. Luttrull found himself feeling more relaxed than ever.

Then he attended the Indiana Prosecuting Attorneys Council's winter conference in December 2022. Luttrull had served on IPAC's board for fifteen years and on the organization's ethics committee for twelve years. At the conference, he ran into Bob Guy, the soon-to-be former White County prosecutor. Guy knew McLeland. They were friends. He knew how

McLeland worked, what his personality was like. He was trying to find somebody to help the prosecutor out with his case. The idea was to find a senior prosecutor with years of trial experience and a congenial personality that would lend itself to service.

So Guy had a simple question for Luttrull. Would he be willing to speak with the Carroll County prosecutor? Nicholas McLeland might need help trying the Delphi murders case. Luttrull felt honored and anxious at the same time. He was concerned he was rusty from being out of trial work for several years. He did not know much about the Delphi case, other than it was a heinous crime against two children. But he said yes. He would be happy to talk to McLeland.

But it would be some time before he heard anything back.

CHAPTER TWENTY-FIVE

On March 21, 2023, Richard Allen found God. And that is when everything went to hell.

Kathy Allen had been trying to send him a Bible for some time. She finally got one through. Allen had not trusted the text at first. The cover was printed with the words *The Message*. It was a gift from Dr. Dawn Frank, a veterinarian at the practice where Allen's wife once worked.

Allen had taken to reading the Bible—and his studies convinced him that religion could offer a way out. His incarceration, he realized, meant there was a very real possibility that he could never again be fully reunited with his family on earth. But if he made things right with God, then he could be assured they would all be together once more in heaven.

As he understood it, getting right with God would mean taking full responsibility for his sins—including, of course, brutally murdering Libby and Abby. He began confessing to the crime to almost anyone who would listen. He even sent a note to the prison warden, indicating that he wanted to not only confess but also apologize to the families of the victims.

He also needed to tell his wife and mother what he had done. In his calls with them, he told them he had murdered the girls in the same sort of calm, even tones another person might use to describe a trip to the grocery store or the bank.

On the morning of April 2, 2023, Allen reached out to his mother. He complained about being unable to get ahold of his wife. His voice was deadly calm. When Janis spoke, she always seemed on the verge of a chuckle. She mentioned some things that had happened recently, a fire and a few tornadoes. Allen remarked that the prison had been hit by hail. They might have been any other reserved Midwestern mother and son—distant, slightly awkward, reduced to talking about the weather. One thing Allen did not mention was that he had received his legal papers days earlier.

Janis told her son she had started going to church again.

"That's good to hear." Allen got choked up.

Janis told her son that she would not have made it through without God.

"Did Kathy tell you that I told her the other day that I . . . I accepted the Lord Jesus Christ as my savior?"

"Oh, no. That's so wonderful." Janis nearly squealed with delight.

Allen wept. "I didn't know if she told you or not, but God's really important to me right now."

Despite his tears, Allen had much to rejoice over. His family was a gift from God. Come what may, he would see them again, maybe in six months, maybe when they all reunited in heaven. He knew they would love him "no matter what."

On April 3, 2023, Allen caught his wife by surprise.

"I just wanted to apologize to you," he said, over the phone.

"What's going on, sweetheart?"

Allen's voice was calm, controlled. "I did it."

But Kathy Allen spoke at the same time, her polite question sailing right over her husband's murder confession: "Are you not feeling well?"

"I did it."

"You did what?"

"No, I did it."

"What?"

"I killed Abby. I killed Abby and Libby."

"No, you didn't."

"Yes, I did." His tone was even. He needed her to believe him, to accept what he was.

Kathy Allen sounded like a wife scolding her husband for a joke that went too far. "No, you didn't, dear."

She fiercely rejected her husband's confession. She declared that prison officials were messing with his medication. She did not make it clear whether she got that unsubstantiated accusation from Allen's defense team or her own imagination.

"Why would you say that?" she demanded.

A note of worry crept into Allen's voice. He had lost control of the conversation. "Because maybe I did."

"They are messing with you. They are messing with your mind." Allen's wife revealed that she and Janis also suspected the prison staff were lacing his food with some unknown substance, effectively poisoning an inmate. When Allen did not completely back down on his confession, she started loudly crying.

"I just wish they would kill me or let me apologize to the families at least," he said.

"Dear. Don't talk anymore. Just don't talk anymore, okay?"

That same day, Baldwin and Rozzi visited their client. As far as the correctional officers were concerned, those visits always seemed to exacerbate Allen's condition. Baldwin told people later that he no longer trusted the Westville officials who had once been so nice to him. That day, they would not allow him and Rozzi to personally inspect Allen's living conditions.

Baldwin claimed that he and Rozzi had found Allen unresponsive and unable to discuss matters with his attorneys. But the defense team had already gotten a lot of ammunition from their client. They had noted the size of his cell, the round-the-clock suicide companions, and details about his interactions with staff. They were planning to hit the state hard.

On April 5, 2023, Allen's attorneys filed a motion that would bring their client's mental state to the forefront of the case.

The "Emergency Motion to Modify Safekeeping Order," signed only by attorney Brad Rozzi, would mark another turning point in the continually deteriorating relationship between the defense attorneys and the prosecution. Purportedly it was an attempt to get Allen moved out of the Westville Correctional Facility and into the Cass County jail, which was almost across the street from Rozzi's office. But those who knew about Allen's confessions wondered if the motion was more about the defense lawyers trying to get in front of an obviously unexpected challenge in their representation of Allen.

Rozzi went on to describe some of Allen's recent behavior, omitting the fact that he had repeatedly confessed to murdering Abby and Libby. Allen, wrote Rozzi, "appeared to be suffering from various psychotic symptoms which counsel would describe as schizophrenic and delusional." He suggested that the poor state of Allen's mental health was directly attributable to his incarceration at Westville. Allen would even wet down and eat his own discovery materials, although Rozzi did not mention that behavior in the filing.

The filing was accompanied by a picture of Allen wearing a dirty shirt and looking very sad.

Instead of making a straightforward case for Allen to be moved, Rozzi used charged and inflammatory language that seemed more designed to attract press and social media attention than to persuade a judge. Allen, said Rozzi, was being subjected to conditions similar to those of "a prisoner of war" and was being kept in a cell "no larger . . . than a dog kennel." Furthermore, he was "required to wear the same clothes, including underwear, for days and days on end, all of which are soiled, stained, tattered and torn."

The primary problem with all of this was that little of it was true.

CHAPTER TWENTY-SIX

The filing surprised McLeland. Legal filings are typically dry, written for an audience of one: the judge. But Rozzi and Baldwin had thrown in colorful, dramatic language, and even helpfully included the striking pictures of Allen for article thumbnails and news broadcasts, a major boon for the media. The goal seemed to be reaching an audience beyond the courtroom. The prosecutor felt the defense attorneys were preying on emotions rather than focusing on the facts.

In his response filed on April 14, McLeland pointed out—for instance—that Allen was not forced to wear the dirty clothes day after day. He had clean clothes in his cell. The reason he wore a dirty shirt in the photo was because he had just returned from his recreation period and had not yet changed into a fresh garment. McLeland also pointed out that the Cass County jail had fewer mental health resources than Westville, so if Rozzi was truly concerned about his client's well-being, then perhaps he would be better off where he was.

McLeland also noted a bit acidly that "the State believes that the current status of [Allen's] mental health is due to the status of the case, not due to the location of his incarceration."

Allen trusted Wala. He confided in her about his life, his marriage, his drinking. He shared his plans with her, such as how he wanted to use his time in prison to get in better shape and lose weight. On May 3, 2023, he even offered her a fairly complete and detailed account of the murders.

According to him, on the morning of February 13, 2017, he went to visit his mother and sister in Peru, Indiana. The women invited Allen to stay and have lunch with them, but for some reason, he chose to decline. Instead, by his account, he drove back to Delphi. But he did not go home.

Instead he got a six-pack of beer. He drank three of them. And then, with his gun, he went to the trails. His plan, he told Wala, was to lie in wait until he found a woman to stalk. His plan was to kidnap and then rape her. But then he saw Abby and Libby.

He told Wala he thought they were older than they were. In any case, he decided they were the ones he would take. He followed them out to the bridge, where he kidnapped them and forced them down the hill, down to where he would soon murder them.

Allen was a bit hazy on some of the details. He said he did something with his gun, which had caused the unspent round to be ejected. At some point after he had the girls under his control, he saw a white van pass by on a nearby access road.

The sight made Allen uneasy. It scared him. It made him worry he was about to be caught. So he decided to kill the girls. He flicked out a box cutter he stole from work at CVS. He cut their throats. He lingered to make certain they were dead. Alone with the bodies and the blood, he threw some sticks on them and hurried off.

Wala carefully and faithfully recorded the whole story in her notes.

Allen could sense the growing distance with his wife, and it frightened him. On May 10, 2023, Allen even asked Wala to help him call her. After Wala dialed the number for him, he asked her to stay in the room. He wanted the psychologist to hear what he was going to say. He wanted her to understand.

Kathy Allen was on her way to a gas station when her phone rang.

"Hi, honey." She explained that she was also going out to meet Brad, presumably Rozzi. She and her husband commiserated. They both felt as though they were losing their minds. Allen had an odd question for his wife. Could he trust Baldwin and Rozzi?

"They're our lawyers, honey." Her voice was tired. She seemed to regard Baldwin and Rozzi as the family attorneys, rather than strictly her husband's legal representatives.

"I need you to know that I did this," Allen said.

His wife's response sounded a little irritated. "What? No. No, you didn't, dear. There's no way. There's no way, dear—"

"I hope you still love me."

Kathy Allen cut him off. She thought her husband was unwell. She would always love him. But there was no need for him to confess to something he did not do.

Calmly, Allen told her of a dream he had had. In the dream, he knew he needed to let her go. But he could not.

"Well then you're dreaming stuff again, okay? That's all it is."

The call ended with Kathy insisting that Allen was innocent.

Allen called her back right after the first call ended .

"I need to know if you still love me, baby," he said.

"Yes, dear." Kathy Allen was crying.

"Okay. And everybody else will as well?" Allen's wife was silent. "Honey?"

"Yes."

"'Cause I may have to spend the rest of my life here." Allen's voice was completely flat. "I just got to know that everybody's still going to love me."

He and Kathy Allen got into a back-and-forth from there. Allen insisted that his confessions were true. She denied it. Around and around they went in some morbid approximation of an argument between little children.

Allen changed the subject, opining that he might get the electric chair, a method of execution not used in Indiana since 1995. His wife promised him she would not let that happen.

"If it does, will you be there for me?"

"This isn't right. They messed you up so bad."

"It's okay, honey. I did it. I did it, dear."

"Stop."

"I cannot stop." Allen told his wife that somebody was there listening. That person was Wala, who he had asked to accompany him for the confession. He seemed to be letting Kathy Allen know that his statements were irreversible, that he wanted everyone to know what he did.

Allen said he was trying to let her go. But what he really seemed to be doing was trying to solicit sympathy, trying to push his wife into telling him that her love was eternal, that no matter his sins, she would adore him forever. She wept, unable to speak for a moment.

Allen's question was gentle. "Will you always love me, baby?"

She did not answer. "Who's with you? Who's with you? Who's with you? Who's with you? You need to stop talking." Kathy Allen wept as the call ended.

Kathy Allen did not want to hear it. Nor did Wala. She told Allen that he should not be talking about his case with anyone except his attorneys, that doing so was not in his best interests. But Allen kept talking.

On May 17, 2023, Allen told his mother that he guessed he felt all right. Janis chuckled at that.

"It's good to hear your voice," she said.

Allen casually tossed out a question: "So did Kathy tell you that I did it?"

"We're not gonna discuss this, okay?" Janis chided. There was a pause. "Are you there?"

"Yeah, I'm still here."

"Yeah. We love you. You know that, don't you?"

"Regardless?" Allen did not care for the proffers of conditional love. He wanted to know if their love would endure despite his sins.

"Yes."

Allen asked if his wife was okay. Janis said they were "holding each other up."

"I'm just worried that you guys weren't going to love me because of the fact that I said that I did it."

Janis told her son that claiming to have killed the girls did not mean he had really done so.

"Well, it does when I did."

"Rick, don't talk like this. I think they're just messing with you."

"No, Mom, they're not." He paused. "I love you, though."

Janis was adamant. "I just know you don't have it in you to do something like that."

Allen's reply had an edge of exasperation. "Mom . . . I wouldn't sit here and tell you I did it if I didn't."

"Well, if they're messing with your meds and all that, yeah, you would." Like her daughter-in-law, Janis seemed to have adopted a rather specific theory explaining her son's confessions. "But we're not going to discuss the case anymore."

"So if I did do it, then you guys wouldn't love me anymore?"

"There's nothing that would ever make me stop loving you."

Janis changed the topic to the letters she wrote her son every day. Allen said he was not receiving them. His tone became sarcastic. "Great, that's something else to share with my therapist."

At least Allen had one person in Westville he could trust.

On June 5, 2023, Allen called his wife. They talked about coffee. Sounding numb, Allen said talking to his wife felt weird. He felt he had fallen down into hell.

"But you know that I done it, right?" Allen asked her.

"Dear, I don't want to talk about that. Okay? Want to have a good conversation between us?"

For Kathy Allen, a "good conversation" with her husband was any one where he was not begging her to consider that he might be guilty of murdering two teenage girls. Her husband expressed his frustration, but agreed to move on.

"I don't know why nobody will talk to me and be honest with me," he said later.

Kathy Allen seemed to assume he was talking about prison officials. She said that those who worked in corrections viewed him as just another number. But Allen seemed to be talking about those closer to home.

"I just don't feel like anybody's willing to be honest with me anymore." Allen sensed his family pulling away from him. They did not take his calls. They were tight-lipped in conversations. "Like everybody's afraid to hurt my feelings or something."

Kathy Allen offered to arrange to have a chaplain pray with her husband. Allen said he had done just that recently. It had not helped.

"Praying to yourself is going to be very helpful. It's helped me immensely. And I know there's plenty of people out there praying for you so, you just got to pray the bad thoughts away, hon. And try . . . the demons are fighting hard to get you."

"I know," Allen said. "I feel like they've already gotten me. I'm already in hell."

By June 11, 2023, Kathy Allen had finally had enough.

"I did it," Allen told her. "Kathy?"

Kathy Allen said nothing for a moment. "What?"

"I did it." Kathy Allen sighed. "Do you still love me?"

"Yes, dear, but you didn't do it."

"Why do you say that?"

"Why do *you* say it?" his wife echoed.

"I don't want to upset you."

"I'm already upset."

Screaming from the other inmates filled the endless gaps in the conversation.

"I'm sorry." The cold response from Kathy Allen was her husband's cue to back off. "I don't know what I'm doing. I feel like I lost my mind."

"Honey, you can't call me and talk like this, okay?" Acid had crept into her voice. Then, she whispered, "You're killing me."

"I'm so sorry, baby." Allen listened to his wife start to cry.

"I can't talk to you right now."

"I didn't want to do this," Allen said.

His wife just cried.

"Honey, I'm sorry," Allen said. "You're not going to do anything to yourself, are you?"

"No. No."

Suicide threats had always worked as a control before, so Allen decided to throw that in. "Probably going to have to kill myself now."

"Stop. You can't be calling me and talking like this."

"You don't have anything to do with it."

"It doesn't matter."

Allen's question came out like a whine. "Why are you so mad at me?"

"I'm not mad. I'm upset."

Allen repeated that he felt like he was in hell. He claimed to not understand what was going on. He said he was waiting on another Bible from her. "I guess I'm just going to have to stop calling."

CHAPTER TWENTY-SEVEN

Of course, Allen made incriminating statements to people beyond his therapist, his wife, and his mother. He was also talkative with his inmate suicide companions, and later the correctional officers posted outside his cell to make certain he remained alive.

Again and again, he told them he had killed the girls. Allen told one correctional officer that he wanted to rape Abby and Libby, but since he was scared, he killed them instead. He insisted his wife had no knowledge of his actions, and that he had acted completely alone. He repeated that he wanted to confess and appeared baffled that nobody seemed to want to hear it.

"I am ready to confess," he said. "I swear to God, I killed Abby and Libby. Fuck me running."

Allen claimed he molested Abby and Libby, as well as childhood friends named Chris and Kevin. He said he was raped by a babysitter when he was eleven. He claimed his grandfather had molested him too. He said he might have touched his daughter and sister sexually.

He requested Kentucky Fried Chicken and a camping trip and the sacrament of last rites.

"I swear I never cheated on a cigarette while I was eating pizza," he declared. He ran in place naked, declaring that he was sorry for wasting God's time, and promising to never again smoke or cheat on his wife. He masturbated near his door while belting "Mammas Don't Let Your Babies

Grow Up to Be Cowboys." He masturbated a lot in general. He also enjoyed singing "God Bless America."

He said his wife was dead and that his actions killed his future grandchildren and set off a nuclear holocaust. He said he ought to burn in hell. He claimed he killed Abby and Libby to allow himself and his family to live.

"God, I am so glad nobody gave up on me after I killed Abby and Libby," Allen said.

He jabbed his own genitals and rear end with a spork. He urinated on a mat. He sipped toilet water and spat it out. He lined up balls of his own feces on the floor. He said he was not crazy; he was only acting crazy.

Correctional officers wrote down everything he said. They did not think his behavior was due to mental illness. They had all seen plenty of that in prison. But mentally ill inmates lacked Allen's calculatedness.

He would roll back and forth or lightly bang his head on the wall, then stop when a correctional officer started paying attention to him. He would sample his feces, but quickly give up on eating it.

"I won't be doing that again," he muttered once, after smearing it all over his skin.

When no one reacted to the excrement on his face, he quietly wiped it away. He would hover over the toilet, as if working up the resolve to stick his face inside, like a man getting ready to jump into freezing water.

In prison, especially in maximum security units, inmates have very little control over their lives. Acting up can be a method of exerting power and a strategy for negotiation. To the correctional officers, that is what Allen's behavior appeared to be. He wanted attention from them and his family and an in-person visit from his wife.

Once, Allen licked the window of his cell door. His words rang through the little cell.

"Kathy, I did it, I'm guilty," he called. "Run, Kathy, run! I did it!"

Allen's confessions had not gone over as he hoped. From the calls to his family, it was clear he very much wanted them to believe he killed the girls; but he also craved the assurance that they still loved him anyway. He did not get either of those things. His wife and mother tended to grow upset and distant whenever he began his confessions, and they sometimes hung up on him. It became clear to Allen that, as he once put it, he would need to choose between God and his family. Ultimately, the choice was easy for him. He needed his family, so he abandoned God.

Meanwhile, Allen exhibited disordered thoughts, and his behavior deteriorated markedly. Wala and other staff noticed that his behavior seemed worse after visits from his attorneys. It also did not escape their attention that his behavior would suddenly improve whenever he communicated with his family. They wondered if his aberrant acts reflected a real mental breakdown or if he was, for some reason, just faking it.

At a hearing on the safekeeping order on June 15, 2023, McLeland was blunt. He told the judge that he and the Carroll County Sheriff's Office did not care where Allen was housed, provided he was not kept in their understaffed jail. That said, he was not going to let the defense get away with their conspiratorial insinuations. Point by point, he dismantled the defense's arguments in the safekeeping order. In response to the prosecutor's questions, Cass County Sheriff Ed Schroder noted that despite Rozzi's assertions, he did not want Allen in his jail. He would simply comply with any court orders. He said that his county jail, despite being a new facility, would offer fewer mental health resources to Allen than Westville. Galipeau also arrived for some terse testimony, in which he explained the special privileges Allen received. When other inmates broke their tablets, they lost that privilege until they could pay for a new one. When Allen smashed his device in a fit of anger, he got a replacement free of charge.

One thing that played in the defense's favor was Allen's appearance at the hearing. The chubby man the world had glimpsed in a mug shot was gone. Allen had implemented a strict diet for himself in prison, although he was sure to never skip enough meals to trigger a hunger strike response from the staff. As a result, he had dropped a considerable amount of weight. To the public, he appeared pale, fragile, and delicate. That alone prompted much concern about his safety in prison.

Regardless, after a somewhat unassured start over the PCA, McLeland dominated the safekeeping hearing. He had spent hours and hours preparing. The Pattys were impressed. They began to warm up to McLeland. He seemed to know his stuff.

As time passed, other people also began to grow more confident in the prosecutor. Superintendent Carter once found himself sitting at the command center with McLeland and Holeman. He brought up a fact of the case, and his two companions got into a fierce debate. To prove his point, McLeland hurried over to a particular box and opened it up. Out of all the containers and cabinets, he knew immediately the exact location of a paper Carter casually brought up. He read it, and smiled. He was right, to Holeman's chagrin.

Rozzi's performance at the hearing, in contrast, was bombastic and with a slightly desperate edge. Instead of narrowly focusing on the law or highlighting the lack of objection from the state, he and Baldwin made Allen out to be the worst-treated inmate in the history of the world. The defense's strategy prompted plenty of click-worthy headlines, but it backfired.

Gull decided to leave Allen where he was. As if that loss was not bad enough, Gull threw in something more.

"The evidence presented at the hearing," she wrote in her order, "did not support many of the allegations advanced by defendant counsel." She was using polite, professional, and legalistic language, but her meaning was clear: She felt Rozzi and Baldwin had lied to her.

CHAPTER TWENTY-EIGHT

Baldwin had access to thousands of pages of discovery in the Delphi case—police reports, interview transcripts, crime scene photos, and more. Many web sleuths following the case would have given anything to paw through such a trove. Despite that, Baldwin still went to YouTube.

While on the site, the attorney started looking up videos associated with the Delphi case. He recalled seeing patches on some correctional officers' uniforms at Westville, patches that seemed to suggest an allegiance to Odin. Perhaps the memory of those patches inspired him to tailor his search a bit; in any case, he somehow found a YouTube video that posited with no evidence that the murders were committed by associates of a motorcycle gang called the Sons of Odin.

Something about the video got Baldwin's mental wheels turning. In the days to come, he would recommend that people who wanted to learn about what really happened to the girls give the video a careful watch.

Todd Click still could not figure out what to do. He had doubts about the case against Richard Allen and was concerned investigators might be overlooking what he considered far stronger evidence: everything he, along with Murphy and Ferency, had turned up about the Rushville connection.

He finally decided to ask a friend for his advice as to what course of action to take.

The person he turned to was Paul Barada, a high school acquaintance who was a former Rush County prosecutor and now an area defense attorney. Barada advised him to write a letter to McLeland and voice his concerns. That would put Click on the record. The investigator readily agreed. He was determined to share his strong opinions about an investigation he was only marginally involved with.

Click mailed the letter on April 28, 2023.

The defense assembled a team. In the beginning, they hired Jason Jensen, a private investigator out of Utah. Jensen did not last long. Baldwin told people that he talked too much. But Jensen's Indiana-based associates Erica Morse and Christine Salzer lingered, although their roles on the team were often unclear.

Brian Alvey was an investigator for Baldwin's Criminal Defense Team, the law firm Baldwin had cofounded. He had worked on the Delphi case. Another investigator the defense team selected was not really an investigator at all. A large man with a thin beard of gray gristle, Matt Hoffman had once served as the fire chief of Carmel, one of Indiana's toniest cities. In the billing, he was listed as an assistant and was paid fifteen dollars an hour. But he was investigating nonetheless. Baldwin loved his dedication.

When it came to the defense's recruitment, strong loyalty and enthusiasm appeared to be valued over experience and sober-minded critique.

In one pretrial hearing at the Carroll County Courthouse, Hoffman ended up on the elevator with Holeman. As Holeman went on about how his knees popped, Hoffman gave the police investigator a tense smile. Then Hoffman watched Holeman exit the elevator and walk away. Slowly, Hoffman extended his middle finger and held it aloft at Holeman's back.

People close to Hoffman described him as a true believer. Men like Holeman were his enemy. That alone made him a good fit for the defense team. The usual nuances, the gray areas, the complications of professionals working on opposite sides of the common goal of determining some approximation of the truth—they were all falling away fast. The defense team saw itself in a battle between light and darkness.

In any criminal case, a defense attorney must be prepared to argue that the prosecution or the investigators had made mistakes which led them to arrest the wrong man. But Baldwin went beyond that. He told people that law enforcement had not simply made some errors but that they had consciously chosen to arrest someone they knew was not guilty. Baldwin claimed that police had known who the real killers of Abby and Libby were by no later than February 1, 2018 (the significance of that date was uncertain) and had then for some presumably nefarious reason chosen to direct their attention elsewhere. The defense attorney even went so far as to say that when the story of the case was written, the villain of the piece would be Tony Liggett.

Baldwin claimed he had proof beyond a reasonable doubt of the guilt of his suspect and proudly noted privately that he had even convinced the skeptical Brad Rozzi of what he was saying. But, of course, persuading a jury would be far more difficult than winning over his cocounsel.

It also seemed possible that Baldwin's judgment may have been clouded by his increasingly emotional connection to what he saw as Allen's plight. The attorney claimed he often wept and became overwhelmed when he pondered what his client was going through behind bars. He professed that it left him feeling helpless and all he could do was hope and pray that Allen did not suffer what he described as "a Jeffrey Epstein–styled 'suicide.'"

CHAPTER TWENTY-NINE

While all of this was going on, the Kegan Kline story moved to a close. As always, the case was complicated by Kegan's unpredictable behavior. As his oft-delayed trial date neared, Kegan decided he did not want to face a jury of his peers after all and switched his plea to guilty. But then—before he was sentenced—he had second thoughts. He fired his defense attorney Andrew Achey and announced he wanted a new attorney. He might not want to plead guilty after all.

A pair of fresh lawyers, William Berkshire and Eric Huneryager, was duly appointed. The ever-shifting Kegan consulted with them and chose to stand by his guilty plea.

Miami County Deputy Prosecutors Courtney Alwine and Jennifer Kiefer were working on the case against Kegan. Alwine was originally going to be the second chair for Diedrichs. But when Kiefer joined the office at the start of 2023, there was a reshuffling of cases, and the two women teamed up to try Kegan. A native of Peru with a slight frame and large eyes, Alwine and her wife had just welcomed a daughter. Kegan's crimes against children sickened her. Alwine could be fiery, with a passionate and forceful courtroom style. Bespectacled and wearing her dark hair in a sleek bob, Kiefer was icier, excelling in legal writing. Beyond that, the two found their approaches were very similar.

Once, Kiefer told Alwine, "I don't think that you and I should work very well together, but we work really well together."

Despite the early tension between Miami County and the state police, they also got along great with Vido, and worked closely with the lead detective. Together, they had hurtled toward a much-anticipated trial. Then Kegan surprised everyone with his guilty plea.

The two young attorneys now had some choices to make.

Sentencing hearings were typically brief and simple affairs. But the prosecutors wanted to ensure Kegan received the longest sentence possible. That meant making sure Judge Timothy Spahr got the relevant information about Kegan's offenses, the specific details that qualified under the statute as aggravating circumstances. With that knowledge, Spahr could then pass a lengthy sentence.

Had there been a trial, Spahr would have learned all of that information through direct witness testimony. But Kegan's plea had short-circuited that. Typically Spahr would now access that information by reading detailed reports. Alwine and Kiefer did not think that was good enough.

First, Kiefer penned a brief explaining in detail why Kegan's crimes statutorily warranted decades in prison. Then, the prosecutors chose to call their witnesses at sentencing so that Spahr—and the world—could hear firsthand exactly what Kegan had done. And so, in the ten-hour-long sentencing hearing, the public learned the horrible details. Kegan had emotionally manipulated young girls into sending him nudes—even convincing one girl to do so when she was in the hospital with her ill mother. He even had videos of toddlers being molested by adult men.

As Alwine spoke in court, the anger in her voice was palpable. Kegan refused to look her in the eye.

Spahr had presided over the Kegan Kline case with an air of affability and tolerance, even when facing a gallery full of social media sleuths. The gray-haired, smiley judge was patient and genial enough to answer an unrelated scheduling question a local woman shouted out in the middle of a hearing, rather than remonstrate with her or order her removal. Toward the end of the sentencing hearing, he left to observe the images and videos on Kegan's phone When he returned, he was ashen-faced. The amiable tone was gone. He had seen things most people can scarcely imagine. Spahr sentenced Kegan to forty-three years. He would have to serve at least twenty-six years before becoming eligible for parole.

Alwine spent the next day with her one-year-old daughter. She did not have to worry about the girl now. She was safe, always with people Alwine loved and trusted. But Alwine knew that safety would not last forever. Her daughter would grow up, and at some point Alwine would not be able to protect her from the world. All she could do was teach her. But her daughter would be twenty-seven years old when Kegan got out of prison.

I can't protect you from everyone, thought Alwine. *But I just protected you from Kegan Kline.*

CHAPTER THIRTY

McLeland agonized over the prospect of seeking help. He had never tried a case with other attorneys. He had always struggled with delegation. The idea of bringing on deputy prosecutors to work on the Delphi case filled him with dread.

But toward the end of the summer of 2023, McLeland accepted that he could not do the whole trial alone. Just getting himself and his witnesses prepared for the one-day hearing on the safekeeping motion had been a challenge. He could not imagine trying to handle a weeks-long trial. So he went to get help.

Some lawyers go back and forth between the prosecution and the defense. McLeland himself had started his career as a defense attorney. But when it came time for him to select two new lawyers to work with him in the case against Richard Allen, McLeland chose people who had spent almost their entire careers as prosecutors.

As a child, Stacey Diener spent plenty of time in courthouses. Her mother worked as a legal secretary, so she grew up around lawyers. She was always struck by the soaring, historic buildings, the intelligent, sharp-dressed attorneys. Even at a young age, she was drawn to the professionalism she encountered visiting her mother at work.

Soon after graduating law school, she started as a prosecutor to gain trial experience. But she soon found she had a special affinity for it. She worked for decades in Indiana's Pulaski County. She joined the office in the nineties, at a time when the sexism in the legal field was still so overt that her female boss ordered her to wear skirts, not pants, in court. In Pulaski County, she eventually rose to serve as the county's elected prosecutor. Diener was slender with sandy-brown hair and a commanding air about her. When she moved down to White County, she worked in prosecutor Bob Guy's office as a deputy prosecutor for years. That is where she met McLeland, back when he was a defense attorney. Diener felt she was good at spotting lawyers who took the job seriously. He had struck her as highly organized and prepared. Even though they were on opposing sides, they became friends. Diener was one of the people who had encouraged him to put his name in for prosecutor in 2017. They stayed in touch.

In the years since, she faced a series of political woes. After losing a contentious judicial election, Diener found herself ostracized by the White County political establishment. In 2022, she lost her bid to succeed Guy as county prosecutor. Prosecuting crimes had been a core part of Diener's life for nearly three decades. It influenced how she viewed the world, how she had parented her children, how protective she had always been of them. But after all of those years, she was out of the job. She started her own practice and got to work tackling family law because she felt she could rely on her experience prosecuting cases concerning child welfare and domestic violence.

After the arrest of Allen, Diener's calls with McLeland would drift into the Delphi case. She had not followed the story closely. Over the years, whenever her husband had tried to tell her about news coverage of the murders, she would caution him that media reports were often inaccurate. She was vaguely aware that the case had elicited a lot of attention, and the idea that others might view the murder of two kids as entertainment bothered her.

Diener would offer to go work for McLeland. She felt she could help him. "I don't know," he would say. "Do you really want to be a part of this?"

He would tell her about all the negative public attention, the endless speculation, the messages from other prosecutors second-guessing McLeland's every move. Diener did not care about any of that. Two girls had been murdered. A trial was looming. It was work that mattered, and work she felt she was good at. She wanted McLeland to know she was there if he decided he needed help.

McLeland's hesitation about the possibility of accepting help thawed in the spring. Bob Guy kept pushing him to meet with Luttrull.

"Trust me," he kept saying. "You guys are going to get along."

In May 2023, McLeland finally reached out to Luttrull. The two men met at the prosecutor's office in the Carroll County courthouse. Then they went out to Delphi's Sandwich Shop. McLeland bought Luttrull a burger and fries and told him about the case.

Luttrull listened. At first, he did not quite grasp the meaning of all the facts laid out in the PCA. McLeland could tell just from the expression on his face. In time, the significance of the sequence of events and witness sightings laid out in the filing would dawn on Luttrull. In the meantime, his mind grabbed a hold of the case and would not let go.

Luttrull liked McLeland and the way he talked about the prosecutor's role. In his view, a good prosecutor was not a lawyer for the victims or law enforcement, but focused on securing justice for victims and working well with law enforcement. They should not be primarily driven by political or reputational concerns, but instead work on being trustworthy above all else. Prosecutors did not make the facts, and good ones did not force them to fit a particular theory of a case. Throughout his career as a prosecutor, Luttrull felt his knees always trembled a bit whenever a judge called on him to stand and speak on behalf of the state. It was a job that carried immense power. In his mind, McLeland took the work seriously, but the Carroll County prosecutor did not seem to take himself too seriously. That resonated with Luttrull too.

At the end of August 2023, Click got a call from Steve Mullin, an investigator for the Carroll County Prosecutor's Office. He invited Click to the Indiana State Police post in Lafayette to share what he had on the Rushville theory of the crime. But Click seemed to assume the meeting had another purpose: that at some point, the people in charge would share everything they had against the defendant so that Click could be convinced that Allen was indeed the guilty man.

Click agreed to the meeting. When he arrived at the post, he got the first of several surprises. Mullin was not there. Carroll County prosecutor McLeland was also not there. Holeman *was* there, but only to greet Click. At some point in their exchange, Holeman casually mentioned a major problem with Click's theories. According to Click, the primary person responsible for the killings was a man named Brad Holder. But, Holeman pointed out, records from Holder proved beyond all doubt that he was at work on the day of the murders and had then gone straight to the gym. His alibi was airtight; he could not have done it.

To Click, things were not quite that simple. True, thanks to the video Libby had taken on her phone, investigators did have a time stamp of the exact moment the girls were kidnapped. But was it not possible to argue that they were actually killed much, much later? And if they had been murdered hours later, wouldn't Holder's solid alibi become much less relevant?

After speaking with Holeman, Click was sent to an interview room with Vido.

Once the two men were alone, Click offered a little explanation. "Yeah. When I saw [the arrest] on the news, I just didn't get that warm and fuzzy feeling."

Vido got down to business. "Start from the beginning," he told Click. "And just work all the way to the end." Click spent the next hour or so doing just that, giving the detective a summary of his efforts on the case.

Dumbfounded, Vido sat and listened. He had been intimately involved with the Delphi investigation and knew the details of it as well as anyone. As Click spoke, it became increasingly clear to him that the Rushville policeman just did not know much about the facts of the murders he claimed to have spent so much time investigating. But Click did not let his lack of information prevent him from feeling certainty that his elaborate theory of the crime should be given more credence than the one the actual investigators painstakingly developed and based upon actual evidence. Furthermore, Click's theory seemed downright bizarre and involved a substantial number of people who had somehow managed to keep it all a secret for years. To Vido, the theory was clearly nonsense.

"Well," Vido said when Click was finally done, "we appreciate you coming in and talking with us. You're free to go."

Click seemed genuinely surprised by the dismissal. "I thought you guys were going to tell me what you guys had on Allen to help put my mind at ease on this."

Vido shook his head. "We can't talk with you because of the gag order."

Around this time, Holeman strode into the room. "Vido gave you the politically correct answer," he said. "I'll give you the not so politically correct answer. Allen has confessed numerous times on telephone recordings." This information, of course, was not secret. It had been disclosed in court filings and hearings. "We're confident we got our guy."

The two troopers reminded Click he was free to leave, and they walked him from the interview room to the lobby. What Click saw there brought him to a dead stop. Sitting patiently in a chair was none other than Brad Holder, Click's suspect.

Holeman nodded at the man. "Brad, you want to come on back?"

They were going to formally interview Holder! Click knew this angle of the case better than anyone else; he would know how to handle it better than these guys. He turned to Holeman. "Let me sit in on this."

Holeman refused. "No," he said, his voice firm. "We've got it. Thanks. You're free to go."

The state police did not need Click. But Richard Allen did.

And so, one Sunday morning, Click drove over to Franklin, Indiana—the home of the Criminal Defense Team. There, he met with Baldwin and Rozzi and a room of their colleagues. They kept him there for nearly four hours, asking him about every last detail of his investigation.

Despite all of Click's work on this case, Holeman and Vido had only given him an hour. They had not taken him seriously. The defense gave him half a day. They told him that he, Murphy, and Ferency had done an exemplary investigation. They became emotional when he spoke.

CHAPTER THIRTY-ONE

Baldwin worked on the Franks memorandum for months, even sharing early drafts with colleagues like Johnson County Prosecutor Lance Hamner. Ostensibly a request for a hearing on the defense's allegation that police had lied to obtain the search warrant for Allen's home, the memo somehow metamorphosed and grew into a detailed, 136-page presentation of Baldwin and Rozzi's theory of the case. There was a reason for this.

Up until June 2023, much of the court filings in the Allen case had been kept sealed and unavailable to the public. Áine Cain and Kevin Greenlee, journalists and hosts of *The Murder Sheet* podcast, believed this was a violation of court rules and filed into the case to request greater public access. Gull agreed with their reasoning, unsealed hundreds of pages of court records and indicated that future filings would be made available to the public.

Baldwin saw this as an opportunity. In a June 2023 discussion of the then unwritten Franks memo, the attorney said the defense team could alter the public's view of the case through filings. He clearly intended to make the most of that, writing the memo with such passion that he claimed he got angry as he typed it.

As he worked, Baldwin struggled to try to make the complicated story he was trying to tell easily understandable to people not familiar with the case. He even went to the extent of sharing the work in progress with wives of friends of his. The end result, he said, was that there were now some very upset women out there who wanted Richard Allen released from prison.

In essence, the memorandum contended that the girls had been murdered by a cult of Odinists as part of some ritual. It was not clear why the defense believed that, as they offered no proof and could not even produce evidence indicating that any Odinists had ever committed murder as part of a ritual. In fact, the lawyers seemed to have little grasp of the very concept of Norse paganism.

In their behemoth memorandum, Rozzi and Baldwin used the term *Odinists* generally to refer to all Norse pagans. But the defense attorneys got some crucial facts wrong. The subject was far more complicated than they seemed to realize.

All Norse pagans worshipped an ancient Germanic religion and celebrated a whole pantheon of gods. Followers of this faith live all over the world.

In the United States, certain terms referred to specific groups associated with Norse paganism.

Inclusive heathens practice a progressive, non-racialist form of the faith and welcome all worshippers.

Saying someone followed Ásatrú usually meant they had adopted an exclusionary, racist, whites-only form of Norse paganism, although the term only recently took on those connotations and did not have such associations abroad.

Odinists were a violent gang of white supremacists largely linked to prisons.

If Odinists were like a violent gang inspired by the racist, antisemitic Christian Identity movement, then Ásatrú were more like non-criminal members of a Christian church that preached racist ideas. That left inclusive heathens as members of a mainline Protestant denomination that welcomed everyone. Each of those groups followed the cross and worshipped Jesus Christ, but they could not be more different in practice.

In other words, worshipping Odin did not guarantee someone was dangerous or even a racist. That was a problem, because the memorandum also accused specific correctional officers of possibly being involved in a vast Odinist conspiracy. The defense attorneys reported that two officers had been spotted wearing patches. One read, "In Odin We Trust." The other patch showed an American flag cut with a valknut. The symbol of interlocking triangles is common within heathenry and may symbolize Odin or those who have fallen in battle. White supremacist groups occasionally use it, but the symbol is also favored by nonracist heathens.

Even more confusingly, the defense team referred to those who followed Odin as *Odinites*—but that term refers to a rare mineral and not a believer in a particular faith. It seemed clear that the defense did not fully understand what they were writing about. Their filing had done the equivalent of accusing a person of being part of the white supremacist Christian Identity movement simply because they wore a cross. Members of a racist and violent Christian group might adopt the cross as a symbol; but one could not jump to conclusions about their specific beliefs based on a highly ubiquitous symbol alone.

Furthermore, the defense team suggested that the words of Professor Jeffrey Turco, a crucial expert uncovered by the police, had been twisted. The state police, after speaking with Turco, filed a report indicating that the academic was skeptical of claims of Norse pagan symbols being present at the crime scene. But Baldwin suggested that Turco secretly supported the defense's theory. His hypothesis seemed largely based upon the fact that the prosecution had not provided the defense with Turco's name as quickly as Baldwin wished. Therefore, his reasoning seemed to be, the state must be trying to hide Turco and, presumably, they would only do that because Turco would somehow damage the case. But Baldwin's guesses were incorrect; after the state managed to dig Turco's name out of the investigative files, the academician clarified that Holeman's summary of his words had been accurate.

The memorandum also included a lengthy and detailed description of the crime scene. Now, for the first time, the public had become privy to exactly how the girls died. The reason for including such disturbing information in the motion was unclear, as the facts had, at best, a tenuous relationship to the legal points being argued.

At times the memorandum devolved into out-and-out fantasy. For instance, Baldwin complained that the circumstances of Allen's incarceration would make it difficult for Allen to tell his attorneys: "The guards are telling me that my wife and family will be killed unless I call my wife and tell her that I killed those girls."

An accompanying footnote casually conceded that "Richard Allen has never spoken these words to his attorneys."

Another footnote included a citation for a YouTuber whose main claim to fame was threatening to blow up the memorial park dedicated to Abby and Libby. But this YouTuber had done something perhaps even more troubling that had not received the same level of attention. Somehow he had gotten a copy of a picture of McLeland spending Christmas Eve with his young daughters. He posted the image, accompanying it with a question for McLeland. How would he feel if the strange YouTuber came to town and harmed those little girls? The posting deeply offended McLeland. It remained unclear why exactly the defense had singled out this YouTuber to mention in the memo.

For the defense, the most crucial evidence of Odinism amounted to certain details from the crime scene. Some sticks had been tossed onto the bodies of the girls. Most had concluded this was done to help conceal them from view. Profilers from the United States Marshals Service's BAU believed it might be a sign of "undoing," or a killer's attempt to distance himself from his actions. The defense claimed the sticks had actually been carefully arranged in order to create runes—symbols, they said, of those practicing Odinism.

Libby's blood had also been left on a tree near the bodies. Baldwin argued that it, too, was a painstakingly created symbol, yet another sign of Odinist involvement in the crimes.

But for many readers, the biggest takeaway from the memorandum was the incessant drumbeat of negativity directed toward the investigators—particularly Liggett. Phrases like "Liggett concealed," "Liggett lied," "Liggett flat out lied," and "Liggett behaved recklessly" were littered throughout the document—accusations with little or no proof. On the other hand, the memorandum was full of wildly effusive praise for the work of Todd Click, Greg Ferency, and Kevin Murphy. They were "honorable law enforcement officers" whose "dogged pursuit of the truth is what we citizens, and those accused of crimes, should expect out of law enforcement."

Baldwin knew the contents were dramatic enough to generate much media attention. The attorney relished the prospect.

When night fell over his office in Franklin, old standard melodies could sometimes be heard drifting out from the windows. He told people he believed his life, and the lives of his family members, could be in danger. He talked to his relatives about how his work could set bad men after them. Speaking to others, Baldwin framed releasing the memorandum as a necessary protective measure. If the world knew the truth, they would pay attention to him, and to some of his chief suspects. That could help Baldwin stay safe.

He told people he was not out to punish anyone. But when the memorandum was released, he said, lives would change.

CHAPTER THIRTY-TWO

As the release date for the Franks memorandum grew closer, Baldwin reached out to the various stakeholders to let them know what was about to happen. To some people who received those calls, Baldwin came across as grandiose, dramatically predicting that his words about the Odinism theory would land like an atomic bomb.

To others, he raised the possibility that perhaps the Franks memorandum would never need to be released at all. The attorney spoke of a plan that resembled something out of a not-terribly-plausible movie. The defense would go to McLeland, let him know everything they had on Odinism, and then tell him this was his opportunity to drop the whole case, walk away, and save face. If McLeland eschewed that deal, the defense would go ahead and release the memorandum.

No such chat with McLeland ever occurred. The case against Allen continued, and on September 18, 2023, the defense team filed the memorandum.

As Baldwin fully expected, the filing attracted a firestorm of attention—though not all of it the kind the attorney hoped for or wanted. Privately he had been using extravagant language about how the information in the filing would bring light to a case that had been in darkness. He imagined that the media would take up the cause and investigate the unfounded allegations about conditions at Westville, that parents of African American inmates would be outraged and demand answers about the supposedly racist guards Baldwin claimed were there. The defense attorney even openly dreamed of the inevitable day Richard Allen would be set free, sue for wrongful arrest and receive enough money that he need never work again.

None of those things happened.

Click could not even finish the memo. He was upset about the publication of the details of the girls' deaths—and by the general tone and thesis of the piece. In his mind, Baldwin had distorted the truth. Click issued a statement about it to the press. "No one in law enforcement believes Abby and Libby were killed in a ritual sacrifice," he wrote. "That is the defense twisting facts for sensationalism." Behind the scenes, Baldwin did not appear to consider the possibility that Click's criticism had been sincere. Instead, he suggested that Click had only said what he did about the memo in order to keep people in law enforcement from attacking him.

Having one of the investigators he had praised in the memorandum come out against its central thesis was a blow to Baldwin, but there were other critics. Publicly laying out his theory in detail did not inspire the country to rise as one and demand Allen's release. Instead, it motivated scores of internet sleuths and reporters to comb through everything and look for holes in the argument, much like they had done with the PCA. The chatter largely focused on the alleged runes on the girls' bodies and the purported symbol on the tree. Many of the true crime fanatics were eager for something to decode from the comfort of their own homes. Others were skeptical of the over-the-top claims.

Barbara MacDonald, a reporter who had migrated to Court TV after HLN's demise, broadcast an illustration of what she claimed to be an accurate rendition of what had appeared on the tree. The drawing was not terribly accurate.

But the defense could not point out that the illustration was off. They could certainly not provide the public with an image of the bloody tree; such crime scene materials were under a protective order from the judge and could not be shared.

In early October, a picture of the bloody tree was posted on Facebook by a man named Mark Robert Cohen. He did not explain how he got the image, but most people (correctly) accepted it as an actual photo of the tree at the crime scene. The photo proved that MacDonald's drawing had not been accurate. Some who saw the photograph commented that the blood on the tree was nothing but a smear, but others thought Libby's blood appeared to form the letter *F* or a Nordic rune—just as Baldwin claimed it did.

As far as the defense was concerned, the issue of the blood on the tree had been resolved. That left the matter of the sticks left on the bodies of the girls.

CHAPTER THIRTY-THREE

The text came in late. "I can show you the bodies."

The message was from Mark Robert Cohen, a Texas tattoo artist who had become obsessed with the Delphi murders. On October 4, 2023, he messaged Áine Cain and Kevin Greenlee, journalists and hosts of *The Murder Sheet*, a true crime podcast that covered the case. Cohen was the one who had also recently posted the picture of the bloody tree.

Now Cohen was offering to show them more. Cain and Greenlee had a policy of generally saying yes whenever a tipster asked if they wanted to see something explosive: irrefutable proof of the rot in Carroll County, never-before-seen search warrants, or conclusive evidence of a grand conspiracy involving Ronald Logan, Kegan Kline, and Richard Allen. Asking for substantiation had served the reporters well when it came to debunking misinformation and sifting out cranks. Anyone who failed to deliver could be written off as a waste of time.

Well past midnight, Cain and Greenlee replied to Cohen. They wrote that they were "interested in seeing whatever pictures you have." They agreed to keep Cohen's information confidential.

Cohen sent the pictures. There was no question about the authenticity of the photographs. The images were graphic. Abby and Libby were there on the screen, pale upon the forest floor. Cain began to cry.

Setting down their phones, Cain and Greenlee decided to inform both parties of the massive breach. They would need to act with caution and secure permission from Cohen before making any major moves. It was far too early to alert anyone. In the morning, they would get to work.

They reached Holeman soon after waking. Greenlee told him: "Somewhere in the system there is a pretty substantial leak."

"The *F* tree' photo?" Holeman asked. The investigators were already aware of that. After spotting Cohen's post, Becky had texted McLeland, reaching the prosecutor while he was out barbecuing with friends. Her granddaughter's blood was all over Facebook. McLeland was scrambling to figure out what had happened. Everyone was trying to figure out how Cohen had accessed discovery.

"That's part of it," Greenlee replied. "We got the '*F* tree' photo. And in addition to that, they sent us crime scene pictures, which show bodies."

"Oh, God," Holeman said. "Just so I can start preparing this, how many photos?" he asked. "Of Liberty? Or Libby and Abby?"

Cain and Greenlee listed the images they had received: Libby's body, Abby's body, a close-up of Abby's hair, two unreleased suspect sketches, the blood-smeared tree, and an image of two clothed women covered in sticks that had been lifted from Brad Holder's Facebook account.

"Okay," Holeman said. "Fuck." He sounded tired and angry. He dwelled on the possibility that one of his own colleagues had torpedoed the case. But he did not believe anyone he worked with would release discovery.

Then again, if the leaker was indeed a colleague, Holeman would need to act fast. The authorities would have to identify and fire the culprit as quickly as possible. But even if they acted swiftly, Gull could punish the prosecution by tossing evidence. She could even dismiss the case entirely.

Cain and Greenlee had little information to share with Holeman beyond the fact photographs had leaked. They would need to consult with Cohen to find out how he wished to proceed, but because he had published the image of the tree through his own personal Facebook account, he all but ensured that law enforcement would soon be looking at him.

The reporters also sent an email to the defense team that day, alerting them to the existence of a leak and the published bloody tree photograph. If fault lay with the prosecutor's office or law enforcement, then the defense would need to demand a full investigation. For whatever reason, the defense team seemed far less interested in running through the details of the leak than Holeman. Greenlee sent them yet another email, underscoring the likelihood of a major leak and providing examples of internet chatter around the situation. Until he and Cain talked to Cohen, he did not feel comfortable passing on too many details or identifying his source. Still, they wanted to give the defense team a chance to launch their own investigation.

Word spread within the case. McLeland was desperate to plug the leak. He called Holeman again and again, asking for updates. Becky and Mike Patty had seen the bloody tree photo when it was first posted. When she learned there were worse pictures circulating, Becky was determined to protect her granddaughter's privacy. Libby was a modest girl. The leak felt like an insult to her memory. Over the years, she had become plugged in with some of the truly well-meaning internet sleuths. One of her contacts got to work piecing together what was happening.

Cain and Greenlee did not succeed in reaching Cohen again until after eleven o'clock at night. They told him the police had noted him posting the bloody tree photo on his Facebook page. Standing safely within the borders of Texas, the tattoo artist felt himself being sucked into the tornado forming hundreds of miles away in Indiana.

"I don't have any bad intentions or anything like that," Cohen said. He wanted to cooperate with law enforcement and the legal parties, but he wanted Cain and Greenlee to act as a barrier. Cohen said his wife had just left him. He said his daughter suffered from chronic illness, and that in March 2021, she had undergone kidney and liver transplants. The one event he had to look forward to was taking her to Disneyland later in October. He could not let the leak tear his life apart. Not now.

He told the reporters the name of his source for the images. It was a man named Robert Fortson, whom Cohen believed was an attorney working with Baldwin.

With Cohen's permission, Cain and Greenlee shared the name with Holeman.

The next afternoon, a YouTuber named Rick Snay told his small audience that he had been leaked crime scene photos, but he insisted he would not share them. This seemed at last to snag the attention of the Allen defense team. At 4:13 P.M., Rozzi sent an email to Gull, Baldwin, and McLeland, attaching to it a screenshot of Snay's post about the pictures.

"Andy and I wanted to touch base with you before the end of the work week," Rozzi wrote. "The issue revolves around the possibility that some of the crime scene photos have been leaked, so to speak, and are in the hands of the public."

He said that while the image of the blood of a child murder victim on a tree was "not overly disturbing," the breach was certainly worrying.

"Of greater concern is the fact that a local content creator, by the name of Rick Snay, has apparently communicated to the public that he has copies of the crime scene photos," he wrote.

Rozzi claimed that he and his team had "just learned of this in the last hour" and had "immediately called Nick." That was not entirely true, given that Cain and Greenlee had reached out the day before, only to receive a strangely incurious response that resulted in their next-day follow-up. Still, Rozzi griped that McLeland had "known about this for the past twenty-four to thirty hours or so."

"The primary purpose of this email is to communicate our concerns with the situation," Rozzi wrote. "We most certainly did not leak this information. We wanted to make sure we got out ahead of this and informed the court, as well as Nick, in the event these pictures found their way on the internet.

Behind the scenes Andrew Baldwin claimed to suspect that the photos were most likely leaked by the police as part of a win at all costs mentality and that whoever did it should be hung by their balls.

CHAPTER THIRTY-FOUR

When Cain and Greenlee finally reached Cohen late that evening, Cohen was worried and wanted to know if he was in trouble. The podcasters assured him that everybody—the judge, the prosecution, the defense, and law enforcement—simply wanted to know the truth. They also asked him if he had leaked to Snay.

"I didn't send anything to Rick Snay," Cohen said, seemingly taken aback. Much later on he revealed that he had shared the photographs with a Florida YouTuber who then spread them far and wide.

Cohen offered to send Cain and Greenlee screenshots of his entire message history with Fortson on Reddit and Facebook. He had one caveat: Cain and Greenlee would need to share the images with law enforcement. They agreed.

As the conversation went on, Cohen began sending the relevant screenshots. The images allowed the podcasters to pinpoint Fortson's Facebook account. He seemed to be a random suburban dad with no obvious links to Baldwin or his team. How did he get access to crime scene photos in the highest-profile case in the state?

Cain and Greenlee once again asked Cohen about Fortson. How had this man gotten involved in the leak? Why had he leaked discovery materials? What was his motivation?

"He said that he didn't know if Allen was guilty, but the people that he's close with are working to make him not guilty," Cohen said. "So he just wanted to see what the prosecution had. So, what did he say? Whatever help that they needed from him or input they needed from him, he would feel morally okay about it." Cohen paused. "Like I said, he's a good guy, but I don't know why he picked me to share that shit with."

Fortson had a friend who told him secrets. That friend was hooked up with the defense team in the Delphi case. That friend gathered intelligence and was generous enough to share. He knew Fortson was intrigued with the case too. Both men were fascinated with Delphi—obsessed, even.

Fortson's career was solidly situated with the Air National Guard. He had enlisted right after graduating high school. He did a total of four deployments in the Middle East.

Beyond his deployments, he stuck with the National Guard. He worked at the Fort Wayne Air National Guard Base. He lived in Fishers, Indiana, a northern suburb of Indianapolis. He was married and had a daughter.

Fortson also had an obsessive side. Many of those around him knew this, but few of them knew the extent of his fascination with the Delphi murders. On Facebook and on Reddit, under his own name and aliases, he joined a variety of Delphi-focused groups. He first met Cohen there. Together, the two men picked over every detail of the Delphi case.

The messages between them showed that by the end of September, the two Delphi aficionados were in touch every day. On Wednesday, September 27, 2023, Fortson sent Cohen the bloody tree photo. He would later send the images of the bodies to Cohen over Reddit.

Fortson claimed he had somehow accessed those materials due to his association with Baldwin's firm, the Criminal Defense Team. He further claimed to have been an attorney on the "short list" to represent Allen, and even now he was connected to the defense team as an unaffiliated sounding board. But none of that was true.

Yet Fortson was easy to believe. He came off as a confident and connected insider, casually tossing off a variety of confidential tidbits. He told Cohen, for instance, that Baldwin and Rozzi had received the discarded phone of Johnny Messer, one of the suspected Odinists. And Fortson clearly had things no one else did; he had images of unreleased suspect sketches, the bloody tree photo, and the pictures of the dead bodies. It just was not clear how he had gotten them.

On October 8, 2023, at five past eleven o'clock on a Sunday morning, Gull replied to Rozzi's email, addressing the attorneys as "Gentlemen."

"Thank you for passing this troubling information along to me, I am quite disturbed by this new development," the judge wrote.

She proceeded to send a numbered list of "assumptions," which read more like marching orders that demanded responses. She asked if law enforcement was investigating. (Holeman had been digging into the leak for several days.) She asked if Snay had been interviewed. (Not yet.) She asked if Cain and Greenlee had been interviewed. (Not formally, though they had been the ones to tip off law enforcement and the parties to the extent of the leak.) She asked if law enforcement had "demanded the return of the photographs." (Not yet.) She "assumed" that Baldwin and Rozzi had turned over the names and contact information of their trusted staffers to law enforcement. (They had not.)

She even offered a theory of her own about the possible source of the leak, recalling a "bill received from Brad and Andy for a duplication of exhibits by a vendor which I disallowed . . . Is it possible that vendor is involved? Brad and Andy should share the name of that vendor and the date that vendor was hired to Nick and/or law enforcement for investigation as the possible source of the leak."

The judge included more than suggestions in her email.

"These local content creators are not journalists and have no right to claim any type of privilege," Gull claimed. "They should divulge to law enforcement who they got these photographs from to allow law enforcement to continue to investigate. The photographs must be returned to law enforcement. If they refuse to turn them over voluntarily, I will issue an order directing the immediate return or they will be subject to contempt of Court. That contempt will result in an immediate arrest and incarceration until such time as the photographs are returned. This is a drastic measure I should not have to take but will if necessary."

With Cohen's permission, Cain and Greenlee had already cooperated with law enforcement and shared everything with Holeman. They viewed Gull's casual suggestion that they be incarcerated with concern. At times, the judge appeared more focused on exerting power over the press—directly through threats about destroyed phones, and indirectly through secrecy and a lack of seating accommodations for media outlets—than on the behavior of the attorneys in the case. Much like many internet commentators, Gull seemed content to give in to her own bias and assumptions and then blame the messengers.

Over the weekend, Cain and Greenlee dug into Fortson's online history. They wanted to know who he was and how he was connected to the Delphi case. Greenlee found what he was looking for in Fortson's list of Facebook friends. Scrolling through, he stopped on a familiar name: Mitch Westerman.

Cain and Greenlee knew Westerman—or, at least, they had interviewed him back in March 2023 for a profile of Baldwin. Westerman had previously served as the Criminal Defense Team's operations manager. Baldwin himself had once described Westerman as one of the men who best knew how Baldwin operated as a lawyer. During his interview with Cain and Greenlee, Westerman came off as talkative and enthusiastic about his affection for Baldwin, a man he counted as a mentor and close friend.

On a phone call with Holeman, they mentioned Westerman's connection to Fortson. The connection, they knew, might simply indicate that Fortson worked for Baldwin in some capacity. Perhaps Westerman had just introduced them. But the tie was worth mentioning.

CHAPTER THIRTY-FIVE

On Monday, Mitch Westerman got a call from Holeman. He did not take it.

Later that day, Westerman approached the Criminal Defense Team headquarters in Franklin. Although he had not worked there in years, his appearance was routine. The married father had a girlfriend in town, a woman who worked in the Johnson County Prosecutor's Office. When Westerman traveled south to visit her, he also liked to swing by and greet Baldwin and his other former colleagues. Sometimes, he and his old boss would even hang out.

Baldwin valued Westerman as a strategist and as a close personal friend. They would sometimes talk about the Allen case. Westerman was not a lawyer. He earned his law degree from the now-defunct Valparaiso University School of Law but had never managed to pass the bar. Working with Baldwin, even as an intern or operations manager, was like living in a blistering courtroom drama. Now he worked as an ethics and compliance officer for a healthcare company. But nothing beat the rush of criminal defense. Going back to the old office was a bit like going home.

Westerman walked up the steps, opening the front doors with the lozenge windows, and then crossing the threshold into a workplace he always loved to revisit. The Franklin office occupied a spacious Victorian house with red brick and green trim. Years before, Tom Jones—one of Baldwin's mentors—had kept his office there. Jones's daughter, Jennifer Auger, still practiced law in the area. A couple of years after Jones's death, Baldwin's firm took over the building, trying to send the signal that they now occupied the same honored spot in the legal community that Jones once had.

Westerman made his way deeper into the office. On the lobby walls, framed newspaper clippings extolled the team's exploits. So did an *Animal House* parody poster, featuring caricatures of the teammates. A long hallway led deeper into Baldwin's domain. A copy of Norman Rockwell's *Freedom of Speech* painting hung on the wall. The hallway led off into different rooms, where attorneys and staffers worked diligently, typing on laptops or printing out documents. The last door on the left was Baldwin's personal office. The room was dim and messy. There, Baldwin kept large poster boards of possible trial exhibits, with names like Theresa Liebert and Carl Abbott written on them.

Next to that was a conference room with a large, glossy wooden table. Shelves of leather-bound law books lined the walls. There were chairs and stacks of boxes on the floor. Approximately 90 percent of the discovery in the Delphi case was kept in the Franklin office—all the materials from the twenty or so hard drives the team had obtained. The conference room functioned as "home base" for Baldwin and Rozzi. Westerman was very familiar with that room. He had done something very bad inside.

On that Monday afternoon, Westerman asked for a "few minutes of Andy's time." During their conversation, Westerman "acknowledged he had made a mistake."

He took Baldwin back to the dead heat of August. Back then, the defense had been preparing to depose law enforcement officials. One summer's day, Westerman was waiting to meet Baldwin. His old boss was preoccupied. Westerman did not know what Baldwin was doing. He could have been meeting with a client, or talking to somebody on the telephone. Either way, Baldwin's office door was closed. Westerman headed into the conference room. He only wanted to find somewhere to wait, he said. He got more than that. Spread on the table in front of him was a plethora of printed images related to the case, including suspect sketches not released to the public and photos of the bodies of the girls.

Westerman pulled out his phone and took pictures of it all.

His tale grew worse. He admitted to sharing those images with a "military friend." That buddy shared them with a Texan named Cohen, and maybe some other people. Now the police were onto the whole mess. Westerman had dodged a call from Holeman earlier that day. Everything was coming apart.

Westerman apologized. He told Baldwin he would do "whatever was necessary to make things right." He volunteered to talk to the police.

A few days earlier, Baldwin had said the person behind the leak should be hung by their testicles. But his view softened now that he knew that person was Westerman. The forgiveness came immediately. He would remark that Westerman had betrayed him, but they were still friends and Baldwin felt awful for him. It was a curious attitude to take about a person who had done such damage not only to the case but also to the families of the victims.

The grim task of informing his cocounsel fell to Baldwin. He composed an email describing Westerman's treachery and sent it at 4:48 P.M. Rozzi was busy that afternoon, attending a meeting of the Logansport Community School Board. He served as the board's attorney. After the meeting adjourned, he spent the rest of the afternoon and evening with his children. Baldwin apparently never called to alert him of the impending disaster. He left his cocounsel to read over the email the following morning. When he read the message from Baldwin, Rozzi got in contact immediately.

The defense attorneys knew what they had to do. After weeks and weeks of hinting at all manner of improprieties on the part of the prosecutor and law enforcement, they had been confronted with a calamity of their own making. They needed to ring up McLeland. Then they had to face the judge.

That same day, Holeman journeyed to Fort Wayne to talk to Fortson at his workplace, the Fort Wayne Air National Guard Base. The two men had a brief conversation. Fortson did not seem pleased by the detective's presence, but Holeman explained it was necessary. "I have to get to the bottom of this."

"I don't feel comfortable talking to you without an attorney."

"Well, the judge said if you don't turn everything over, you could go to jail for contempt."

"I don't have anything," Fortson said. "I deleted everything."

"Well, she wants to know two things. How many people did you send it to? And where'd you get it?"

Fortson refused to say. That was the end of the discussion on the base.

Holeman tried calling Baldwin and Rozzi. Baldwin would not pick up his phone. Rozzi answered but refused to cooperate. Holeman passed the investigation to Ben Rector, a young detective at the Lafayette post, whom Holeman regarded as one of the best. Westerman refused to provide access to his phone, but during a search of his home, police managed to get hold of a device with some of his messages. During that search, Westerman's relatives cursed the name of Jerry Holeman.

When Rozzi and Baldwin finally consented to an interview with Rector, they were adamant about having nothing to do with the leak. In their telling, they were Westerman's victims too.

McLeland had been surprised that day when Baldwin and Rozzi dialed him up. He was even more shocked when they pulled him into a solemn conference call with Gull. The defense attorneys confirmed to the judge that Westerman had been responsible for the leak. They characterized the leaker as having "snuck" into Baldwin's workplace to take photos of the discovery on his phone.

After Baldwin and Rozzi finished talking, there was a pause. Then the judge broke in. "Fellas, I'm speechless," Gull said.

McLeland wanted them disqualified. He wanted them gone from the case before they could do any more damage. He said so.

A flurry of exhortations came down the line. Baldwin and Rozzi tried downplaying the breach. Gull ignored them. She told McLeland she would do some research, and that she tended to agree with him.

Baldwin and Rozzi would have to wait to learn their fates. For all of the defense's bloviating about corrupt sheriffs and pagan guards, one of their own—a trusted confidant, one of Baldwin's treasured protégés—had apparently dealt them a mortal blow.

On October 11, 2023, Richard Allen voiced his own opinions on the leak—or, at least, he signed his name to a letter he purportedly wrote in Westville. Addressing his letter to Gull, he wrote that he had communicated with Rozzi, who had told him about the leak.

"I am aware that images of crime scene photos and other related documents were taken by a friend and former employee of Attorney Baldwin, at Attorney Baldwin's office," he wrote.

"Attorney Rozzi has also communicated to me that the Prosecutor has requested that my Attorneys be disqualified from representing me in this case. I do not want this to happen. I want Mr. Baldwin and Mr. Rozzi to continue to represent me until this case is resolved, one way or the other. I believe they are acting in a manner that is in my best interest."

The revelation of the breach drove away sleep for Holeman. Usually, four to five hours of rest were enough for him. But the chaos of the leak left him four to five reports behind on paperwork. Work ate into his evenings and weekend hours too. October 11, 2023, was one night where Holeman was exhausted enough to break his typical routine and actually head to bed at a reasonable time.

In the early morning hours, a storm rolled over Indiana. The rain and thunder frightened Holeman's Great Dane, Khaleesi. That was around three o'clock in the morning. Half-asleep, Holeman rose to tend to the dog. He picked up his phone and glanced down at his email. A message from the Lafayette post's dispatch popped up. A detective from the Fishers Police Department wanted to talk to Holeman about a suicide investigation.

Holeman knew what had happened before he even called the number. There was only one case he knew of that involved a man from Fishers. Fortson was dead.

The Fishers detective filled in the details. Time of death was around 9:00 p.m. on October 11. The victim had sustained a single gunshot wound to the head. The case was a clear suicide. Holeman did not ask for details.

Still, the detective passed along some backstory. While combing the scene, the Fishers detective found a scrap of paper. There, Fortson had scribbled a lawyer's name. After ringing up the attorney, he told his wife that the lawyer had just advised him to decline speaking to the police. The attorney assured him that everything would be okay. He seemed to calm down.

Then, on Wednesday night, Fortson shot himself.

Holeman hung up the phone. Fortson might have been looking at a contempt of court charge at the very worst. But even that was highly unlikely. He had not been the target. He was not even the original leaker. He was just a link in a chain between the defense and Delphi case obsessives who were desperate for the latest "clue." The lawyer had been right; things would have probably been okay in the end. Outside, the storm faded, drifting onward into the darkness.

CHAPTER THIRTY-SIX

Seven minutes to four o'clock in the morning, McLeland typed out an email that read like a scream into the void. At seven minutes past four, he sent it to the judge and the defense attorneys.

"I just got off the phone with ISP," he wrote.

Holeman had called him at a brutal hour. McLeland's daughters were asleep. He ought to have been resting too. Instead, he was reeling.

"At 10:00 PM. last night, Robert Fortson committed suicide," McLeland wrote. "One self inflicted gun shot wound. He is married and has a teenage daughter. The initial information that I have is that his wife stated that he was worried sick about being in this situation and the last info that I have is that Fortson stated to his wife that 'if I just be honest or "come clean" about where I got the photos I will be ok.'"

McLeland pleaded with the defense attorneys to tell the truth. "This is getting serious and way out of control gentlemen," he wrote. "If you have additional information about this leak, please forward it on to me or ISP Detective Holeman immediately. I do not want to get another phone call like this that Mitch or someone else involved in this leak has hurt themselves or someone else."

The defense attorneys did not reply. In the morning, Gull did.

She wrote back one minute before seven o'clock. "This is beyond tragic . . . once again I'm at a loss for words. I'm deeply concerned that Mr. Allen's defense is being compromised by all these recent events." She wrote that her staff would schedule a hearing in a week, on October 19. That would take place in Fort Wayne, in Gull's usual domain, the Allen County Courthouse. She asked the defense attorneys to "cease work" on Allen's case until the hearing.

Before the beginning of the public hearing on October 19, Rozzi asked Gull to meet with the attorneys in her chambers. "It's probably obvious that the tension from our side is coming, you know, from the words 'disqualification' that were murmured in the phone conference that we had a couple weeks ago. I'm assuming you understand how that kind of raises the intensity level of the circumstances." He went on to suggest that perhaps the leak should not be discussed in open court.

Baldwin chimed in. He seemed a bit agitated, stumbling over his words. But he also soon focused on the same thing Rozzi did. "So, you know, you had indicated that, you know, when he—when Nick said—don't know if he said the word *disqualification*, but—"

"Oh," said Gull. "He did."

"Okay," said Baldwin. "Didn't know if he just said it in a more generic way. And your response was, you know, 'I'm leaning in that direction' or something along those lines . . . And so that . . . that's, you know, a cause of concern."

Sounding much like a repentant schoolboy, Baldwin went on to assert that he had learned his lesson and from now on would take better care of the sensitive materials with which he had been entrusted. "So," he concluded, "you know, I'm hoping that that can be something that the Court, you know, can say, 'All right. That's fine.' And then let's get on with the trial. But I'll shut up now."

"And I'm not distancing myself from Mr. Baldwin," said Rozzi, as he distanced himself from Baldwin by pointing out that he himself had no connection with Westerman, the alleged original leaker. He repeated his view that they should not discuss the issue of the leak in open court.

He concluded his remarks in an especially memorable fashion: "And if, you know, the point here is, is I'm gonna say this maybe a little loosely, but forgive me. I don't care. I don't care that all this stuff is out there, because it's been out there for five or six years."

Of course, the crime scene photos of the bloody—and in Libby's case, naked—bodies of children had not been "out there" for five or six years. They only reached the public after Baldwin's friend Westerman leaked them. The defense had been on the case less than a year at that point.

When Gull addressed the matter, she did not hold back. "It pains me to say this," she said, "but the totality of these circumstances demonstrate gross negligence and incompetence on the part of the defense team. I am unsatisfied with your representation of Mr. Allen. I am gravely concerned about his rights to have competent, non-negligent representation. He currently doesn't have that right now, because what you have demonstrated is negligence and incompetence."

After delivering that devastating blow, Gull nudged the defense attorneys toward exiting the case. "Now, I am sharing my thoughts with you privately. I don't want to say this in open court. I would encourage you to talk privately about what you wish to do." She was, in short, telling them that if they left the case now then she would not humiliate them in front of the world.

Rozzi looked for a way out. "I'm [a] team player and I'm not the kind of guy that just bail out on somebody just for the sake of doing it, but I think it's obvious that, you know, he can speak differently, but I'm not as connected to some of, you know, this most recent circumstances as [Baldwin] is." Perhaps, he posited, Baldwin could go and Rozzi could stay?

"No," said Gull.

Rozzi was plainly outraged. "I've seen lawyers disqualified and there is process for that and it's not this, with all due respect, where you walk into somebody's office, a judge's office, and they read a prepared statement to you and, essentially, that statement is an indictment on my professional, you know, activities, and then you're handed, you know, essentially, a sheet of paper with two—you know, with two options and one of them is, is 'I'm gonna go out here and shame you or you can quit.' I just—you can understand how upset that would make any lawyer, and I just think it's—I don't think it's the right way to handle this from a due process standpoint." Rozzi was correct. Typically, in cases where a judge disqualifies an attorney, there is a significant record looming behind that decision. In the Delphi case, there was only a single backroom meeting. "So I have no choice but to, you know, withdraw my appearance, 'cause I'm not gonna go in there and take public shaming."

Baldwin then orally moved to withdraw his appearance. "So we're gonna leave, I guess, and you're gonna, how is this—you're just gonna get up on the bench and say—"

"I'll just say we've had turn of events and defense counsel is withdrawing and that's all I'm gonna say," said Gull.

Baldwin had a final concern. "Can you wait for us to get out of here?"

A few minutes later, Gull walked out on the bench and told the packed courtroom that Rozzi and Baldwin had withdrawn from the case. She did not explain why or indicate in any fashion that she had pressured them.

It seemed for a moment as if a page was being turned in the case, and that things would soon become very different.

But that did not happen.

CHAPTER THIRTY-SEVEN

Almost immediately after agreeing to depart the case, Rozzi and Baldwin changed their minds and began trying to get put back on it. The two attorneys even took the unusual step of offering to work for free. So Rozzi filed into the case once more, declaring his intent to stay on. Rozzi's move seemed to motivate Baldwin. He also filed back into the case, arguing he had not really meant it when he made an oral motion to leave the case.

But, in their version of events, Gull was at fault for their deception. She had coerced them, threatening to embarrass and disqualify them in front of the press. Baldwin and Rozzi asked to be reinstated to the case pro bono. The idea seemed to be that Gull would only enjoy the power to remove them if they were public defenders being paid by the county; if they worked without pay—as retained counsel—Gull would lack the authority to fire them.

Gull nixed the filings from the record. As far as she was concerned, Baldwin and Rozzi had withdrawn. They no longer had a right to file into the case. She appointed Bill Lebrato and Robert Scremin to represent Allen. Lebrato and Scremin were mainstays of the public defense scene in Allen County. Tasked with running the county's public defender agency, Lebrato had practiced before Gull for years. They knew each other well. Scremin was a well-respected criminal defense attorney who had once been a narcotics detective and a member of a special weapons and tactics, or SWAT, team.

Despite all of this, Rozzi and Baldwin signaled that they planned to attend the next hearing in the case, scheduled for October 31, 2023.

Snow clouds hung over Halloween. Court convened in Carroll County. Fort Wayne had drawn a crowd, but fewer stragglers turned out for Delphi. Those who did awaited the confrontation.

Baldwin and Rozzi were the first lawyers to arrive in the courtroom. The latter had dropped his despondent gaze. Baldwin looked ready for battle. The assembled deputies and bailiffs had not tried to prevent him or his cocounsel from storming the courthouse. Apparently, Baldwin and Rozzi were welcome inside. Accordingly, they made themselves at home. They occupied the prime seats at the table designated for the defense.

Kathy Allen quietly traipsed in with her mother-in-law. David Hennessy, an Indianapolis attorney representing Baldwin's interests, sat next to them. Hennessy was a veteran barrister who—at least according to him—was known as "Mr. Murder," presumably because of the high number of murder trials he had been a part of. But, as the decades slipped by, many legal observers began to whisper that the once whip-smart attorney had lost a step or nine. Recently, Hennessy spoke of retiring, suggesting that a triple murder case he and Baldwin were working on together—and would ultimately lose—would be his last.

Now, as everyone waited for the hearing to begin, Hennessy loudly held court, blasting out his opinions to anyone within earshot. He candidly shared his views about the new defense team. None of what he said had much to do with relevant legal issues. He claimed Scremin was lazy and not up to the task of defending Allen. He said Lebrato had a "PI report" on him, referring to a 2005 public intoxication charge. As far as attorneys with addiction issues went, Hennessy himself had incurred a drunk driving charge in 2018, after being hauled to jail, red-eyed, and sporting a shirt splattered with food stains.

The new attorneys came into the courtroom shortly before the hearing began. Lebrato was a short bald man. Scremin was taller and bespectacled, with his dark, curly hair tied up in a bun.

Scremin remained standing. He looked vaguely out of place, hovering around the overcrowded defense table. Then, suddenly, he grinned. He approached the railing to greet Hennessy. The men clasped hands and addressed each other warmly. Smiling, Hennessy asked the allegedly lazy lawyer about his children.

When Gull arrived, those gathered stood. Her face was completely blank as she gazed out at her lopsided court, at the two prosecutors—McLeland and his new deputy James Luttrull—and the four defense attorneys—Baldwin and Rozzi and Scremin and Lebrato. The choreography of the hearing was off from the start. Normally, Allen would have been brought out before the judge took her seat at the bench. This time, however, after an awkward pause, McLeland had to ask an usher for the shackled Allen to be brought in. The prisoner's chains clinked as two body-armor-wearing law enforcement officers guided him to his seat next to his old defense attorneys.

Allen looked well. He had gained weight. His skin was a healthy, pinkish hue, a change from his usual grayish pallor. His walk was less uncertain, although his eyes still bulged with apparent shock.

First, Gull addressed the prosecution and the new attorneys. Scremin and Lebrato had already filed to continue the case. McLeland offered up no objection to that motion.

Hennessy came in with a stage whisper. "Mr. Allen objects! Come on, fellas!"

Allen turned his head in the direction of his wife, Kathy. He mouthed, "It's okay." He nodded and scrunched up his face, a look meant to comfort and reassure.

Gull next addressed the two original defense attorneys. She asked if anything had changed since the previous hearing. Her voice was icy. Even Rozzi sounded unsure of himself as he talked in circles, explaining that the old defense had chosen to withdraw as a "strategic move." Baldwin tried speaking up too, but his deflated attitude quickly returned. At one point, Gull told him not to interrupt her.

She told the old defense they were guilty of gross negligence. She asked for McLeland's input, and he noted that Rozzi and Baldwin were guilty of telling "outright lies." Gull did not want them in her courtroom, either as public defenders or private counsel.

As this went on, Hennessy clutched the empty row of wooden seats in front of him, like a man holding onto a thrilling roller coaster. He was stuck in the stands with the observers, but his actions and mannerisms were more akin to an aggressive stage parent or a nervous Little League coach. He would hiss Baldwin's name at various points, trying to attract his client's attention. When Hennessy could no longer sit still, he leapt up and made a move for the well of the court. A deputy shooed him away. He stalked in front of the gallery, leaning over the railing near where Baldwin was sitting. Another deputy told him he needed to sit down.

Baldwin requested that Hennessy be allowed to come in and make a few comments on his behalf. Gull permitted that. When Hennessy finally got the chance to properly address the court, he was smooth. He only added a few ridiculous touches, calling the Franks memorandum a work of art. He raised numerous relevant points, decrying Gull's lack of a record and noting that Allen ought to have access to the meeting in chambers where the defense was dismissed. Gull heard him out. Then Hennessy sat down.

Gull turned to Allen himself. She apologized to the defendant, saying that what had happened was unacceptable. She knew he wanted to keep Baldwin and Rozzi as his attorneys, but she could not, in good conscience, leave him with defenders she considered "grossly negligent." She disqualified Baldwin and Rozzi. The trial was pushed back a year, to October 2024.

The whole hearing was anticlimactic. The pro bono trick had not paid off. As Baldwin swept out of the courtroom with Rozzi and Hennessy at his heels, he left with a condescending exhortation. "Journalism!" he called out to the news crews, many of whom had been waiting in the cold for hours to cover the case. Baldwin's blue eyes bulged in his head. "It's time for you guys to start being journalists."

The battle of the legal egos had only just begun.

CHAPTER THIRTY-EIGHT

A week later, attorneys Mark Leeman and Cara Weineke entered the case on an appellate level. Leeman was a well-respected lawyer from Logansport, Indiana. He would do most of his talking in court.

Cara Wieneke was an appellate attorney based out of Brooklyn, Indiana, a community of about twenty-five hundred people in Morgan County. She enjoyed an especially active online life. On her blog, she wrote about attorneys who went on YouTube, claiming it was possible for lawyers to make a million dollars if they became top "LawTubers." On her personal Twitter account, meanwhile, she suggested the United States may have faked the moon landing and subsequently had been blackmailed over it by Russia. She later claimed that was a joke, but tweeted, "I wear that [moon landing denier] label like a badge of honor." In months to come, she would share defense talking points on Twitter and as a guest on YouTube channels.

Together, the pair filed an original action in the Indiana Supreme Court claiming that Gull violated Allen's rights when she removed Rozzi and Baldwin. "No Indiana court," the attorneys claimed, "has ever tolerated a trial judge removing a lawyer from a case, over the client's objection, based on the judge's subjective belief the lawyer is negligent, or even 'grossly negligent.'" Therefore, the lawyers asked that Rozzi and Baldwin be reinstated as Allen's attorneys. But that was not all. They also wanted Judge Gull to be removed from the case.

"A new judge," they wrote, "should also be appointed to avoid the appearance of bias that will otherwise permeate these proceedings." Their argument was that since Gull publicly slammed Rozzi and Baldwin as grossly negligent at the most recent hearing, the public might question her impartiality in the future. "To restore the public's trust in the integrity of the judicial process in this high-profile case, a new special judge should be appointed."

Gull, predictably, took the opposite view. Her attorney, Matthew Gutwein, argued in his brief that Gull's removal of Rozzi and Baldwin had been necessary. They had done such a poor job of representing Allen, he maintained, that she needed to fire them from the case to preserve Allen's right to effective counsel. And, of course, he also made clear that there was no reason to remove Gull from the case, that she had not indicated bias in any way.

Loretta Rush, the chief justice of the Indiana Supreme Court, scheduled the oral arguments in the case to be held on January 18, 2024.

After being removed from the case, Baldwin became almost Nixonian in his desire to expose—and potentially punish—those he saw as his enemies. He reported having heard presumably damaging rumors about Judge Gull, Nicholas McLeland, Jerry Holeman and pretty much anyone else involved in the case. During this period, he also wrote to a pair of journalists he perceived as his enemies, claiming that some of their reporting on him was "possibly actionable." The journalists interpreted his words as a not-so-veiled threat to sue.

Baldwin also let it be known that he also had doubts about Allen's new lawyers, Scremin and Lebrato. He complained that they had not reached out to him even though he was on the verge of completing a task that could move the case to a resolution. Perhaps inspired by their lack of homage to him, Baldwin claimed to have done some research on them which had left him with concerns. It was unclear if this research amounted to the same criticisms Hennessy loudly raised about the newly appointed attorneys in the courtroom or if Baldwin imagined he had something different on them.

Around this time, McLeland began to face an unexpected crisis much closer to home. His mother was diagnosed with breast cancer. McLeland's father had already passed away. He was close with his mother. Seeing her suffer pained him.

In the weeks and months to come, while McLeland's mind would be with her, his ongoing work on the Allen case would constantly interrupt. He planned to take his mother on vacation. Then a hearing got rescheduled, and he had to postpone those plans.

McLeland was determined to make the vacation happen. He finally got a moment to take his mother on a family trip. They headed to Florida. But the radiation had taken a toll. She collapsed almost as soon as they arrived at the condominium. They spent most of the vacation in the emergency room until she recovered enough to go back home.

The leak was a grueling ordeal for all those involved. But that time came with one bright spot for McLeland. By the end of the autumn, he was no longer alone.

In September 2023, Lutrrull told the Carroll county prosecutor that he would work the case as a deputy. In the latter half of the month, he went to the Command Center in Delphi. There, in a meeting with plenty of food courtesy of Kathy Shank and McLeland's staff, Luttrull met the investigators.

Over the course of the discussion, Luttrull found himself struck by the toll the investigation had taken on those at the center of the case. The idea that he had been entrusted with something so precious to McLeland and the investigators weighed on him. He began working out of the Command Center, getting himself caught up on the case.

Around that time, Diener called McLeland to ask how things were going. "How are you holding up? Do you have help yet?"

He told her the news. McLeland received the funds to hire deputy prosecutors for the Delphi trial. Now Luttrull was going to help him with the case. Diener did not know the former Grant County prosecutor personally, but she had heard of him and they had both sat on the board of IPAC. He had an excellent reputation. But she was still annoyed. Diener had offered to join the case plenty of times before.

"I wish you would've asked me to help you. Unless you feel like I can't be helpful. Why don't you want me to help you with this case, Nick?" she finally asked.

McLeland seemed taken aback. He said he would love Diener to join him as well, but he had not thought she would throw away her new career just to work on the Delphi case. "Seriously? I thought you were making money hand over fist." He had apparently not taken her previous offers all that seriously.

Diener told him that the financial rewards were not enough to make her prefer private practice over prosecutorial work.

"Well, I do have money for an additional prosecutor," McLeland said.

"I'm serious," Diener said. "I will close my practice tomorrow."

That time, McLeland took Diener up on her offer. Quietly, she began withdrawing herself from all her cases. To avoid any overlap, Diener held off on filing an appearance in the Delphi case until she had fully unwound her practice. She had been in family law for about ten months. But that was over. Diener was a prosecutor once again.

The three prosecutors would spend many hundreds of hours preparing to try the Allen case together. That would require them to work as a team. Luttrull and Diener knew what serving as an elected prosecutor felt like. They had both done it, so they were able to leave their egos out of the process. McLeland was the one who would face the fallout of the case's outcome. If they made a mistake, it would reflect on him. Meanwhile, McLeland kept signing all the filings. The case was his responsibility. That strategy also kept most of the ire of the case obsessives firmly trained on him.

That fall was an intense one. At the time, the trial was scheduled for January. There was much work to do. Most of the earliest meetings were conference calls. The three prosecutors would also meet at the Command Center. The big table there was spread thick with documents related to the investigation.

For McLeland, the first step he took with his deputies was one of the hardest. They had to divide up the case. McLeland knew every piece of evidence, every witness. Now, he would have to trust the others to take over some of those responsibilities.

When it came to the division of the case, Luttrull was the most easygoing. He told the others he was happy to handle any portion of the case. McLeland was more adamant. He wanted the investigators and most of the law enforcement witnesses. Diener opted for the civilians, the families of Liby and Abby, the trail witnesses, the mental health professionals, and the local searchers. That left Luttrull with forensics.

McLeland's unease would fade in time. He would sit in on their meetings with witnesses. He found his new deputies to be excellent communicators. They were the kind of attorneys he could envision spending countless hours with, stuck in a room, analyzing evidence, poring over exhibits, and debating the order of witness order. He started feeling like he could let go.

When a hearing in the Allen case took place in the Carroll County Courthouse, it seemed to dominate the entire building. Deputies provided extra security at the door and in the halls. A throng of reporters and members of the public gathered outside and then hurried up the winding staircase and into the gallery, eager to see what was happening in the small courtroom. Things were different at the Indiana Supreme Court.

For one thing, the Court did not have its own building; instead it occupied a portion of the Indiana Statehouse. The crowds there were just as likely to be protesting for a ceasefire in Palestine, meeting with lobbyists, or touring the building as they were to be attending the Allen oral argument.

But all the familiar faces were there, even if they did not have a formal role in the proceeding. Brad Rozzi, Andrew Baldwin, Nicholas McLeland, Jerry Holeman, Doug Carter, and Mike and Becky Patty were present, all intensely interested in seeing for themselves just how things would go.

In the oral arguments—which lasted an hour—both sides had the opportunity to present their case to the Court. Perhaps more importantly, the individual justices could also pepper the attorneys with questions about possible weak spots in their presentation. The most striking example of this came in the presentation given by Leeman, who was speaking for Allen.

After a person is convicted of a serious crime at trial, one of the most common ways they argue they deserve a new trial is by claiming they had ineffective counsel. In the Allen case, Gull herself suggested Allen's counsel was negligent and wanted to replace them; if his efforts to keep them were successful and they returned to the case, would he in essence be giving up the chance to later make an ineffective counsel claim?

Leeman largely tried to sidestep the issue; the court seemed to do so as well. Just a few hours after the arguments, they issued an order. Rozzi and Baldwin were back on the case. And Gull would stay on as well.

CHAPTER THIRTY-NINE

One of the first things Rozzi and Baldwin did when they returned to the case was to again ask Gull to walk away from it. In a filing for her to recuse herself, the attorneys tried to make the case that her efforts to remove them were so egregious that no one could rely on her to be impartial moving forward. "Here," they argued, "there is no recognizable legal rationale which supports Judge Gull continuing to preside over this case . . . Judge Gull should recuse herself and in doing so, restore any sense of impropriety that is clouding the system of jurisprudence in the State of Indiana and in this very proceeding because of the Judge's prior actions."

Gull denied their motion without a hearing.

The next major motion would not go away as easily. On January 29, 2024, McLeland made a filing asking Gull to hold Rozzi and Baldwin in contempt for their role in the leak. It was a step the prosecutor felt he needed to take, especially after seeing how the spread of the crime scene images affected the families.

For his motion to succeed, McLeland would need to meet a high evidentiary bar—in short, to prove beyond a reasonable doubt that the defense had willfully and intentionally leaked the crime scene photographs.

Gull set a hearing on the matter for March 18, 2024. As that date drew nearer, a couple of things became quite clear.

Rozzi and Baldwin did not want the hearing to happen. Their attorney in the matter, David Hennessy, filed a flurry of motions seeking to delay or complicate it. In separate filings, Hennessy requested that the prosecutor be recused, and that Gull recuse herself. He also filed something he called a "motion to stay all ancillary proceedings and get this case to trial," which was essentially a request for the hearing to be delayed until after the completion of the murder trial. Still not done, Hennessy—in a separate filing—asked to delay the hearing because a favorite aunt of his had died recently and it was possible her funeral might be scheduled on the same day.

Gull denied it all.

Perhaps more significantly, the preparation for the contempt hearing would underscore the close and growing ties between the defense team and a virulent group of YouTubers and other social media influencers who had become fans of Richard Allen.

Certain figures in the mainstream media reliably carried talking points that delighted the defense. On February 13, 2024, MacDonald went on Court TV and declared that the cartridge evidence was essentially worthless. In her telling, law enforcement secured the crime scene for three days, cleared it, and then resecured it the following day.

"My understanding is that unspent shell was discovered during that second search after the scene had been resecured," MacDonald claimed. "And it was found under the dirt. It wasn't just laying out in the open. It had been somewhat buried whether intentionally or through time or the elements, we don't know."

MacDonald had long been a major proponent of Logan's guilt. Once she joined Court TV, she brought with her a decidedly sympathetic stance toward Allen. MacDonald's claims about the cartridge elicited much consternation, along with calls for the CSIs involved to be fired. None of it was true, of course. But such misinformation still added to the growing cloud around Delphi. In the face of such allegations, many members of the public wondered if the investigators were even halfway competent, if the prosecution even had the right guy.

Mainstream media figures often ran coverage overtly sympathetic to Richard Allen's team. But others went even further.

The fact was, the defense team had been in touch with YouTubers almost from the very beginning of their involvement with the case. Even after Gull's gag order was issued, there was—in theory—nothing wrong with this, assuming it was handled professionally. The YouTubers had obsessed over the case for years; their brains were filled with trivia and theories, and it could behoove the defense to listen to them. But problems could arise if the defense took inaccurate claims to heart or if the interactions became anything more than a one-way street—if, in short, the defense shared theories and ideas of their own with YouTubers who would then pass those talking points along to their audiences. That would be a clear violation of Gull's gag order.

The team seemed to grow less concerned about any appearance of impropriety in terms of contacts with YouTubers after Rozzi and Baldwin were thrown off the case by Gull. For instance, the team gave a YouTuber named Bob Motta Jr. a reserved seat at the Supreme Court hearing and then dined with him afterward. Motta Jr. then went on his channel and Court TV to provide analysis favorable to the defense.

Motta Jr. was an Illinois-based criminal defense attorney whose biggest professional asset seemed to be that his father, Bob Motta Sr., was successful in that field. Joining his father and his wife, Ali, Motta Jr. landed what was arguably his biggest case—the defense of Nebraska serial killer Anthony Garcia.

It did not go well.

The Mottas seemed underprepared, objecting to the admission of boxes full of damaging evidence by uttering only one word—"403." The local attorney the Mottas worked with asked to be removed from the case because of his concerns over the Mottas' ethical violations. After the county attorney declared that the Mottas were "inept or intentionally acting to mess up the criminal justice system," the judge ordered Ali Motta off the case. And, perhaps worst of all, their client was convicted and ultimately sentenced to death.

After this, when Motta Jr. decided to enter a new field, he again relied on his father. The senior Motta had once represented notorious serial killer John Wayne Gacy. At some point during that relationship, Motta Sr. had recorded hours of conversations with the murderer. The senior Motta eventually turned those tapes over to his son, who concluded that he could use them to create a true crime podcast. Subsequently, Motta Jr. seemed peeved whenever others did their own projects about Gacy. A critical tweet about a Netflix documentary on the case would remain pinned to the top of his Twitter page for years.

When he exhausted Gacy, he moved on to cover other cases. He also seemed to shift his focus from the audio podcast to its associated YouTube channel. The different medium made it easier for Motta Jr. to interact in real time with his audience—and solicit financial support from them. In fact, whenever a viewer would send a few bucks to his YouTube channel, Motta Jr. would cry out with near orgasmic delight that he had just received a "five dolla holla."

One of the new cases he covered was the Delphi murders. Whenever he did an episode on it, his audience numbers would spike—so he did as many programs on it as he could. Behind the scenes, he did even more. But as the contempt hearing would make clear, the defense was also deeply interested in YouTubers who had a much smaller reach on the platform than Motta Jr.

Gull's courtroom boasted ornate columns and walls of green marble. The color gave the room the look of a submerged grotto. The glass ceiling that soared overhead muted the sound, though, garbling the testimony of witnesses and speeches from the attorneys. It seemed appropriate that the slow, difficult fight between the parties and the judge would appear to take place underwater.

Hennessy hobbled up to the prosecution table before the start. Stacey Diener had been working on the case in the background for months, but the contempt hearing would be her first appearance in court. She and Hennessy had met before, in deposition. Glibly, he asked Diener if she was the court reporter.

Prior to the hearing, Hennessy, as he was required to do, gave the court a list of witnesses he might call. The list included names familiar to those who got their case news from YouTube. Steven Wood was best known online for having loudly advocated that the real murderer was a young witness who fully cooperated with police. Julie Melvin, of course, was an online crank who had spent years floating around the case. She and Hennessy had spent some time together in the bar at their hotel the night before the hearing, and were even spotted gallivanting along the sidewalk. Angela Michos Sadlowski, the social worker from North Carolina, would eventually receive a letter of concern from her board regarding her online harassment of people involved in the case. Courtney Parsons was a pet food company employee from Texas who—a few days earlier—had falsely claimed that a court employee was a secret source for a podcast she did not like. The harassment inspired by that claim forced the employee to delete her social media altogether. Rick Snay was a local YouTuber with a small audience who was the first to publicly post about the crime scene photo leak.

It was unclear what the defense hoped to get from these witnesses.

As it happened, they did not get much—other than the public perception of being united with some of the cranks who monopolized the case discussions on YouTube. For whatever reason, Sadlowski and Parsons did not appear in court. Melvin and Wood both testified for only a few moments before their words were deemed immaterial to the matter at hand. Melvin trembled as she testified. Snay was present but did not get called to the stand; during a break in the hearing, he got into a physical confrontation with a YouTube rival. As a result, he was banned from Gull's courtroom.

The contempt hearing largely revolved around Baldwin's behavior rather than Rozzi's. Westerman, after all, had been Baldwin's friend. He was said to have photographed crime scene pictures that were left lying on a table in Baldwin's conference room. At least from the outside, it appeared Rozzi's direct involvement in that was minimal.

Yet it was Rozzi who chose to testify under oath in the contempt hearing. Reporters in the gallery quietly wondered if Baldwin's seeming lack of interest in offering sworn testimony about the leak meant he was not especially interested in being honest about what had occurred.

In court, Hennessy stumbled. He forgot names and details and often seemed confused. At one point, he dropped the battery pack to his microphone. Holeman had to step in to help him pick it up off the floor. Even Baldwin later remarked that he felt the older man had not done a good job of articulating his legal arguments. But, fortunately for the defense, Gull did not take Hennessy's performance into account when reaching her judgment a few weeks later.

"The Court," she wrote, "now finds that the State proved by a preponderance of the evidence that defense counsel was sloppy, negligent, and incompetent in their handling of discovery materials. Counsel failed to properly secure evidence and discovery material in this matter . . . Counsel has described Westerman both as a criminal and a valued consultant and confidante. Despite this Court's findings of sloppiness, negligence, and incompetence, the State is required to prove that Counsels' conduct was willful and intentional beyond a reasonable doubt for the Court to find Counsel in contempt. As the State has not met that burden, the Court declines to find them in contempt of Court."

It was a clear win for the defense. At least, it was as much of a win that a team publicly branded as "sloppy, negligent and incompetent" could hope for.

For his role in the leak, Westerman faced a misdemeanor criminal charge, which was dismissed after he completed a pretrial diversion program. Legally speaking, there was not much of a path to address a man taking pictures of crime scene photographs of children that he then shared with others on the internet. Westerman's wife divorced him over the course of the scandal. He never reached out to the families of Libby or Abby to apologize. Speaking with Fortson's relatives at the man's memorial service, he blamed his late friend for sharing the images.

As far as the families of Libby and Abby were concerned, the leak was devastating. Most of the YouTubers and online sleuths who received the photographs did not delete them. Instead, they traded them with friends, eager to opine on the sticks, the injuries to the girls, the positions of the bodies. The families knew that it was only a matter of time before somebody published the images of their dead children on social media.

All the while, they were forced to say nothing. Through all the vile accusations from the defense's online fandom, through all the chaos and heartbreak around the leak, they kept silent.

Soon after the contempt hearing, the defense team welcomed a new member to their ranks. Attorney Jennifer Auger formally joined Baldwin and Rozzi when she entered a limited appearance on March 27, 2024. According to her filing, Auger would only be working the case in a few specific areas, such as digital forensics.

The daughter of one of Baldwin's mentors, Auger practiced in the same small town. Despite this history, Baldwin could be negative about the woman now signing on to the Allen effort. When discussing her with at least one person, Baldwin pointedly made sure they knew that Auger had represented Judy Kirby, a wrong-way driver who killed seven and received one of the longest sentences in Indiana history. This, he joked, was the type of person he was getting to work with him.

The sky over the forest was cloudy as two men made their way down the ravine, searching for the crime scene. One carried with him containers of his own blood.

The first man was Rich Davies, the former FBI agent who had come back to the case as a special deputy after retiring from the Bureau. The other was Major Pat Cicero of the LaPorte County Sheriff's Office. He was there to learn the truth about the Delphi crime scene.

Like the case's original crime scene investigators, Olehy, Datzman, and Page, Cicero was a CSI who had trained under Dean Marks of the state police. He had testified at trials as an expert in bloodstain pattern analysis and crime scene reconstruction. Page brought Cicero into the case, connecting him with Luttrull. He joined the team in February.

Davies was there to guide Cicero to the appropriate spot. He knew the way, but the path was treacherous. Going down the slope, Cicero almost lost his footing a few times. The ground was wet and slippery. He clung to trees and saplings for support as he descended.

Mostly bald and bespectacled with a gentle voice, Cicero had worked diligently to become a competent CSI. He attended and later taught trainings at the University of Tennessee Anthropological Research Facility, popularly known as the Body Farm. He also played as a drummer for his church, and for two bands in his area.

Once the ground leveled out, Davies knew the way to the shallow depression in the earth. Cicero recognized the place from the crime scene photographs. He got to work. He had already spent so much time studying the scene from afar. Now he could witness firsthand the shift in elevation, the space between the trees, the layers and layers of leaves and sticks on the forest floor. The branches were bare, allowing Cicero a clear view of Deer Creek. He could see the opposite bank.

It was unusual for a defense team to outline their entire theory in detail. The Franks memorandum gave Cicero plenty to work with. He could put the defense's claims to the test.

A third person was in the forest with Cicero that day. A test subject, a person around Libby's height. That test subject would be helping with a few experiments. Cicero produced non-anticoagulant vacutainers containing his own blood. Human blood allowed for the most accurate testing. Selecting a nearby tree—the same species as the one with the alleged rune—Cicero dipped his finger in his blood. He attempted to paint the so-called symbol on the bark. He also tried doing so with a stick. The painting process was difficult, and the alleged rune was difficult to recreate. Cicero found that somebody could replicate a similar shape through painting, but it would require the killer to continuously have to go back to the nearest substantial pool of blood about ten feet away, dip his finger in to reapply, and hurry back to the tree without dripping too much, again and again, until the pattern was complete. It was a slow-going, arduous process.

Then, the test subject dipped a hand in the blood, and pressed it up against the tree. Cicero stared at the blood on the bark. There, glistening, was a marking that looked remarkably like the one found at the murder scene.

On April 30, 2024, Judge Benjamin Diener announced he was resigning, effective immediately. The bench in the Carroll Circuit Court was empty.

That was the kind of opportunity that McLeland had waited years for. Becoming a judge had long been his dream. Early in his career, he could barely contain his ambitions. Two years out of law school, he unsuccessfully ran for judge, losing to Benjamin Diener.

Then in 2020, he forfeited another chance. After Judge Fouts resigned from the Carroll County Superior Court, McLeland did not run. The Delphi murders case was unfinished. He felt he could not leave at that time. So instead, he held back and watched as Troy Hawkins, his deputy prosecutor, got the nod from Governor Holcomb.

But the resignation changed things for McLeland. By then, he had served as a public defender and a county prosecutor. Becoming a judge felt like the next step. He felt ready for it. And another shot at the bench might not come up for years. He met with the families of Libby and Abby to talk about his plans. He told them all that he had always wanted to be a judge. He had already missed one chance. He had to think about his career and his own family. In a way, he was asking their blessing to move on. The families gave it readily. They told him that they wished he would stay on. McLeland had come a long way with the relatives of the girls. By then, they were confident about his abilities and the dedication he had for their case. But they understood why he needed to leave. McLeland left the meeting with the support of the families of Abby and Libby. He was free to pursue his dream.

The weeks passed by. When he first became prosecutor, McLeland had vowed to do his best to get answers in the Delphi murders and the unsolved Flora fire. Now that the Delphi case had broken open, he would have to depart before a trial. That bothered him. The thought of handing things over to somebody new was almost painful. He found he could not let the case go, or else it would not let him go. He let the time slip away. He did not seek the judgeship. Once again, McLeland stood aside and watched Governor Holcomb appoint his deputy prosecutor—Shane Evans that time around—to the bench. The families did not realize until they saw the news about Evans. But the meaning was very clear. McLeland was staying on the case.

CHAPTER FORTY

In the lead-up to the contempt hearing, the defense had filed a flurry of documents, most of which again seemed designed more for the public than for Gull. The one that would have the most lasting impact on the case was a "motion for parity in resources," signed by Rozzi and Baldwin. The bulk of its seventeen pages was a long complaint about money; the attorneys claimed they were not getting paid quickly enough and that Gull was not giving them money to hire experts to testify on Allen's behalf.

As usual, the truth was far more complicated than that. Gull complained the lawyers or their staff were not filling out paperwork correctly.

Their proposed solution to the money issue they identified was outlandish: "The defense requests that this Court order the State of Indiana, through Prosecutor McLeland, to assume the expenses of all experts, law enforcement officers, administrative staff and any other expenses arising out of the prosecution of Richard Allen, from this point forward, from his own personal finances." There seemed little possibility indeed that Gull would demand McLeland use his own savings to pay the expenses of his government office; the suggestion seemed another ploy to get press attention.

But then someone—apparently a YouTuber—had another idea on how to exploit the issues raised in the parity motion. Why not create an online fundraiser so people could donate money for the defense to pay experts?

On some level, the notion seemed ridiculous. Rozzi and Baldwin were public defenders. Their work was being financed by the taxpayers of

Indiana. There seemed no valid reason to convince devoted followers of the case to send their own money to pay for something that was already being paid for. But that did not stop the team from moving forward with it. The fundraiser was duly set up; the website indicated that it was being run in some fashion by Hennessy.

But much of the planning for the fundraiser seemed to take place in a Twitter group chat that included appellate lawyer Cara Wieneke, attorney Michael Ausbrook (who represented Rozzi and Baldwin alongside Hennessy), and YouTubers Bob Motta Jr., Angela Michos Sadlowski, Courtney Parsons, and Nicole Mazzochetti Miller. That group brainstormed the precise language to be used on the fund's home page, picked the most sympathetic-looking picture of Allen they could find (in which the defendant donned a lilac polo and cradled a small dog, because, as Miller noted, "people love dogs"), discussed their contact with the defense attorneys, and griped over their regular annoyance with Hennessy as they helped him deal with the many, many technical problems he encountered. ("David is OLD," wrote Motta Jr. at one point. "That's a real thing. Technology has lapped him three times over.")

Despite the participation of two attorneys who represented either Allen or his defense team, the tone of the conversations was ribald, profane, and enthusiastic; derisive toward Gull, McLeland, law enforcement, and even the victims' families; and oftentimes deeply misogynistic toward the judge in particular. In between peppering his new friends with updates on how his day at work was going, Ausbrook would slyly refer to the judge as "Miss Gullch," a nod to the Wicked Witch of the West's Kansas counterpart. The YouTubers were more blunt. Motta Jr. called her a "ratchet bitch" because the judge's rulings nearly interrupted his "vacay" in Mexico, and Sadlowski, Parsons, and Miller followed suit.

In Delphi-related online spaces, a strange phenomenon took hold. Anytime a well-known or moderately well-credentialed figure like an attorney, a journalist, a former law enforcement officer, or a YouTuber would voice an opinion in line with the Delphi defense, case obsessives would lavish them with effusive praise. Postulants could go from toiling in relative anonymity to enjoying exuberant "appreciation posts" from strangers. Love bombing, a technique favored by cults and narcissists alike, refers to over-the-top expressions of admiration and affection deployed to draw a victim into an abusive or troubling situation. This weaponized flattery seemed to coax many of these targets deeper into the Delphi space, where they often espoused even more radical opinions to keep up with their adoring new fans.

In that way, portions of the online Delphi community functioned a bit like a funhouse. The attention-starved and the lonely were led through the darkness to a warped mirror, one that showed them whatever they wanted to see. In the reflection, they glimpsed truth-tellers, crusaders, warriors, legal giants, and fabulous celebrities. Walking away from the case became impossible. All their friends, those random people on the internet who said they were intelligent and fearless and beautiful, would vanish. And they could not say or do anything to anger those lovely friends.

Ensconced in their private Twitter message group, the Delphi defense's brain trust began doing whatever they could to promote the unnecessary fundraiser. Motta Jr. tweeted about it from the account associated with his YouTube channel. "Look," he wrote. "This IS NOT a fundraiser declaring that Richard Allen is innocent."

Motta Jr.'s tweet contradicted the text on the fundraiser's web page, which said, "Richard Allen was arrested for a crime he did not commit." That text was later revised. But that was not the biggest problem with Motta Jr.'s tweet. At the end of it—just above the link people could use to send money to Richard Allen's team—Motta Jr. used the hashtag #JusticeforAbbyandLibby.

That hashtag had been specifically created by the families of Abby and Libby to not only spread awareness of the case but also share happy memories and images of the girls. Motta Jr. and the other defense team fundraisers had now hijacked it to raise money for the man charged with killing the girls the hashtag was created to honor.

The move sparked a furor online—and Motta Jr. ended up apologizing. But the uproar did not keep people from donating. By the time the fundraiser stopped accepting money, a total of 709 people had given $40,220.76. Since no funds were needed to pay for experts, what actually happened to the money remains unclear.

The filing for funding did more than inspire a problematic fundraiser. It was the latest iteration of the defense's ongoing attempt to create a narrative around the case. To them, the contest seemed to be more than prosecutors and defense attorneys going up against each other in court; in their minds, this case was something different. The prosecutors—perhaps in collaboration with Gull and the investigators—were supposedly doing everything they could to rig the system, to stack the deck unfairly against Allen. In short, everyone except the defense attorneys was hopelessly corrupt—or, at the very least, completely incompetent. That was the subtext of the complaint. Why, the system would not even give the man the opportunity to get his own experts and mount a defense!

Most troubling about the defense's unfounded suggestions of corruption and conspiracy was not just that they were untrue, but rather that so many uninformed people across the country believed it all. And they acted on their ill-founded beliefs.

The prosecution, investigators, and even Gull herself were subjected to waves of unthinking and angry harassment from case followers naïve enough to accept the defense's claims at face value. This was not just idle name-calling either; the online crowd were tracking down and threatening the family members of people connected to the case. They would spread ridiculous rumors—people falsely claimed, for instance, that McLeland was best friends with alleged Odinist Holder, and that Gull was being blackmailed by high-ranking Norse pagans. The Facebook page of Liggett's late son was also vandalized with comments about how corrupt the sheriff allegedly was. All of this was considered justifiable as part of the fight against the nonexistent corruption that had overtaken Carroll County and the multiagency murder investigation.

These sorts of things happened to virtually everyone involved in the case who was not part of the defense. Perhaps recognizing how awful this made them look, some with close ties to the defense occasionally tried to suggest such things happened to them as well.

On one memorable occasion, Sue Wright reported that her former co-litigant Sadlowski called her growling like a dog and slurring some threats. Wright thought Sadlowski might drive to Indiana to harm herself or others. Concerned, Wright ended up getting in touch with Holeman.

There was little Holeman could do, given that Sadlowski was in New York at the time. He let local law enforcement know, and they did a welfare check to ensure that Sadlowski was not a danger to herself. In a four-hour marathon live, Sadlowski recounted the incident in a YouTube video, claiming that she had been "swatted." She spun it as Holeman and her enemies conspiring to have her killed for seeking the truth.

This utterly untrue claim—like all the untrue claims before it—only inspired more and more hatred and harassment of those in law enforcement. And it did nothing to help Richard Allen.

Rather than avoid those engaging in bizarre and antisocial online behaviors, the defense team often embraced them. In her messages with various group members, Sadlowski proudly shared information about her contacts with Hoffman. She posted screenshots of her text conversations with him. She shared that she and Parsons had met him in person when he was off the case, likely at a low-turnout rally they hosted in Indianapolis to support Allen. They told others that he showed them evidence in the case. She said Hoffman suspected shadowy forces were blackmailing Gull. Nobody questioned her statement. The cranks had a strong grip on the defense team. And the defense seemed happy for the unquestioning support. Not as long as Sadlowski, Parsons, and their friends created memes extolling Baldwin and Rozzi as swoon-worthy "defense daddies."

―

Rozzi and Baldwin, meanwhile, continued making filings that were increasingly trivial. A prime example of this was the filing the defense made on June 18, 2024. In this motion, Rozzi and Baldwin—two middle-aged men—essentially told Judge Fran Gull she needed to smile more at them.

The lawyers conceded their complaint "may seem petty or trivial," but they offered it anyway, mentioning her so-called "disdainful facial expressions." They then discussed something that had happened in a hearing over a year earlier (which would suggest the incident had been stuck in their minds for quite a while).

While the hearing was in progress, McLeland had asked for a break to use the restroom. Gull wanted to ask him how long he needed for his upcoming witnesses, but McLeland misunderstood her and assumed she wanted to know how long he would be in the lavatory.

"No, no, no," said Gull. "I mean in your witnesses, with your evidence, ding dong. I don't care how long it takes you to go there. No, I don't care about that."

The defense contrasted this with an incident that had occurred at a hearing on May 7, 2024. On that date, the defense asked for a brief recess and—before granting it—Gull had asked why the defense was requesting it. This, apparently, was a huge problem. "Judge Gull," wrote the defense attorneys, "did not playfully call Brad Rozzi 'ding dong,' but instead questioned Rozzi's reasons for seeking a recess . . . The fact that Judge Gull treats the defense differently on such a basic matter as requests for a recess provides a rational inference of bias."

Like so many of their other filings, this one ultimately went nowhere.

The "ding dong" filing was just one of many from the defense team that seemed inexplicable. The defense also did other things. On one occasion they rather memorably included the prosecutor's private cell phone number in a document. The prosecution team struggled with how to respond to such filings.

Often McLeland would prepare a first draft of a document in which he allowed himself to vent and freely express his feelings on the defense tactics. He would fully intend to soften it before filing it with the court. Diener would encourage him to leave some of that emotion in the final version while Luttrull would urge McLeland to take the high road and make it sound more professional.

Since McLeland was the elected prosecutor and it was his name on the document, the final decision on such edits would be his alone.

As was the norm, in the Allen case the lawyers for both sides got the opportunity to depose witnesses prior to the trial. Parties testifying in a deposition would be sworn in, much like in court. The process was intended to give attorneys not only the opportunity to learn information but also to measure the credibility of various witnesses. In the Allen depositions, there was also a great deal of strategy involved.

Baldwin and Rozzi, for instance, were concerned that their questions could possibly alert witnesses to what their trial strategy might be. For that reason, they chose to play dumb in their first deposition of Liggett. They were convinced that the sheriff walked out of the experience completely fooled by their act.

In fact, Liggett figured out their deposition strategy was just an act. But he had concerns of his own. Since he had won the election and become sheriff, he had had much less to do with the Allen case on a day-to-day basis. He had not had the time to refresh his memory before being deposed. As a result, he was not as sharp as he would have liked to have been on the topic. He believed the defense attorneys picked up on that and he wondered what it might mean for what he could expect in the trial.

At times, the depositions could drag on and on—and tempers could grow shorter and shorter. As the deposition of Dr. Monica Wala stretched into its fifth hour, Diener told Rozzi that she had an appointment she needed to get to and asked if they could schedule the rest of Wala's testimony for another day. Rozzi initially said that that would be fine but then backtracked.

"I don't give a damn about your schedule," Rozzi told Diener.

He said it was his deposition and he was going to keep going. Ultimately, though, Rozzi relented and the meeting was rescheduled. Despite such incidents, Diener became known as the prosecution team's diplomat, the only one who could really work with Rozzi.

At times, the mood in the deposition room could grow contentious. McCleland would tell the defense team they could not ask a particular question. The defense attorneys would insist that they could ask whatever the hell they wanted. McLeland would retort that they could indeed ask what they wished but that did not mean the witness would answer them. Despite all of that, the defense team only rarely asked Gull to intervene to force witnesses to answer particular questions. That actually surprised the prosecution team who felt that Gull had been liberal with what she allowed the defense to do.

Things could grow tempestuous for witnesses as well. At one point in their deposition of Holeman, the defense brought up the topic of Stephanie Thompson. In 2022, Thompson, a twenty-three year veteran of the Indiana State Police, had been killed with her seventeen-year-old daughter Mya in a tragic house fire. Holeman had known Thompson well. They had come up as detectives together. They had been friends.

Thompson had given a few polygraph examinations in the case, including some related to the Odinists. Now the defense made allusions to her death, suggesting that she had actually been deliberately murdered by Odinists and that the Indiana State Police had covered it up. Holeman could not believe what he was hearing. The accusations made no sense. And they were infuriating. Without evidence, the defense was accusing him of having a hand in the death of a good friend and her daughter. At one point during that exchange, Holeman threatened to just leave.

Another issue about the depositions that left the prosecution team annoyed was that they continued to happen even as the trial date got closer and closer.

CHAPTER FORTY-ONE

As the trial date approached, Gull had a backlog of motions she still needed to rule on. She scheduled a three-day hearing to give both sides an opportunity to present their arguments.

The final day of the hearing was arguably the one most crucial to the defense. That was the day the court considered a motion in limine filed by McLeland.

A motion in limine is a request for a judge to order that certain evidence not be admitted into the trial. In this instance, McLeland wanted Gull to forbid Rozzi, Baldwin, and Auger from mentioning at trial anything to do with Odinism or ritual murders.

Ever since they had filed the Franks memorandum nearly a year before, the defense made it clear that the Odinism hypothesis would be the cornerstone of their case. If McLeland's motion in limine was granted, they would not be able to use that theory in the trial. So it all came down to this day, this hearing. If they could not convince Gull of the connection between Odinism and the murders, their hypothesis would be inadmissible. Everything was on the line; it was time to play all their cards.

The first witness Baldwin called was Dawn Perlmutter, who declared herself the director of the Symbol Intelligence Group and an adjunct professor of forensic medicine at the Philadelphia College of Osteopathic Medicine. As Baldwin presented his witness, something about his manner was guarded, like a boxer bracing for a punch to the nose. At the conclusion of his long, meandering presentation of Perlmutter, she testified that she was convinced the murders of Abby and Libby had been a textbook ritualistic killing. According to her testimony, she seemed to base this opinion largely on the murders having been committed outdoors, in nature, with a knife. Her methodology, by her own account, centered around searching for symbols her clients wanted her to find. For that, the defense paid her thousands of dollars, $5,000 to Perlmutter herself and a total of $13,525 to her Symbol Intelligence Group. The team had scrambled to find an expert after Turco backed the state police. Perlmutter had the look of a bespectacled academic—and some of the buzzwords—but seemingly none of the rigor.

McLeland's cross-examination was a long gauntlet with a trap at the end. "Have you ever," he asked, "seen a racist Odinist group target two young white females?"

Perlmutter tried to dodge the question. "They will do that if they can—"

"It's a yes or no."

"No," said Perlmutter. It was a major concession. The defense expert was admitting she had never seen an Odinist group do what had been done to Libby and Abby.

But McLeland was just getting started. Within a few minutes, he also got her to admit she had based her conclusions only on the materials the defense had given her—and they had left out such items as police interviews with their Odinist suspect and evidence of that suspect's alibi.

He pressed her on the blood found on the tree near the bodies. The defense claimed this was crucial evidence, that it was a rune—a symbol intentionally painted there by a group of murderous Odinists using Libby's blood. Perlmutter made it clear she agreed with that analysis.

"The blood on the tree," asked McLeland. "How confident are you that that is a symbol, as opposed to blood spatter?"

"I'm extremely confident," said Perlmutter. "It's an intentional mark; in my opinion, it's an intentional mark."

"You have no training—or you have minimal training in blood spatter?"

"Correct."

In short, she conceded that she was not qualified to make the assessment she was offering.

McLeland was still not done. "You talked about . . . some of the evidence you used . . . to make a determination of whether or not this is the—I think you used the classic or textbook ritualistic killing; is that correct?"

"Yes."

"And is it important for you to examine that evidence before you make that finding?"

"Yes."

"How important?"

"It's important to examine the evidence."

"I mean, common sense says it's important to examine that stuff before making an analysis so your analysis is correct."

"Yes."

McLeland had a secret weapon—something devastating Luttrull had found in his research. He asked Perlmutter if she had gone on Court TV on September 19, 2023. She said yes.

"And you gave an analysis of this killing at that time; is that correct?"

"Yes."

"And prior to giving that analysis, had you observed any evidence from this case?"

"I just read a Franks memo."

"Did you observe any of the evidence from this case?"

"No."

"And on that television show—I hope I get this quote right—but you told them that this is a classic ritual murder; correct?"

"From the description, yes."

"And you told them that before examining the evidence the defense had given you?"

"Correct."

"Now, you're in the business of consulting and testifying in these type of cases, you testified to that, that you get paid to do these things; right?"

"Yes."

"And so if you were there on Court TV, a national program, and say, 'This is a classic ritualistic murder,' then you change your story, that may hurt your business; correct?"

"That is not what happened. I reviewed the report, which was very specific, and I gave my opinion and, looking at the evidence, if it was different, I would have changed my opinion."

"Is it in your practice when you're examining crime scenes to look at motions filed by the defense to make an analysis of a crime scene?"

"That was given to me by the Court TV people."

"I understand that. Are there any other cases where you've examined a crime scene where you've looked at a motion from the defense to make an analysis of whether or not that crime scene is a ritual killing?"

"That was—no, no. That was—"

"Goes outside your standards; correct?"

"Yes, yes."

"Okay," concluded McLeland. "I don't have any other questions, judge." On top of everything else, he had established that Perlmutter had reached her conclusions about the crime scene months earlier, after only a cursory examination of one defense filing. It was the final, fatal blow to her credibility.

Afterward, even Baldwin had to concede McLeland had done his job well. During a break in the hearing, he drifted past the prosecutor. "Good cross, man."

The defense did not just rely on Perlmutter; they also brought in Click and Murphy, the two investigators who had provided them the blueprint for their Odinism theory. By that time, Click had retired from the Rushville Police Department and was working with the Department of Child Services. Murphy had retired from the Indiana State Police and now served at the Beverly Shores Police Department.

Each man's testimony was strikingly similar. To bolster their case for cult involvement in the killings, each man offered a hypothesis built on supposition tottering on guesswork. But, on cross-examination, each man readily conceded he had no evidence putting his suspects in Delphi at the time of the murder.

If even the defense's own witnesses admitted they could not place their suspects in the city the murder happened on the day the murders occurred, then it seemed clear that Rozzi, Auger, and Baldwin had failed to establish a link between Odinism and the murders. Beyond that—despite the thousands of dollars they received from Carroll County and enthusiastic donors, despite their team of private investigators, despite everything else—the defense team had truly failed to build upon, expand, or corroborate the lead that Click, Murphy, and Ferency put together.

The prosecution also produced an expert witness—Major Pat Cicero of the LaPorte County Sheriff's Office. Cicero, who refused to take any payment for his services, was there to testify about the crime scene, to indicate, for example, if the so-called bloody symbol on the tree was put there by Odinists or if it had a simpler explanation.

Before prosecutor James Luttrull got to the substance of Cicero's testimony, he walked the major through what he had done to analyze the crime scene. The difference between Cicero's preparation and Perlmutter's was stark. While Perlmutter arrived at a conclusion before examining anything—then took a look at a few items the defense shared with her—Cicero studied files full of crime and autopsy photos, police reports, diagrams, and postmortem reports. Cicero also visited the crime scene. Additionally, he had studied physical pieces of evidence such as the clothes Abby had been wearing. As part of his analysis, the major had also done tests, using his own blood.

To explain his conclusions about the bloody tree, Cicero needed to discuss what the crime scene told him about what had happened to the girls. Absent surveillance footage, there was only so much he could conclude about a scene. He had to stick to what the evidence showed.

Abby did not seem to have moved—other than perhaps to have turned her head—after she received her wounds. The clothes she wore were saturated with her blood, especially the hood and upper back of the sweatshirt.

Libby's blood was present in small accumulations throughout the murder scene. That—and the bloodstains on the bottom of her feet—told Cicero that the girl had been mobile for a while, at least after receiving her first injury. There was also a great deal of blood on Libby's hands. Cicero told the judge this meant that as the girl was standing and staggering about—her life's blood gushing out of her—she had tried desperately to staunch the wound with her own hands.

It finally became time to talk about the blood on the tree. Cicero testified about using his own blood to try to paint a symbol on the tree—which, of course, is what the defense contended a group of Odinists had done. They believed the blood on the tree was a carefully crafted rune, a sign that the crime had been committed by Odinists. But Cicero found it difficult to replicate the marking on the tree by painting blood onto the bark.

Cicero concluded it was indeed a transfer stain, but not one made by meticulous painting. Instead, he believed there was a simpler answer, that something covered with blood was pressed up against the tree. As the spectators in the packed courtroom listened, spellbound, Cicero explained that the imprint on the tree was consistent with the shape of Libby's hand.

What the defense claimed was a rune was instead the bloody handprint of a dying girl as she leaned against a tree for a last bit of support.

CHAPTER FORTY-TWO

By the time the hearing ended, it was clear the defense had utterly failed to demonstrate any connection between Odinists and the murders. Perhaps the biggest surprise had been simply how poorly the defense had done. The prosecution team assumed that for some reason the defense had simply chosen not to bring their best game, that they were holding something back.

Considering how they actually performed in court, it did not come as a surprise when—a few weeks later—Gull ruled that their Odinism theory would not be permitted into the trial.

In some ways, that was perhaps a boon for the defense. Shortly after the hearings, one of their star witnesses imploded. On September 26, 2024, Click was charged with official misconduct, forgery, and falsifying child abuse or neglect records. In his role as an investigator for the Department of Child Services, he was accused of pretending to check in on at-risk kids, then forging parental and guardian signatures for his records. The alleged actions would have put children and their families at risk.

The Delphi case was rife with individuals—law enforcement officers and civilians alike—who took their own theories quite personally. They would become emotionally invested in a specific outcome or person of interest. When the members of Unified Command tacitly or directly rejected their ideas, these individuals did not take that as investigators making a choice likely informed by access to crucial case information.

They took it as an insult. Many regarded the inner circle of the investigation with a scorn that seemed to indicate some level of jealousy. They felt cast out, rejected. Fortunately, there were others who were happy to step in and boost their egos.

Internet cranks would eagerly speculate about Click's woes. Reflecting that Ferency had been murdered by a prison guard, they would argue that perhaps everyone who got too close to the truth in Delphi was being targeted. It did not matter that Click's troubles occurred in Ripley County, many miles away from Delphi. They regarded him as yet another martyr in the case. Rolling into trial with a witness credibly accused of forgery would not have been ideal for Allen's team though.

But the news was not all bad for the defense. As the three-day hearing ended, Gull did hand them a victory. She removed the safekeeping order. Allen could be transferred to the Cass County jail, something his attorneys had been clamoring about for over a year. Allen smiled as he was escorted out of the courtroom. Only he was alone in his quiet celebration. Kathy and Janis Allen had fled the courtroom before Cicero's testimony about the brutal nature of the girls' deaths. Apparently, hearing about a crime they were ostensibly convinced their Ricky was incapable of committing was far too taxing for them.

According to the defense team, Allen's move to Cass County would be a boon to his mental health. But it did not work out that way. Just a few weeks into his stay in the jail, something went very wrong for Allen.

Sitting on his bed during lunch, Allen was calm one moment. Then, he erupted. Screaming, yelling, shrieking, he declared himself innocent. He threatened to kill the deputies on guard. Then, staring at the camera in his cell, he drew a finger sharply across his throat. A slit throat, of course, was the cause of death for Libby and Abby.

In a matter of moments, Allen was back to normal. He protested that he did not need to be restrained and hauled to a padded cell. He was quiet and complacent once more.

Allen's entire outburst had been caught on surveillance footage. McLeland, Diener, and Luttrull were struck by what they saw. They believed that if a jury witnessed the angry Allen making threats and miming the murders, then they would likely vote to convict him in minutes. The problem was that the footage—as damning as it was—had nothing directly to do with the crime. So, even though it seemed to reveal something crucial about Allen and his instability and his temper, it was not clear if Gull would ever allow the jury to see it.

Stacey Diener was about the last person Becky expected to see at the racetrack. The Pattys had gone there that night to support their grandson Josh Lank Jr. He was a race car driver, and he was competing at the track that evening.

Becky approached Diener. "Strange to see you here." The deputy prosecutor and the families had gotten to know one another professionally. It was Diener's task to prepare them for the trial, which meant plenty of conversations about the worst day of their lives. Becky admired Diener's ability to balance sensitivity with a tough sort of competence. But she seemed so refined that she looked a bit out of place at a car race.

As it turned out, Diener's daughter was dating another race car driver. As the cars tore around the track, the Pattys sat down next to Diener and talked. For that one night, they were not a victim's family and a deputy prosecutor preparing for a daunting murder trial. They were just people who ran into one another at the track, talking about racing, talking about anything else other than what lay before them.

Long before he joined the prosecution team in the Richard Allen case—back when he was the elected prosecutor of Grant County—James Luttrull had a saying he used in the courthouse. On occasion, he faced opposing counsel that favored what he liked to call "the Beach Boys defense." Those defenses centered around suppositions that did not match the facts, to the refrain of "Wouldn't it be nice?"

Whenever that occurred, Luttrull would find himself stopping in the hallway and stomping his foot on the floor. "This case will be tried on terra firma!" he would declare to his startled deputies.

To the Delphi prosecution team, it seemed like the defense had long ago blasted off terra firma, and disappeared beyond the stratosphere. But despite the loss of their vaunted Odinism theory, the defense still projected strength. Lawyers in the Franklin area heard things. The talk was that Baldwin was confident about his case. In Logansport, Rozzi was rumored to be filming himself working, in anticipation of a documentary deal, even as those who knew him from the legal community whispered that they never would have thought he would push such a bizarre conspiracy theory in court. Defense investigator Matt Hoffman told people that he dreamed of attending law school to help prevent wrongful prosecutions.

The bluster reached McLeland and the investigators. The prosecutor felt his case was strong. But McLeland was a worrier. Sometimes he would grab Holeman and ask him what they were missing. The two men would sit around and ponder whatever secret weapon the defense might be preparing to unsheathe. Holeman feared that the defense's plan was to just drag the matter on forever. As summer turned into fall, as the leaves reddened and fell away, he expected a continuance.

None came. It was perhaps the most surprising news of all. The defense was ready to go in October.

PART FIVE

THE TRIAL

"We've had this discussion
a thousand times"

CHAPTER FORTY-THREE

Rows and rows of prospective jurors filed into Gull's green courtroom. On the first day, fifty-two Allen County residents were called inside and split into four panels of twelve with four stragglers. On the second day, there were three rounds of twelve. The court was seeking to sit twelve jurors and four alternates. The jurors needed to be open-minded, available, and undecided about the high-profile Delphi murders.

In voir dire, Allen was at his most calm, his most placid. Gone were the glares and stares of the pretrial phase. At least for the time being, he seemed intent on making a decent first impression.

At the start of both days, each side launched into a mini opening statement. McLeland's presentation mirrored his planned opening statement, centering around Bridge Guy, a bullet, and the brutal murder of two girls. He told the story of the murders in a forceful, concise fashion.

In a loud voice, Baldwin hooked his audience with a declaration of his own: Allen's confessions were false.

"He confessed to crimes he didn't commit and facts that are not true," Baldwin said.

After the mini opening statements, the selection process started. In each round, a new panel moved into the courtroom's jury box. Attorneys on both sides were allowed to pepper the panels with questions, and then use their limited number of strikes to knock out anyone whose answers proved concerning.

There were a few surprises. On the first day, a dark-haired man in a blue shirt proclaimed he was a psychic who might be able to help out with the case.

"I am valuable not as a juror but as a help to the prosecution," he said.

The man explained that he could preternaturally sense the emotions of others.

"Thank you very much for your candid response," Gull told him. At the end of the round, the psychic was dismissed. Not long afterwards, the self proclaimed psychic reached out to McLeland on Facebook to once again offer the use of his supernatural powers to the state. The prosecutor never responded, likely to the relief of Luttrull and Diener. They felt McLeland had spent too much time engaging with the eccentric character during jury selection.

For McLeland, voir dire was about introducing himself to the jurors. He took on all the rounds on behalf of the prosecution. The defense team took the opposite approach, splitting the responsibility between them. Each attorney led with a certain style. McLeland charmed. Baldwin beseeched. Auger inquired. Rozzi floundered.

McLeland told the panelists he was nervous. But despite his self-deprecation, he never sounded anything short of personable and self-assured. He enjoyed talking to people and so he considered the process of jury selection to be one of his favorite parts of a trial. Of course there were a few extra wrinkles this time. While the trial would be held in Carroll County, the jury selection was taking place in Allen County. That meant McLeland was in an unfamiliar courtroom. There were so many cords on the floor that the prosecutor feared he would trip and fall on his face.

But whatever concerns he felt were not reflected in his performance. His voice boomed despite the poor acoustics in the room. McLeland relied on easy-to-understand examples about the burden of proof, taking the panelists through the story of a melting snowman. Smiling a bit mischievously, he would ask the more skeptical panelists if they believed beyond a reasonable doubt that he was, in fact, an attorney. Hour after hour, he went out of his way to be courteous to the men and women on the panels.

"Every single one of you is a good juror," he told them. "You might just not be a good juror for this case."

For some reason, Rozzi was tasked with the most rounds for the defense. His questions to prospective jurors sometimes veered into outright interrogations. In one round, he started off by assuring the panelists that he "tried to dumb this down" while hoisting a poster board emblazoned with the definition of burden of proof. In another, he quizzed those gathered about whether they could define the word *levity*.

That was part of a stretch where Rozzi was keen on explaining why the jurors might expect to see Allen and his attorneys guffawing and grinning during the murder trial. Gallows humor was key.

"Sometimes you just have to smile or laugh," Rozzi said.

The defense team was apparently dedicated to keeping their client as entertained as possible.

"Does anyone have a problem with that?" Rozzi wanted to know.

In one particularly excruciating moment, he singled out an older woman sitting in the jury box.

"Did you report you had an intellectual disability?" Rozzi's tone was blunt.

The woman stared at him, clearly startled. "No."

Rozzi skulked off, muttering about his jumbled seating chart notes. Later, he called a grown man—the sole African American member of a four-person panel—a "bad boy" after learning about his past trouble with the law. In contrast to McLeland's charm offensive, Rozzi's approach proved to be heavy on the offense and light on the charm. He never fully recovered with the jury.

On her sole round, Auger asked the panelists about wrongful convictions and reasonable doubt. Along with Baldwin, she would counter McLeland's example by asserting that a man in Johnson County had once faked his way through a legal practice before getting busted. She also wanted to know what the prospective jurors thought of her.

"Sometimes defense attorneys like myself get bad reps," she said. "People think we're shady."

One of the men in the panel asked her if the reputation was earned.

Auger's answer was measured. "I like to think not." Auger's presence in the trial confused members of the prosecution team. Originally, she signed on a limited appearance to handle only certain issues but during the trial—with no explanation—she took on a much larger portion of the workload. It was not clear if she had somehow aggressively commandeered a greater share of the case or if Rozzi chose to take a lesser role out of a desire to separate himself from parts of the case.

On the first day, Baldwin started his first round by clapping his hands on his client's shoulders. The theatrical move was one he had employed in plenty of jury selections in other courts.

"Look at this guy right here," he begged the panelists.

Allen gave those seated in the jury box an awkward smile.

After imploring the prospective jurors to search their hearts and minds, Baldwin jumped into talk of confessions. "Is it really possible he's innocent?"

McLeland felt Baldwin was getting dangerously close to preconditioning the jury. In quick succession, he made two requests to approach. After a quick visit to the bench, Baldwin continued in a more muted fashion.

Baldwin threw in yet another twist on the second day. In his mini opening, he claimed that hair that did not belong to Allen had been found on Abby's hand. News outlets ran with coverage of the exciting new clue.

Of course, Baldwin knew the hair meant nothing. Bozinovski had tested it and found it belonged to a female relative of Libby. After that, police had not spent time on it. They dropped it. There was no evidentiary value in the presence of the hair. It had likely gotten stuck on Libby's sweatshirt and then transferred to Abby's hand when she put the garment on.

Baldwin would later claim his mention of the hair centered around police incompetence, because Indiana State Police had only recently confirmed that the hair belonged to Kelsi, as opposed to another of Libby's female family members. But Baldwin had written a check he could not cash. He had gotten the prospective jurors' hopes up about intriguing forensic evidence, all seemingly in exchange for a few favorable headlines and startled cries from credulous television talking heads. Again and again, members of the defense team treated their own credibility as an infinite resource, an ever-replenishing spring rather than a scarce and already polluted pool.

Voir dire wrapped up a day early. The parties met the following morning for one final pretrial session. Then the jurors were each sworn in and ferried off to Delphi. The sixteen men and women were ripped from their everyday lives and flung straight into a storm.

Outside the Allen County Courthouse, a woman named Lana Oriani wandered around the sidewalks. She confronted passersby as she ambled about. She had a YouTube channel. She had commented on other criminal cases, often taking up conspiratorial talking points. She shared a room with Motta Jr., a fellow YouTuber, at the nearby Bradley Hotel.

Yelling intermittently, she approached pedestrians, asking if they were jurors on the Delphi case. She even shot footage of herself trying to scan license plates of nearby cars. In Fort Wayne, her goal was to identify the jurors and sell that information to her fellow internet sleuths.

Allen's supporters were not content to let the trial play out. They wanted to know who the jurors were. They wanted to investigate them, to ensure they were not crypto-Odinists or prosecution plants.

The defense needed them. Allen needed them. The hunt was on.

CHAPTER FORTY-FOUR

The line formed early on the eve of trial. Lumpy forms bundled in sleeping bags or slumped in lawn chairs huddled on the cement ramp leading up to the courthouse's main entrance. Gull's rulings on public access meant that news cameras were not permitted to broadcast the trial, live or on a delay. There would be no audio-feed, either. Attendance was required in order to glimpse the trial at all. Some of those who waited in line were affiliated with podcasts and YouTube channels, along with a few case enthusiasts who had followed the mystery for years. Still others were true crime tourists, whose hobby involved attending high-profile trials.

Members of the media consortium—handpicked by Gull and her team at Allen County—underwent regular lotteries to draw press passes for specific sessions. Everyone else had to wait out in the cold. Unlucky journalists who lost at the lottery and ended up stuck in the line found themselves grumbling about having to compete for seats with rubberneckers.

Gull owned the chaos. Not only had she barred attempts to broadcast the trial, but she had also refused to implement any compromises, such as an audio-only feed, a media room, or a spillover space for the public. There were plenty of options that may have reduced the pressure on the courthouse itself.

Under Indiana law, the decision to allow cameras was entirely under her purview. There was nothing legally improper about barring them. But from a practical standpoint, Gull's actions seemed to feed right into the conspiratorial narrative about the case. The American public was used to on-demand access to most court cases. The Delphi trial stood out as an aberration, which convinced some people that a cover-up was afoot.

Liggett came to the courthouse that first night. He occupied a strange position within the case now. As one of the investigators, he was due to take the stand and testify. As sheriff, he was tasked with ensuring the whole show ran smoothly. He relied on Deputy Mitch Catron for assistance arranging court security and organizing the team. He stood near the doors, staring down the crowded ramp.

"This looks like a homeless encampment," he said with some sadness.

Liggett's main concern was safety. Plainclothes officers were on standby around the courthouse, ready to intervene if the line became unruly. Meanwhile, two entire sides of the grand limestone building were barricaded. Plastic orange barriers and police cars blocked the roads. On the far side of the courthouse, tarp-draped fences concealed another set of doors for the jurors. Authorities were not taking any chances. One mistake, and the jurors might be photographed or filmed. Or worse.

Indiana's trial of the century was underway, and the noise got to McLeland. As he prepared, everybody seemed to want to run him down for a talk. He felt like he was dodging questions and platitudes and chatter wherever he went. He only wanted to focus.

Throughout the trial preparation, McLeland had become crankier and blunter behind the scenes. He was exhausted. He was only catching a few hours of sleep a night. Thoughts of the case would sometimes wake him up at three o'clock in the morning. Falling back asleep was always impossible.

"Man, you're grumpy today," Holeman would tell him.

"You're damn right," McLeland would say.

The case was McLeland's responsibility, his priority. He wanted everything to go perfectly. Holeman knew how McLeland felt. Perfection was impossible, but they all had to try.

Holeman would be chatting away about how things were going, only to have McLeland ask him for a moment to concentrate. So Holeman would fall silent. The prosecutor was probably one of the smartest people he had ever met. And McLeland was pouring everything into the trial. Holeman loved him for that.

The prosecutor and the investigator had become as close as brothers. Sometimes they acted like annoying siblings. They would squabble and then go back to being fine a few minutes later. Holeman would try to hug McLeland just to irritate him, because he knew the prosecutor hated hugs. But they trusted one another implicitly.

Over time, McLeland started to seek out Holeman when he needed solitude.

"Hey, don't let anybody in my office," he would say. "I just want to be in here by myself."

Holeman stood guard outside. Most of the time, only Diener and Luttrull were permitted inside. The three prosecutors had decided on three pillars that would hold up their case. They needed the jury to understand that Allen was Bridge Guy, by his own words and the observations of key witnesses. They had to explain the cartridge, and how that tied him to the murder scene. And they would emphasize Allen's confessions about the vicious murders. For years, the dominant narrative in the public was that the case was weak, flimsy. The prosecutors disagreed. If they could successfully construct those three pillars, then they were confident they could secure a conviction.

The prosecutors each put so much pressure on themselves. Holeman could see the burden weighing on McLeland in particular. As Holeman stood guard outside the prosecutor's office, McLeland worked and worked—all alone with the case he could not walk away from.

CHAPTER FORTY-FIVE

The circuit courtroom in Carroll County was beautiful, with its stained glass skylight and walls trimmed in pale blue. But it was also very small. Instead of separate tables for the defense and the prosecution, both sides worked at a line of desks pushed together. Holeman found himself seated on the end of the prosecution side. Allen's transport team—four imposing men in matching dark suits—sat Allen right next to him. That seemed rather awkward to Holeman.

"How you been?" Allen asked the investigator who arrested him.

Holeman responded reflexively. "Good, you?"

Allen stared back at him. "Not so good."

"Well, considering the circumstances . . ." Holeman looked away. On his other side, McLeland was trying not to laugh.

Gone was Allen's prison garb. Throughout trial, he would favor button-downs in pastel shades and reading glasses mostly left perched atop his head. On the first day, his shirt was a pale pink, a contrast with his pallid, clean shaven face. The intent seemed to be making Allen look harmless. A bright orange uniform might cause the jurors to prejudge him. Allen's transportation team was also disguised. A group of uniformed officers hanging around a defendant might give an unfavorable impression. One of the law enforcement officers on that team was Michael Hobbs, a young detective with Carroll County. He and his colleagues wore suits, to blend in and avoid drawing scrutiny from the jury. Their mission was to protect

Allen, and ensure he did not do anything dangerous. Every morning, they met at six o'clock for a briefing. Then officers from Cass County would drop off Allen at the courthouse. By then, the transport team—along with a few bomb-sniffing dogs—had searched and cleared the basement. That was where they would sit around with the defendant until it was time for trial.

In the hallway outside the courtroom, deputies stopped Bob Motta Jr. from walking inside. He told them he was with the Allen family. The deputies replied that the Allens were on their way up, so he needed to wait for them to confirm his story. In a few moments, Rozzi burst through the doors. He gestured for Motta Jr. to come in. The defense's unofficial spokesperson sauntered over to the row of seats reserved for their team and took his place. Rozzi hung around to ensure he got a spot.

The YouTuber claimed later that Kathy Allen had invited him. After all, another YouTube commenter named Christine Zentner-Calderon, who had dyed her purple hair a more sober black, had received the same courtesy. But unlike her, Motta Jr.'s role throughout the trial was to be more public-facing, part of a fruitful media campaign for the defense. With a designated seat ensured, Motta Jr. did not have to wake up early or brave the line. He was free to join Court TV for panel discussions in the evening. There, he would rattle off defense talking points to help shape the public narrative. Throughout the trial, he functioned as a spokesman for the defense, a voice for Richard Allen. The arrangement was a boon for Motta Jr. himself and the defense. Also there to offer their support in the defense rows were Salzer and Morse, two private investigators who continued to hang around the defense team and provide some aid to Hoffman. Within a few weeks, Morse would incur three charges of animal cruelty after deputies serving an eviction notice discovered a dead cat and neglected kittens in her feline feces-strewn home in Michigan City. Morse believed her legal troubles were in retaliation for her work on the Allen case.

When Janis and Marvin came into the courtroom, Allen smiled and waved at them. The defendant's mother and stepfather were not the only faces showing up to support him. His wife, Kathy, was there too, her graying hair hanging in curls. The rows of hard wooden seats were divided into sections, butting against one another like warring territories, seperating the credentialed press, the victims' family members, prosecution relatives, Allen's kin, defense guests, and the members of the public.

Baldwin seemed to have some scores to settle at the trial. When he noticed Ben Rector—the state police detective who signed on to run errands and wrangle witnesses for the prosecution—he nodded and said, "Oh, there's the trooper that tried to arrest me." Baldwin had not forgotten the leak. He felt persecuted by the police. The police had not forgotten either. Especially not with anonymous figures continuing to plaster the images of dead children all over social media.

When Gull sat down at the bench, she was about ten minutes late. But she looked rather pleased, chuckling as she spoke with attorneys. Her silver hair hung down, long and sleek. She was well-rested. But that was not why she was smiling. Addressing the entire court, she mentioned an incident that explained her high spirits. Deputies had nabbed four cameramen who had gotten too close to the restricted area. Gull said they had violated the decorum order by attempting to film jurors when they arrived at the courthouse. She said their cameras were confiscated and would not be returned. (Later on, they were.) The four journalists would be barred from the trial.

"I think it's important that Mr. Allen get a fair trial free from the nonsense of the media," she said.

Gull's smiling announcement was a clear warning to the rows of credentialed press. She would not tolerate mistakes in her court. In light of YouTubers attempting to film jurors, the strong focus on traditional media outlets struck some journalists as bizarre and misguided.

The rules for the gallery, including the credentialed press, were simple and brutal. There would be no readmittance. If a spectator wanted to protect their seat, they would need to forgo eating breakfast or dinner, drinking water, and other necessities.

Around 9:23 A.M., the jury entered the courtroom to Gull's warm greeting. The judge gave them preliminary instructions and explained the four counts against Allen.

The large touchscreen television loomed over McLeland. The TV was a late purchase, arriving only two weeks before the trial. Before the public took their seats in the gallery, Mullin had tested the device and found no issues. But the thing filled McLeland with dread. He had not practiced on it much. The prosecution team had been too busy preparing for trial. Mullin and Nathan Meyers, the assistant prosecutor's investigator, worked hard to get comfortable with the technology. Meyers even worked through a weekend just to get familiar.

But when it came time for the prosecutor's opening, the glowing monitor failed to respond to Mullin's increasingly frantic administrations. He tried to pull up the drone footage of the trail, which had been specially prepared to add a theatrical flair to McLeland's opening statement. On the prosecution's side of the courtroom, shoulders hunched and pulses quickened. Back in the gallery, Allen's family members smiled and chuckled.

McLeland wondered how long he should allow Mullin to toil over the device. Standing with his back to the jury, he knew he looked like a complete fool, a hillbilly lawyer well out of his depth. His first move at trial involved an excruciating delay and technological incompetence. A bad omen if he had ever seen one.

Finally, McLeland had enough. He whispered for Mullin to sit down and forget the TV.

The first few words were the hardest to get out. Inside, McLeland was rattled, but he did not let that bleed into his emphatic delivery. McLeland quickly fell into a rhythm. He had written out the entire statement first, and then jotted it down a second time in shorthand. He knew it well and was prepared to deliver it with confidence.

Some lawyers are openers. Others are closers. McLeland was the latter. He did not care for opening statements, which he regarded as opportunities to inadvertently overpromise to a jury. In his defense days, he often eschewed them altogether. As prosecutor, he was bound by statute to deliver one, so he aimed to make his statement brief but dramatic.

He asked the jury to focus on three things: Bridge Guy, the bullet, and the brutal murders of two girls. He introduced the victims. "They were best friends. They always were together. They were more like sisters than friends."

McLeland put the entire courtroom in the minds of the girls, describing the chill that Libby must have felt seeing the man on the High Bridge. "Imagine the fear you would have, not knowing what he wanted."

Finishing up, a small stack of papers clutched in his hand, McLeland gestured at Allen.

"The evidence will show that the last face the girls saw before their throats were slit was Richard Allen's face," he said.

Then came the defense's turn. Unlike his opponent, Baldwin was widely considered an opener. His philosophy of trial was built around opening statements. He believed that a lawyer needed to capture the hearts of the jury early on. A case could be won in an opening statement, he imagined. Baldwin was known for his oratorical talents. He could be down-to-earth. He could be dramatic. He could compel a jury. That was his reputation.

But the opening statement Baldwin delivered was long, confused, and rambling. He jumped from topic to topic, never even bothering to truly introduce Allen as a human being deserving of sympathy.

He spoke about reasonable doubt. He railed against the state for the recording mishaps and for the FBI's departure from the case. He extolled the importance of phone data, and how that would make the state's case "start to fall apart." He previewed the defense's argument that the girls were likely killed far later than the state suggested. He knocked Libby's video, saying it was "not very panoramic" and that it did not show Bridge Guy's mouth moving.

He also admitted that the hairs on Abby belonged to Kelsi, but he argued that law enforcement was negligent for not confirming that years ago. All the talk of Kelsi's hair at the scene had set off segments of the online community, inspiring rolling waves of hatred against Libby's sister, who was by then pregnant with her second child. Baldwin hinted that the eyewitnesses who saw Bridge Guy were not to be trusted. He tried to deputize the jury, telling them, "You may see stuff we didn't." Choking up, Baldwin brought up Allen's suffering in prison.

The longer he went on, the more apologizing he did. Baldwin seemed aware that his opening was going on too long and told the jurors he was "going as quickly as I can."

At one point, he stopped, visibly emotional. "I'm sorry. This is so important."

He hypothesized that two killers had murdered the girls with two separate knives, a serrated and a non-serrated blade, based on the findings of pathologist Dr. Roland Kohr. Twice, Gull admonished him for veering very close to argument.

Baldwin addressed the jury with a final plea. He asked them not to make up their minds until the very end. "Please wait. Richard Allen is innocent. He is truly innocent."

CHAPTER FORTY-SIX

The prosecution's case in chief began with the families. One by one, the relatives of Libby and Abby spoke about their last moments with the girls on February 13, 2017. Diener guided them each through direct examination. With her questions, she sought to establish the facts of the day while allowing each relative to convey the sheer loss. She wanted the jurors to get to know the girls through their families, the people who knew them best. In the back of her mind she was worried. She wondered if the defense attorneys would grill any of the family eyewitnesses on the stand.

Becky went first. She recalled Libby wanting to grow up to be a forensic scientist, someone who helped the police solve crimes. She began to cry recounting how she learned the girls had been found.

"I couldn't understand why they wouldn't take me to her," she said.

After lunch, Kelsi testified while the drone footage McLeland had wanted for his opening played on the big TV. Kelsi and the jurors watched along as the footage displayed the wintry path that Libby had last traveled. Kelsi remained calm and impassive on the stand.

Derrick came next. A large man with a puffy orange beard, he wore overalls. He told the court about the murmur he had heard among the searchers around the time the girls were found.

"I just heard Mom screaming," he said. "She had heard something."

Anna came last. Dressed in a black-and-white dress, her expressive face showcased her emotions. When Diener asked her if she was Abby's mother, she smiled slightly. Her answer came in soft and proud. "Yes, I am."

Diener asked her what Abby was like.

Anna's face reddened as she held back tears. "She was a very kind little girl."

Baldwin handled the family cross-examinations. He was not overly effusive with the relatives. To Diener's relief, he avoided harsh questioning. For years, Derrick in particular had been subjected to rumors and abuse. Anonymous internet commentators seemed to have no issue accusing him of being involved in the murder of his own child, or at least possessing guilty knowledge. But Baldwin did not pursue that angle. The attorney kept asking them all about the girls, if they had strong, clear voices, if they stood up for themselves. His questioning seemed to suggest that the girls would have fought back against their killer. And yet no one had heard screams or cries for help that afternoon.

For the rest of the day and the subsequent days, McLeland went through law enforcement witnesses. Deputy Mitch Catron. Investigator Steve Mullin. Detective Darron Giancola. Diener handled civilian searchers Jake Johns and Pat Brown.

All throughout, jurors were permitted to take part in the examination. In Indiana, jurors could submit questions. After review from both the parties, the judge could read those aloud to the witnesses. Even this early on, the jury seemed to be paying close attention. They asked about phone connectivity issues in the woods, the drone footage, and the location of the bodies.

Becky fled the courthouse. Her eyes were wide and red. She hurried across the street and cried. Her grief was not a private event. As a figure in a national crime case, even without cameras in the courtroom, anything Becky did was scrutinized.

That morning, those waiting in line watched her cry. A man in a red, white, and blue sequined suit stood there, sparkling in the early morning light. Some of those in line behaved more like revelers taking part in a block party or a concert than people attending a trial for the murder of two little girls.

Becky did not return even as the courtroom filled up that morning. That was the first of the Saturday sessions. Gull had set a grueling pace for the trial. Court would be in session on Saturdays, but only for half a day. The judge seemed to be signaling that she wanted the trial over with.

Security remained an ever present concern for the state. Witnesses were escorted in and out of the courthouse. On at least one occasion, YouTuber and case obsessive Oriani screamed at a witness from afar.

Sustarsic, the jail commander, was one of the law enforcement officials guarding the front door. She found most people attending the trial were polite—handing over their cell phones, complying with directions, and patiently waiting their turn. But others made the jail commander feel more like a kindergarten teacher. On a few occasions, she and her fellow officers heard about a fight brewing outside. They would rush out the doors and calm things down.

The ever-present fear was that somebody would try to do something in front of the jury. When McLeland saw people like the sequined man, he wondered if the day had come that somebody would scream out a protest chant or try launching themselves over the railing in the middle of court, to get their moment of attention. His biggest fear was that such an incident would occur on the last day of the state's case in chief, forcing a mistrial.

During the testimony that day, the sequin-bedazzled man fell into a coughing fit and fled the premises, never to return. One bizarre trend at the trial featured people driving miles and miles and sitting out in the cold for hours only to spend only a few minutes at the trial.

Allen turned in his seat, looking at the media row. He broke into a wide grin when he saw his family. But the longer he looked, the more his expression clouded. After a few seconds, he gaped at them, as if horror-stricken. At the end of the session, the Allen family's new friend Zentner-Calderon tried to wave at the defendant. She failed to get his attention. Allen seemed to be staring at nothing at all.

The judge permitted representatives of the credentialed media to review exhibits at the end of each session. That day, a dark-haired woman snuck her way past the group of reporters to gawk for herself. Nobody around her had any idea who she was. For all they knew, she might have been a confused and overeager true crime fanatic.

They did not know her name was Ali and that she was a YouTuber, Bob Motta Jr.'s wife and cohost. They certainly did not know she had been booted off her one high-profile murder case for leaking. All they knew was that she did not belong there. One of the young reporters pointed out the YouTuber's presence to Amy Graham-McCarty. A seasoned journalist and editor who juggled four jobs, Graham-McCarty had extensively covered the case for the *Carroll County Comet*. She did not have a problem with informing Ali that the exhibits were for press only.

Ali became surly. Her foul mood lingered, and she ultimately complained of the incident to her social media following, accusing a legacy journalist of tattling on her. Somehow, her followers deduced—or were told directly, behind the scenes—that Graham-McCarty was to blame. The local journalist saw a wave of harassment.

The defense attorneys had certainly courted the mainstream press. But most of their devoted following had little use for journalists or traditional outlets. As far as they were concerned, any attempts at objective coverage were tantamount to disloyalty. Only they—the online army, the YouTubers, the commentators, the moderators—were truly devoted to the truth.

The sky was dark outside the courthouse when the families filed into the room adjoining McLeland's small office. For all the years the prosecutor had spent studying the case, preparing, he felt lost in that moment. Nothing in the boxes of files could tell him how to gather two families and show them images they could never unsee. But McLeland and his deputy prosecutors did not want to blindside any of the relatives, and they secured permission from Gull to brace the families. So together, they all prepared to look at dozens of crime scene pictures, and then more of the autopsy photographs. That was one of the hardest nights of the trial.

The loved ones of Libby and Abby had a few reasons for wanting to see the horror themselves. They felt that Allen—the man who spent so many pre-trial sessions gawking and glowering at them—would take satisfaction from any overt reactions. They did not want to give him that. They did not want the media reporting that they reacted in a hysterical fashion. They wanted to see the images ahead of time, so they could steel themselves in court.

The families gathered around a laptop and clicked through the images. Some broke down. McLeland did not think he would get emotional. He had seen the pictures so many times. But he and Diener found themselves tearing up watching the families react to the graphic images of their children.

Becky had thought she had already gone through the worst of it. A crank from the Netherlands known for evading bans on YouTube had already sent her the leaked crime scene pictures. On vacation, she had opened an email and seen her granddaughter lying naked and dead amid the leaves. But the other crime scene photographs and the images from the autopsy were even worse. Libby and Abby had suffered. They had been scared and tormented and humiliated. They were slaughtered and left to grow cold in the forest.

CHAPTER FORTY-SEVEN

The forensics had fallen to Luttrull. His first witnesses were the trio of state police crime scene investigators.

He started with Sergeant Jason Page of the Peru post.

Pictures of the crime scene appeared on the big TV. The close-up photographs of their faces—Abby's pale, Libby's streaked with dark blood—were the worst, in some ways. In the family rows, Timmons began to cry. At the defense side of the table, Hoffman chewed gum. Allen just stared at the screen. As the day went on, he became more and more agitated. Seeing the pictures of the bodies did something to him.

On cross, Rozzi tried to dredge up the Odinism theory.

He pressed Page on the sticks atop the girls' bodies. Page said they had found nothing of significance regarding the sticks. Then Rozzi moved to the bloodstained tree. The defense attorney asked Page if he had ever heard of the term "the *F* tree." Actually, unknown to Rozzi, Page had been the one who had coined the phrase "the *F* tree" on the first day of the investigation.

Rozzi spoke casually, as if the defense had not tried their hardest to brand it "the *F* tree" in filings and through their online acolytes. "They call it that because there's blood on it in the shape of a *F*."

Page sounded unimpressed. "I think that's the reason some people refer to it as that. I refer to it as a bloodstain."

Duane Datzman came next. He was three years retired from the state police by then. More pictures came on the screen. Allen began swiveling in his chair. To get ahead of the defense, Luttrull had Datzman explain that the police did not collect the sticks at the scene. Mossy, crumbly wood made for a poor source of DNA, and there was no blood on them. But facing pressure back at the post, he had returned on March 3, 2017, and collected them. As predicted, analysts found nothing on the sticks.

Baldwin took on Datzman. The defense attorney complained that the investigators should have videotaped the cartridge as it was picked up, then hinted darkly that the jury could not trust whether the one in evidence was the same cartridge Datzman had noticed at the scene.

Datzman pushed back. He had never before videotaped the collection of a cartridge. That was not part of typical procedure. Too much handling of the cartridge at the scene could have resulted in scratches or lost trace evidence.

Baldwin also asked why Datzman and his colleagues had not taken the body temperatures of the girls. The retired investigator's answer was simple. Such procedures required a rectal insertion. The investigators would not perform a test that could have destroyed evidence of a sexual assault.

"You know, my mother used to take my temp by putting a thermometer under my arm," Baldwin reminisced.

Luttrull objected. He asked the judge why it was at all relevant what Baldwin's mother used to do when he was sick.

Baldwin continued to get cute with Datzman. He asked him if he could have jogged off to CVS to pick up a thermometer.

Brian Olehy was the final CSI called to the stand.

Like Datzman, he had since retired from the state police. Olehy described processing the girls' bodies. The blood all over Libby made swabbing for offender DNA difficult.

To get a better angle on the screen, McLeland moved to a different spot at the table. Sitting next to Allen now, he looked up at what he believed was the man's gruesome handiwork.

The next day, the defense tried to beat up Olehy over the cartridge and the sticks and the lack of body temperatures. The former CSI was nonplussed. He and his colleagues had followed proper procedure in collecting the cartridge. And sticks were a terrible source of DNA. The sticks meant nothing. He did not regret leaving them behind. Had the CSI team collected every leaf in the forest, they would have swamped the laboratory and found nothing. Collecting body temperatures was an imprecise method for ascertaining time of death. One by one, Olehy shot down the defense's claims.

"An attorney's opinion is not relevant to this jury," Luttrull objected when Rozzi would not back off.

The women had each seen Bridge Guy.

Railly Voorhies came first. Her long dark hair hung around her face, the same dark hair Allen had described to Dulin back in 2017. Voorhies was a young woman. In 2017, she had been a Delphi high school student. Much like Abby and Libby, she had enjoyed the day off school by heading to the trails with her friends Breann Wilber and Anna Spath. Her little sister, who was very young, also tagged along.

Voorhies was very quiet, to the point that Gull somewhat sternly told her to speak up. She was clearly nervous. But Diener guided her along, and what she had to say was powerful. Wearing light jackets on the insistence of Voorhies's father, the group of girls left his home around half past eleven and walked the trail to the High Bridge. The day was sunny and warm. They stopped along the way a few times, at Wilber's house or Voorhies's mother's house.

On the way back toward the Freedom Bridge, they ran into a man. His face was covered by a running mask, but the skin around his eyes was white. He was bundled up, overdressed for the weather. Voorhies smiled at him and waved as they passed each other.

The man glowered at her. Voorhies felt a chill. The encounter was unsettling.

"He seems happy," she muttered to her friends at the time.

Voorhies could not identify Allen. But she testified that she was certain she had seen the Bridge Guy from the video.

Wilber was next, a young woman with dark blonde hair pulled into a ponytail. She knew Libby through Kelsi, one of Wilber's best friends. Like Voorhies, Wilber had seen Bridge Guy. She remembered her friend greeting the man and getting cold silence in response. The man was walking with purpose.

"It just kind of gave me weird vibes," Wilber said.

Wilber had taken pictures all along the walk, documenting specific times the girls were there. On the way back, she photographed a bench.

The last witness was not a part of the group of four young women. Betsy Blair, one of the sketch witnesses, had been there separately, walking the trails for exercise. On the day of the murders, her Fitbit kept track of her steps and locations. She described seeing the man on the High Bridge, how she felt he was waiting for someone.

Like Voorhies and Wilber, Blair was certain she had seen the man Libby captured in her video. All the witnesses had different descriptions. The younger women, Voorhies and Wilber, were certain that the man was older. Blair thought he was boyish and youthful. None of them had seen him very long. But what mattered was that they were all confident they had glimpsed the man in the video. They had seen Bridge Guy.

Blair recalled passing by Libby and Abby as they headed toward the High Bridge.

"They were just walking along and chatting with each other kind of quietly, kind of intimately," she said.

She had been the last person to see the girls alive, aside from their killer.

When Sarah Carbaugh took the stand, the sky was dark outside, casting shadows in the courtroom. Her long hair hung loose over her purple blouse.

Confidently, she answered Diener's questions about February 13, 2017. She rattled off testimony about her sighting of the stealthy man walking along the side of the road. Carbaugh even hunched up her shoulders to demonstrate the man's strange shuffling walk. Her manner was bombastic, and a few members of the jury began to grin.

Carbaugh also explained why she had not come forward immediately despite recognizing Bridge Guy on the news.

"I am very traumatized by anything murder-related," she said.

Carbaugh called herself a chicken, a coward. When she ran into a law enforcement roadblock months later, in the summer of 2017, she was ready to talk. She gave in her tip then. Police took her statement and confirmed her location with the Hoosier Harvestore video, and Carbaugh had cooperated ever since. She wanted nothing more to do with the case though.

On the stand, she sounded more like a quip-ready witness in a courtroom drama than anything else.

Things devolved further during Baldwin's cross-examination. He confronted Carbaugh. In the transcripts of her earliest interviews, the word *blood* never appeared. There were thirteen separate mentions of mud. She had also said the man she saw wore a tan jacket.

Carbaugh retorted that she had been nervous and mumbling in that interview. She mentioned blood. The transcript was just incorrect. And looking back, she believed she had mistaken dried mud and dirt for a tan-colored fabric.

On the stand, Carbaugh was a talker, a dream for any defense attorney. Baldwin did not have to say much. He asked Carbaugh questions, then let her go. When silence fell between them, she would fill it. Needling her did not take much effort. By keeping cool and quiet, he was able to showcase the witness's increasingly irritated responses.

"I know you're just doing your job," she snapped at him at one point.

Baldwin kept hitting her with questions in a dull, dismissive tone. He asked her why she told police she believed the man she saw had "effeminate eyes" and curly hair and a funky hat. He asked her why she would not stop to help a man she believed just suffered a fall on the trails.

Carbaugh was indignant. "I'm not going to stop and help a random man."

When Baldwin asked about the distance between Carbaugh's car and the man, she remarked, "I didn't take the ruler out while driving."

Irked, she added that she could not tell Baldwin how many freckles the man had either.

Diener tried to intervene. At one point, she asked Carbaugh to only comment on things she knew about firsthand.

The courtroom was divided over Carbaugh's performance. Baldwin had successfully knocked her credibility with the jury. On a human level, they understood she had not asked to be put in such a position. As jurors on a murder trial, though, they preferred the more stoic witnesses. But many in the gallery loved her. They appreciated that she was outspoken and unwilling to let anyone push her around. Some of Libby's relatives told others that they appreciated the feisty young woman who spoke up for herself.

CHAPTER FORTY-EIGHT

The blade took almost everyone by surprise.

As the prosecutor handling forensics, it fell to Luttrull to call Dr. Roland Kohr. Semiretired now, the forensic pathologist had a gravitas in the courtroom, even when his quiet voice was barely audible. He had testified at so many trials. As a forensic pathologist, his expertise was in high demand when it came to autopsies. He had done over seventy-seven hundred in his life.

"The word *autopsy* literally means to see for yourself," he told the jury.

The jurors, the gallery, and the victims' families would see a lot for themselves that day, as the prosecution flicked through slide after slide of autopsy photographs. The images showed the girls' dead faces, their wounds up close. At the defense side of the long table, Rozzi fidgeted, chewing on a pen and flopping his gold tie. The members of the jury were upset. McLeland had promised the bailiff that the prosecution would give advanced warning about the showing of crime scene pictures. The prosecution team had forgotten to do so that day.

In a soft voice, Kohr shared how both girls took as long as ten minutes to die. In the gallery, Libby's mother and half-sisters cried. One of the older men on the jury scribbled notes, and occasionally rested his head in his hands.

The blade was what gave Kohr pause. He had noted that the wounds on Libby's throat indicated a "serrated-like" sharp-edged weapon. That was a boon for Allen, as far as his defense team was concerned. They were eager to claim that the strange findings could be the result of multiple killers wielding different kinds of knives. But since then, Kohr had spent time puzzling over the kind of weapon that could fit what he observed in the autopsies.

A possible answer came to him in his garage. While working, he happened to see a box cutter. He thought that could certainly account for Libby's wounds.

The testimony was unwelcome from the defense's perspective. A box cutter, of course, was the very type of weapon Allen claimed he stole from CVS to use in the murders.

When Rozzi got up to cross Kohr, he was fuming. He asked Kohr to recall the deposition he gave on February 27, 2024.

"We conducted an autopsy—" he began before correcting himself.

Rozzi was so flustered that he accidentally swapped the words deposition and autopsy once more. Earlier, the prosecution had initiated an unexpected attack on Rozzi's style of questioning. He often started his questions to witnesses with phrases like "you'd agree" and then stated a proposition. The prosecutors objected to that, and Gull ruled that such wording was leading. Forced to abandon his typical way of speaking, Rozzi had seemed shakier on cross ever since. With Kohr, he had to strike two questions from the record. He began to raise his voice.

"You didn't say anything about a box cutter, did you?" Rozzi demanded.

Back in his seat, Baldwin shook his head. Kohr's comment about the weapon had blindsided the defense. Rozzi wanted to know why he had never received a supplemental report regarding the theory. He seemed to suggest that Kohr was colluding with the prosecution.

Unmoved, Kohr demurred. He said the box cutter simply offered a possible explanation based on his observations of the girls' injuries. But then again, it was just speculation on his part.

Luttrull came back with another question for the forensic pathologist. He wanted to know the minimum number of knives used in the murders.

Kohr's answer was ready. "One."

Baldwin's accusation was delivered with venom. "You are so desperate to have this be Richard Allen's car that right before lunch you lied to this jury."

Light flashed in the lenses of Mullin's glasses. The prosecutor's investigator was up on the stand, his face expressionless.

Liggett had been the chief antagonist of the defense's Franks memorandum. Holeman then eclipsed the sheriff as the lead villain in more recent legal filings, the puppet master who spirited away Turco and swore at Allen in an interview. But at trial, Mullin became Baldwin's favorite target. The defense attorney seemed determined to paint him as malicious. That struck those who knew Mullin to be the type of guy who would drop everything to help a colleague with a home improvement project, who walked around asking people, "What can I do to make your day easier?" as particularly ludicrous.

Before lunch on October 24, 2024, the defense cross-examinations were uneventful. Kathy Shank, the first witness, was hardly the kind of figure to draw a defense attorney's ire. As she sat up on the stand, her earrings shimmering, Baldwin politely asked her about the sheer mass of tips. After that Rozzi had tried to impeach Dulin—irritating Gull in the process—but things did not get too heated.

Then came Mullin. McLeland put him on to discuss his interview with Allen, and the early days of the investigation into the defendant. The prosecutor's investigator mentioned that Allen said he could have driven the route that took him west, past the Hoosier Harvestore camera that day.

McLeland objected to the defense attorney's opening charge. Baldwin tried again. "You said Richard Allen said he may have driven the country route."

Sounding disgusted, he added, "Richard Allen's video is available for the jury to watch—his words and body language—but we have to trust your word?"

Baldwin handed over a transcript of the October 13, 2022, interview between Mullin, Liggett, and Allen and demanded that the investigator find where his client said he had gone west on the day of the murders.

After a moment's quiet, Mullin followed up with a mild query of his own. "Is that a question?"

Baldwin again instructed Mullin to find the relevant passage in the transcript. The investigator read through the documents. The silence dragged on and on. Finally, Mullin pointed out that Allen's answer left room for the possibility that he drove the country route that day.

"On that particular day, he said east," Baldwin said.

"He said that was one possible route he took," Mullin said.

Baldwin asked the investigator if words mattered. Tersely, Mullin said yes.

The ensuing questions from the jurors were ambiguous. One wanted to know if Mullin had investigated the number of black Ford Focus vehicles registered in the area.

Mullin had not. But the question gave McLeland an idea.

CHAPTER FORTY-NINE

Liggett was back. The Delphi case meant so much to him. In some ways, the investigation had taken over his life for years. But he had been absent from the courtroom. The separation of witnesses prevented him from attending the trial until the judge released him from the subpoena. On a more practical front, he also had managerial duties as county sheriff. Getting shut out of the whole thing felt strange though.

Now he was up on the stand, a witness for the prosecution. Dressed in his sheriff's uniform, Liggett spoke in a calm, matter-of-fact manner. Briskly, McLeland took him through the whole investigation. Liggett also was tasked with translating the footage that Libby had taken. He had a singular advantage over the jury. As a detective, he had listened to the video hundreds and hundreds of times on headphones. The sounds, the scuffling, the click of the gun, the fear in the girls' voices, were forever stuck in his head.

Rozzi tackled the cross-examination of the sheriff. During the depositions, Liggett had felt the defense had gotten the best of him at times. But since then, he had spent hours preparing for trial. His face set in a grim expression, he watched Rozzi get up.

The defense attorney started off with a reference to the sheriff's election. He wanted to know about how Liggett's advancement nearly doubled his salary. In the defense seats, private investigator Erica Morse vigorously nodded her head. The implication seemed to be that Allen's arrest was politically motivated.

Liggett's voice was firm. "It had nothing to do with me. It had to do with two little girls who were murdered."

Sounding disgusted, McLeland fired back an objection. "Is the defense contending he made an arrest with no evidence to better his position in his election? With no evidence?"

Rozzi's ill-founded allusion to the election was less about the facts of the matter, and more about acknowledging conspiracy theories about Liggett. Rozzi then ran Liggett through a whole host of topics, from the leak of pictures from searchers to the Bridge Guy's weight and height to Betsy Blair's sighting. Sitting next to Baldwin, Allen glowered up at the sheriff.

Next, Rozzi attacked an eyewitness. In some ways, Baldwin had prevailed in his cross of Sarah Carbaugh. But the victory seemed somewhat pyrrhic. By embracing Carbaugh's sighting, the defense could have easily raised the question about the lack of trace evidence found in Allen's Ford Focus. Bridge Guy's pants were soaked in blood, after all.

Mockingly, Rozzi referred to the three weeks Carbaugh spent frozen in fear, unwilling to come forward to police. McLeland objected. Liggett responded with empathy. "Two girls were killed. I understand why she'd be panicking."

From there, Liggett continued to spar with Rozzi. He disputed the contention that the FBI had been forced off the case, saying he could always call the special agents if he needed assistance. He expressed his belief that Allen alone killed Abby and Libby.

"Prior to Richard Allen, I was open to anything. That's part of being a good investigator."

When Rozzi suggested the video did not show the Bridge Guy speaking, and that another unknown assailant had in fact been recorded, Liggett appeared dubious.

"That's a stretch."

When Rozzi claimed there was no digital evidence tying Allen to the crime, Liggett pounced. Allen's missing 2017 phone did not appear in the tower data.

"That's what's interesting. He says he was on the trail looking at his phone. There's no evidence of that either."

Rozzi contended that the cartridge was the only reason for Allen's arrest. Liggett calmly rattled off the Hoosier Harvestore video and the various descriptions of the witnesses.

Rozzi threw out that Blair had seen a man that appeared youthful.

"To her," Liggett replied.

Rozzi noted that Allen had cooperated with the investigation by meeting with Dulin in 2017.

"I don't know why he came forward," Liggett said.

Allen narrowed his eyes. Beside him, a slight smile broke out over Holeman's face. Over by the courtroom door, Baldwin stood in his rumpled gray suit, looking stricken. At least one concerned juror glanced his way.

Rarely is it a good idea for an eyewitness to parry with defense attorneys on the stand. Lawyers are adept at making fools of their untrained opponents. But Liggett managed to repel Rozzi's claims without sounding overly aggressive or long-winded. That night, the defense's pet social media commentators would describe the sheriff as a bumbling bumpkin who crumpled in the face of Rozzi's brutal inquiries. But the reality in the courtroom was far different.

The trial was far from over. There were still logistical matters to attend to. Liggett headed back to work on the outside.

Vido found himself stuck in the hallway outside the court for hours. He spent so much time refreshing his memory on the case. For many investigators, the feeling was that they had to know everything, or they could end up ruining the case. For Vido, the anticipation became terrible. His testimony always seemed to get pushed back. But finally, it was his turn.

McLeland wanted him to talk about the search of Allen's house. Methodical and very polite, Vido projected competency on the stand. He shared his insights about what the state police had collected, as the prosecution clicked through the pictures that had been taken during the search.

When Auger had good material, she could be incisive. Other times, she and witnesses seemed to be talking past one another.

With Vido, things got a bit confusing when she began asking him about knives. Specifically she wanted to know if people used knives to fish. Vido was not from the country. He grew up in Lake County, near Gary and Chicago. But he did fish. He decided to answer her question as directly as possible. "Spearfishing, possibly?" he asked.

Auger had something more like fileting in mind. Vido agreed that knives could be used to gut a fish, or cut a line, although he always used scissors for the latter task.

Auger pivoted to the items the police had not found. There was still the matter of Libby's missing underwear and the one sock that was never recovered. The killer may have taken both as trophies. It was also possible that both garments had washed away down Deer Creek, never to be found.

Vido confirmed that no such items had been discovered in Allen's home. All the time he was on the stand, he was struck by how intent the jury seemed. He could see they were watching him, taking everything in.

Luttrull thought they needed to do something with the gun. He had gone to McLeland and Diener, saying they ought to demonstrate the racking of a semi-automatic pistol to the jury. The prosecutors recruited Holeman because he was the biggest guy on the team, and he had the upper-body strength necessary for the task.

McLeland got him on the stand to answer a few questions about his interactions with Allen during the house search. A box waited on a table nearby.

Then Holeman stepped down and slid on a pair of blue gloves. His next job was to retrieve Allen's SIG Sauer from the box. Armed only with a dull pair of scissors, he sliced at the box until the webbing of tape and seals and stickers snapped apart.

Within the box lay yet another box. Within that was Allen's SIG Sauer.

Holeman's hands trembled as he retrieved the gun. He racked it as hard as he could. The metallic click rang through the courtroom. The gallery hushed. Everyone in the courtroom had heard something akin to what the girls had heard on the High Bridge that day in February. The effect was chilling. Holeman held up the gun for the jury.

CHAPTER FIFTY

Some of the most stressful moments could happen outside the courtroom.

Diener struggled to sleep during the trial. Sometimes she found herself in the courthouse until one o'clock in the morning. She often went to bed at midnight at the earliest, and woke around three or four o'clock in the morning.

So to maintain a semblance of normalcy, Diener had a regular morning routine. She would drive to the Starbucks at Kroger, grab a hot drink and then—during the twenty minute or so drive to work—she would listen to *The Murder Sheet*, a podcast that was doing daily detailed episodes on the trial. But, one morning, she went out to her garage and found that her car would not start. Her husband came out to help troubleshoot and the couple soon figured out the problem.

The day before, Diener's husband had taken her car out to get it washed. But there was a problem; her car and his both had push button starts but the mechanisms were different. When he returned her car to the garage, he believed it would shut off automatically, as his did. But instead it remained running, eventually leaving the battery completely dead.

Diener did not have the time to figure out how to solve that problem; she needed to get to court. "I'm going to need to take your car," she said.

She drove the unfamiliar vehicle to Kroger. She wanted to listen to the podcast over the car speaker but she could not get her phone to connect to the system. Instead, she kept getting a message that the vehicle needed an update. That was not a surprise; her husband did not like to do vehicle updates because he worried it might introduce a virus into the system. But Diener wanted to listen to the podcast and so she hit the update button.

The vehicle shut down, saying that it would not be operable again for twenty minutes.

Frantic, Diener began desperately pushing buttons, hoping she could somehow exit the process. But she could not. She was stuck. All she could do was watch the timeline that tracked the painfully slow progress of the update. She called McLeland to explain she was stranded.

Fortunately, she did not have any witnesses that day—and despite everything she still made it to the courthouse a few minutes before the session started.

Melissa Oberg was back in the line of fire. During her nearly seventeen-year tenure as a forensic firearm examiner at the Indiana State Police Laboratory in Indianapolis, she had worked on so many cases. The Delphi trial marked her 112th time on the stand. Even after departing on good terms to pursue a new career as a data analyst, she still had to come in and testify for some trials. The one difference was she would no longer get paid for her time.

Coming into court, Oberg clutched a large binder. Once she was on the stand, Luttrull took her through the science of forensic toolmark identification and the cartridge found at the murder scene. Her work was to examine how hard tools left marks on softer objects. Oberg compared that to a hand leaving a mark in the sand. Impressed marks were akin to patting down the sand. Striated marks were something like fingers clawing the sand, scratching out lines.

She explained her process. When an examiner found a sufficient agreement of marks in terms of both quality and quantity, then they could make an identification.

Luttrull also had her display the gun itself. Like Holeman had done before her, she slipped on blue gloves, unboxed the SIG Sauer, and racked it. The click was not quite as deafening. Oberg returned to the stand, and Luttrull resumed his questions.

Sitting next to Baldwin, Allen turned and gave a wide-eyed stare to his wife. His lips began to move, although he made no sound.

Oberg carefully explained that basing an identification on pictures of the markings on a cartridge was not considered an acceptable method in the forensics community.

"It would not be appropriate to do that," she said.

Oberg compared photographs of a cartridge under a microscope to a paused moment in a film. One could hardly claim to understand a movie after only viewing a single frame. An examiner had to scrutinize the object itself under a microscope to get a full understanding.

She explained that after receiving Allen's firearm, she had tested four cartridges. She could not get good marks on any except the one she fired and then cycled. That was not surprising. In her experience, firing the cartridge first and then ejecting it led to more pronounced marks that made comparison easier. But the firing did not change anything. The extraction and ejection marks remained the same. A tool mark was a tool mark, she said.

In the past, she had examined cycled unspent cartridges multiple times. Under a microscope, she saw sufficient agreement between the ejector, extractor, and chamber face marks of that cartridge and the one found between Libby and Abby. That tied Allen to the crime scene.

That day, a few of the remaining jurors found the presentation regarding the firearm forensics quite dull. By then, the souls in the jury box had dwindled from sixteen to fifteen. One of the four alternates had to leave because of a family emergency. A few more losses like that, and the proceedings would crash to a halt.

Together, the jurors sat through a direct examination that featured a lot of technical terms and one notable technical glitch that occurred when

Luttrull went to play a video detailing the manufacturing process at a SIG Sauer plant.

"Is our technology working?" Gull asked him.

The answer was a resounding no. After the mishap during the opening statement, the prosecution would always test the technology outside the jury's presence. It would work fine, only to freeze whenever court was in session. Luttrull ended up skipping the first video, unable to get it to play. The setbacks with the seemingly possessed television were agony for the prosecution team. Holeman stood there, smiling awkwardly. McLeland fantasized about throwing the thing out the window.

But finally, after a cringeworthy pause, the second video rolled.

Then came Rozzi's cross-examination. The cartridge linked his client to the crime scene. He was determined to fire away at it with everything he had. He came armed with props. The defense had printed out a series of images of the cartridge at a microscopic level, despite Oberg's warnings about the illegitimacy of such tactics.

Rozzi started out by lecturing Oberg over the definition of *sufficient*. He cited the dictionary publisher Merriam-Webster, throwing out less-impressive synonyms like *enough* and *adequate*.

Luttrull objected.

"So we're talking two different languages?" Rozzi asked Oberg.

She gave him a faint smile. "We appear to be."

Rozzi jabbed at Oberg over the lack of graduate work requirements in the firearm forensic field.

"You could have a bachelor's in physical education," he said.

Oberg replied that her former employer required a college degree in a hard science. Her bachelor's degree was in chemistry.

From there, Rozzi seemed to ask the same questions again and again. When Oberg would answer, Rozzi would often interrupt her. The cross-examination dragged on for hours.

Blank-faced, Luttrull tried to object when he could.

Once when Rozzi started to talk over Oberg, Luttrull snapped: "Let her answer."

He thought Oberg held up well. In Luttrull's mind, if defense attorneys were like hammers, then ISP forensic examiners tended to be like anvils.

That day, Rozzi made a number of reasonable points, prompting Oberg to speak about the controversies around forensic firearms examination and the wider world of forensics. He also had her explain that the cartridge in question was a very common one.

For the most part, though, instead of methodically and succinctly slicing away at the evidence, Rozzi was stuck on a tedious tirade. His court presence could come off as arrogant, loquacious, and lacking in self-awareness. Nowhere was that side of Rozzi more on display than during his cross of Oberg. As the hours dragged on, some members of the jury felt on the verge of tearing out tufts of their hair. Listening to Rozzi was becoming unbearable. Behind the errant TV, McLeland—in the gray suit and pink-and-blue plaid tie he favored—sat watching, chewing gum, and drumming his fingers on the well's wooden fence. The jury often saw him at his most affable and charming. In quieter moments, he kept his eyes locked dead ahead, his posture tense.

Looming on the bench, Gull appeared frustrated. Amid all the back-and-forth, she let out a weary exhale.

"She's answering the question," she admonished Rozzi during one interruption.

In another instance, as Rozzi gestured wildly, she told him, "Nobody can tell what you're pointing at, sir."

In one sidebar, the judge remonstrated with the attorneys. She noted that she had been lenient, but that she would not keep tolerating lawyers hammering witnesses with nearly identical questions. She gazed at Rozzi as she spoke. Luttrull thought she might be referring to him as well. He felt his pace in trial could be plodding with some topics.

Even Rozzi himself appeared ruffled as the hours passed. On the outside, he seemed like a schoolyard bully, shaken that he could not get a rise out of his victim. At one point during his cross, he asked Gull if she wanted him to take a break.

"No," she said.

Later, Rozzi promised to move along.

Gull spoke for the entire court. "Please."

The lawyer frayed from there. He hurried back to the defense side of the table and whispered to Baldwin. The courtroom was silent aside from the sound of ripping paper.

The one person who seemed to remain unflappable was Oberg herself. She answered the endless questions posed to her, although her smile became more wan as the day went on.

Things only got worse after a lunch break. Sounding frazzled, Rozzi provided the court an estimate of how much time he would need to finish his questioning of Oberg.

Wryly, Gull replied, "When lawyers tell me a time, I usually double it."

Rozzi also kept asking the expert to share opinions about images of the cartridge, something Oberg had explicitly cautioned against. The attorney broke out his poster boards again, grilling the witness about how different the images looked. Luttrull threw out an objection, accusing Rozzi of "misusing those photographs." Rozzi repeated one point again and again, saying that studies showed forensic firearm examinations were unreliable. Luttrull objected.

Gull weighed in too. "Will you stop misstating the evidence?"

The defense attorney quickly offered to move on. The questioning fizzled out. Oberg escaped back to the civilian world.

CHAPTER FIFTY-ONE

The night before he was due to testify, Holeman popped an extra blood pressure pill. He knew he was in for it.

On the stand, Holeman was there to talk about his interview with Allen. The jury watched both police interviews for themselves. But there was a problem. The videos were both edited to take out mention of the Klines and polygraph examinations. Letting the jury know that Allen had refused a polygraph would violate his rights and likely cause a mistrial. But in Holeman's interview, that meant the jury would hear a tense but relatively calm interview devolving into a screaming match with a single cut, without any context. In prep, Luttrull had told Holeman that he unfortunately "won" the swearing contest in the interview, letting fly far more profanities than Allen. The prosecutors were concerned about how that would play.

Holeman needed to add context. He talked about his years of experience and the hundreds of interviews he had conducted. He discussed his interview with Allen. In that interview, he had established that the suspect never loaned out his guns, never visited the crime scene. In other words, there was no innocuous explanation for a cartridge from his gun landing between the girls' bodies. That gave police enough to arrest him. Holeman explained that he had used tactics like deception and aggressive mirroring to try to get information out of Allen.

Holeman said that through his training, he could sometimes pick up on signs of potential deception from a suspect.

Baldwin jumped on that. He asked the witness to list signs of lying. Holeman rattled off a few, saying that in certain instances, somebody touching their face, glancing away, or looking down could appear dishonest. But it was all highly contextual. Dryly, Baldwin pointed out that not everybody who touches their face is a liar.

Holeman explained that Allen had only shown subtle signs of deception. But that had not made much of a difference in the interview. In Holeman's mind, he cared about what Allen had said or not said, not so much about how he had acted.

"I saw you looking down quite a bit," Baldwin taunted Holeman during cross. "Was that a sign of deception?"

The defense lawyer turned to the jury. "The nice, calm guy on the stand right here is not the guy Richard Allen experienced."

He pointed out that police had lost proof of Holeman's Miranda warning to Allen.

"We had a lot of technical difficulties a lot of the time," Holeman said.

Baldwin confronted Holeman on the lies he told Allen. Holeman said he thought he was minimally deceptive. Once, he told Allen that experts had matched his voice to that of Bridge Guy. That was not entirely false. The detectives who worked the case, who had listened to the killer's voice hundreds of times, all thought he sounded exactly like Allen. But Bridge Guy had not spoken enough words to elicit an official analysis.

Baldwin also noted Holeman never recorded Allen's strange statements during the search. The court was instead just supposed to believe his contention that the suspect had repeatedly said, "It doesn't matter, it's over."

"He admitted he said it in the interview," Holeman replied.

Baldwin asked Holeman if he believed that only one killer was involved in the murders. Could it really be that a little man like Allen had murdered two kids in the short span of an hour all by himself? Holeman thought back to his drug enforcement days. He said that if a group of killers had been involved, one would have likely flipped on the others to get out of trouble.

Baldwin was aghast. "Do you really think one person did all that?"

Holeman remained resolute. "Without a doubt."

"Would you agree it would be easier for two?"

"No."

McLeland kept up a steady drumbeat of objections whenever Baldwin strayed too far. He especially hit back when the defense attorney claimed that the killer only had an hour to commit the crime.

The girls were kidnapped from the High Bridge at 2:13 P.M. Carbaugh had seen Bridge Guy on 300 North at 3:57 P.M.

McLeland was to the point. "I think Mr. Baldwin mischaracterized some evidence for the jury."

CHAPTER FIFTY-TWO

That day, Becky brought banana bread to the members of the gallery lined up outside the courtroom. Derrick had baked it himself from scratch. She walked around the third floor rotunda, passing out slices.

Sometimes it seemed like Libby's family was single-handedly trying to feed all the trial attendees. Mike would pass packets of peanuts to people during breaks. Tara would show up at midnight with a pot full of chili. Her wife, Amanda, would insist on slipping along all manner of snacks to those sitting around her, to the terror of anyone trying to avoid the wrath of the deputies. Despite their pain, they had all adopted the roles of caretakers of others throughout the process.

Toward the end of the line, Becky found herself face-to-face with Melvin. Over the years, the internet crank had spread all kinds of rumors about the case. Becky had many unkind thoughts about Melvin and her acolytes. But she held out the bread anyway. Melvin reached out and snatched a piece, smiling vacantly at the woman she had once proclaimed to be demon-infested. Becky kept walking all the way down the line.

———

At trial, Bozinovski's role was more to explain what she did not find than what she did. In her even tone, she explained to the jury that in her capacity as a DNA analyst in the state police lab in Indianapolis, she had not discovered a DNA profile for a male offender in the Delphi case.

She found plenty of DNA belonging to the victims. She received three untestable, rootless little hairs that could belong to anyone. She found trace amounts of male DNA, too tiny a sample to even analyze further, that could have easily come from living in a household with a man or boy.

Thanks to television programs like *CSI*, everybody expected more from a brutal crime. Bozinovski was there to explain why the state could not tie Allen, or anyone else, to the crime with DNA. Luttrull had worked with her before. Bozinovski was a capable analyst. She had tried her best. Some cases simply did not yield suitable forensics finds.

In the Delphi case, a few things were working against Bozinovski. The dirt, the damp, and the overwhelming amount of Libby's blood, which would have washed away an offender's skin cells.

The technical elements of Bozinovski's testimony were a struggle for some to sit through. At one point, Gull acidly addressed the gallery.

"I don't conduct court in your bedroom," she said. "I would appreciate you not sleeping in my court."

On cross-examination, Auger tore into the DNA analyst about the focus on male DNA. After all, nobody knew for sure whether the killer was a man or a woman. She took the jury through all the items collected from Allen's house, none of which yielded any meaningful trace evidence. At one point, she nearly seemed to be mocking Bozinovski. "Is it fair to say you put a lot of time and energy and effort into this case?"

Luttrull cleaned up on redirect though. He had Bozinovski restate the bare facts. She had not located any full DNA profiles for Allen, or for any other possible offenders. Nobody had left a suitable DNA sample. But the girls certainly had not been killed by a phantom.

Next, Cicero returned to the stand. As he got started, Abby's mother, Anna, left. Cicero retread much of the same ground he had covered in the three-day hearing. Crime scene diagrams and pictures flashed on the big

TV. One came in upside down. The prosecution's technical issues had not fully subsided.

It fell to Cicero to guide the jury through the barbarous crime scene. Like he did at the three-day hearing, he pointed out the pools of blood and what they told of Libby's desperate last moments. Pictures of leaves smeared with blood came up on the screen. Throughout his testimony, the crime scene expert referred to the girls as "Ms. German" and "Ms. Williams." He wanted to afford the girls dignity and care. They were gone, but they were still deserving of respect. So were their families.

Luttrull asked about a strange pattern of blood on Libby's cheek. Moisture had rolled across her face, diluting the blood.

Cicero said, "Absent a raindrop, it would be consistent with a tear."

Libby had cried. She had suffered. Her final moments were spent in anguish. Sitting at the prosecution table, Holeman blinked. Not even he had known about the tear. He felt like crying too. Members of the gallery began to sniffle. Becky wept. Libby had been crying out there in the woods. Becky had not been there to help her granddaughter, to comfort her, to protect her.

Luttrull left that day, weary. In his years as a prosecutor, he had seen many evil things. A man bound, shot, and slashed in the throat over a little marijuana and a hundred dollars. A young girl, assaulted and impregnated by her rapist. An elderly woman, raped and beaten to death on Mother's Day. Now, the images of Libby and Abby on that forest floor. He never wanted to see the crime scene pictures again.

A parade of prison guards descended on the courthouse. Starting with former warden John Galipeau, the current and former correctional officers testified one by one about Allen's stream of confessions and bizarre behavior.

That day, Allen was all over the place. He seemed animated at times. Then, when Raymond Smith testified to seeing Allen masturbate while belting out "Mammas Don't Let Your Babies Grow Up to Be Cowboys," the defendant let out a laugh.

Between listening to the testimony and sitting right beside the defendant, Holeman sometimes felt he was losing his own mind. The investigator would mostly stare off at some random fixed point in the distance. One day, he glanced over as Auger passed Baldwin a note to give to Allen. Then he heard Baldwin mutter something.

Holeman turned. "What?"

"Quit looking at his notes," Baldwin hissed.

Holeman's eyesight was so bad he relied on reading glasses. Part of him hated the idea that people like Baldwin thought he was such a corrupt liar. An incurable optimist in some ways, Holeman thought if he could just prove to the defense he was a human being, not the living embodiment of evil, perhaps they might listen. During the break, he held up his phone to Baldwin. The text on his screen was massive.

"You see my font on my phone, buddy?" he asked. "I can't read those notes."

Baldwin fumed. "Get away from me. Don't talk to me."

CHAPTER FIFTY-THREE

A juror's single question got McLeland thinking. He and Mullin went to work. They wanted to show the jury that they were taking their questions seriously. Looking at the Bureau of Motor Vehicles data, McLeland realized they could achieve that while also putting together a dramatic little moment.

Calling Mullin on the stand, McLeland had him start with a large pool of data. In the BMV records, Mullin had found dozens of black 2016 and 2017 Ford Focus cars registered in Carroll County and neighboring counties back in February 2017. There were thirty-one in total.

Next, they whittled away the duplicate entries. That left them with eighteen vehicles. The suspense was palpable in the courtroom as the list of registered cars shrank.

Then McLeland and Mullin added the parameter of only showing only Ford Focus SEs, the vehicle's special edition. That was the type Allen owned, a sportier version of the traditional Ford Focus. Mullin found eight such cars.

But only one was registered in Carroll County itself. And that belonged to Richard Allen.

Raising her eyebrows, Auger grimaced at that bit of legal drama. Of course, the vehicle in the surveillance footage strongly resembled Allen's car, down to the rims. But the obvious argument was that the exact model could not be determined for sure. Nor were the license plate number or vehicle identification number visible. Outsiders were also perfectly capable of driving a Ford Focus SE through Carroll County at any time. She brought up those doubts on cross.

Meanwhile, some of the jurors were less than impressed. They wondered why McLeland's investigators had not narrowed down the list of cars already. The jury was a cautious bunch. They preferred calm, methodical work to flashy moments. Generally, that was why they preferred McLeland and his team. Technical difficulties notwithstanding, the three prosecutors projected a far more competent and professional front. Most of the jury looked askance at some of the over-the-top defense rhetoric. But they were willing to critique both sides on any given day.

The witnesses and examinations the lawyers thought would land did not always resonate with Allen's fifteen peers. Some of the quieter moments lodged themselves in their minds. Either way, the jurors were paying attention, taking it all in.

The star witness wore suspenders. Frizzy-haired and goateed, Brad Weber grinned as he made his way to the stand. Weber had become a key part of the case. McLeland called him because, indirectly, he could put Allen at the scene of the crime. The defendant had told Wala that he had seen a van as he abducted the girls, which had scared him.

The van sighting was a particularly damning confession from Allen. Only the killer could pinpoint the location of a certain type of vehicle traveling down a remote driveway at a specific time of day. And nobody could have fed that detail to Allen. The location and significance of Weber's van was never highlighted on social media. The van did not appear in police reports. It was not buried in Allen's discovery materials. That was because investigators had not known the van was important until the defendant made them aware that he had seen it. After Allen had handed the state a confession containing a detail only the killer could know, investigators went and corroborated the detail. But Weber made for an unlikely eyewitness. His testimony would center around what he had done that day, not what he had glimpsed. He had not seen the killer. But the killer had seen him.

Weber told the court he had driven his white van home on the day of the murders. Based on the time he clocked out of work, typical drive times, and the lack of accidents that day, he would have crossed under the High Bridge shortly before half past two.

Baldwin got up and changed topics. He asked Weber about being out of town for a week prior to the murders. McLeland objected on the basis of Baldwin's question being outside the scope of the direct examination. There was a short sidebar, and then Baldwin resumed his questioning.

"You did not drive straight home from work," he told Weber.

Weber did not like people twisting his words around. "Not correct."

"You went to work on ATM machines," Baldwin told him.

Glaring, Weber barked at the attorney. "Not correct."

McLeland jumped in to intervene. "Mr. Weber, hold on," he said, with a nervous laugh.

Angrily, Baldwin snapped, "I'm done."

Weber leaned back in his chair. Baldwin walked up and thrust a subpoena toward him. The star witness had just been served.

Holeman had no poker face. When the defense attorneys said something he thought was stupid or unfair, he would narrow his eyes or wince. The reactions were unconscious. He was not even aware of them until one of the bailiffs told him to knock it off. The bailiff was worried that Holeman would make him burst out laughing.

Holeman was not alone in his reactions. Whenever he was exasperated, Mullin would press his hand over his mouth. Some members of the jury did not care for those habits. They preferred that the law enforcement officials remain stolid.

The jurors noticed other reactions too. Rozzi tended to hinge his upper body forward, bowing slightly from the waist when he was really getting into a line of questioning. Luttrull had a certain gesture he would always do, pressing his arms to his chest and holding his palms upward. One of the jurors even sketched out Luttrull doing the gesture and stuck the image on the announcement board at their hotel. Baldwin always looped an arm around Allen, hugging him closer, making his client look even smaller by comparison.

Then there was Allen. He would gape at the jury, bugging his eyes out. Some of the jurors had taken to staring right back at him, refusing to glance away first. During breaks, Allen would sometimes appear normal, sharing smiles with his family. Other times, he would fix his strange glower on the gallery. A couple of times, he even pointed straight at members of the public, holding the pose for a disconcertingly long time. His affect was mostly creepy, and some worried about what he might do if he got desperate. There were even frightened whispers about Allen possibly lunging for Holeman's gun.

Hobbs disagreed. Behind the scenes, Allen usually behaved somewhat normally. The defendant often greeted his transport team in a friendly manner. "Morning, detective, how's it going?" he would ask Hobbs each day. Allen spent hours with the officers. He ate lunch with them every day of trial. He got to know each of their names. He could be passive-aggressive about following instructions—moving slowly to stall things, pretending not to hear commands—and sometimes came off as manipulative. But that was the worst of it. One subject of conversation made Hobbs less inclined to think Allen would try anything. The defendant would make comments marveling about the height and size and fitness of the members of his transport team.

For his part, Holeman was unconcerned, too. Nobody was going to get his gun from him. He was not afraid to sit next to Allen. There was something pathetic about the man. He was like an overgrown baby, and Holeman found himself at times thrust into the role of caretaker. He brought Allen bottles of water. He picked up and retrieved items the defendant had dropped. Holeman figured that Allen was still a human being, despite what he had done.

Dr. Monica Wala had also treated Allen like a human being. She had done what she could to make Allen's time in Westville less miserable. For that, she lost her job and was subject to online revulsion. In fact, the constant hounding from the attorneys coincided with the time when Wala was seemingly removed from her role at Westville, although she retained her employment with the prison's contractor.

Allen came to trust Wala. He told her he was an alcoholic. He told her he suffered from a sex addiction. He told her he wished he could travel back in time and change his actions. On the stand, Diener asked her to recite Allen's detailed confession to her.

On cross, Rozzi tore into Wala. The defense needed the psychologist to corroborate Allen's mental health struggles, but otherwise they sought to destroy her, portraying her as a dishonest true crime obsessive. They partially succeeded in that quest when they brought out at the three-day hearing that she had looked up Kegan Kline's information in the prison system.

The defense had portrayed her as a case fanatic who could not help but search Kegan's information. In reality, Wala was under the impression that the inmate might move to Westville. Looking up reports on a possible patient was certainly less scandalous than a professional succumbing to morbid curiosity. But the defense's approach to Wala certainly fell into their typical practice of attempting to wreck anyone they felt stood in their way.

Libby German took a selfie of herself and her best friend Abby Williams on the drive to the trails of Delphi, Indiana. Not long after, the girls disappeared. *Credit: Courtroom Exhibit.*

Local teens have long prided themselves on crossing the Monon High Bridge, an abandoned railroad bridge spanning Delphi's Deer Creek. *Credit: The Authors.*

The Monon High Bridge is rickety and treacherous, rising sixty-three feet in the air. It hovers over the creek, the woods, and a private driveway.
Credit: The Authors.

Wild bluebells grow in the clearing where Libby German and Abby Williams died. *Credit: The Authors.*

Found underneath the body of Abby Williams, Libby German's phone contained a video recording of their abduction. *Credit: Courtroom Exhibit.*

Community members and visitors set up a small memorial to honor Libby German and Abby Williams on the trails of Delphi, not far from where they went missing. *Credit: The Authors.*

A sketch of Bridge Guy peers out of a window in Delphi, Indiana. *Credit: The Authors.*

LEFT: A flood of police investigators and volunteers arrived in Delphi to assist with the early days of the double murder investigation. RIGHT: A team of Indiana State Police investigators worked on the Delphi murders case, including David Vido (left), Brian Harshman (second from the left), Steve Buckley (third from the left), Jay Harper (fourth from the left), and Jerry Holeman (third from the right). *Credits: Anonymous.*

Richard Allen, the man accused of murdering Libby German and Abby Williams, was a quiet CVS shift manager in Delphi. *Credit: Courtroom Exhibit.*

Detectives discovered photographic evidence demonstrating Richard Allen's familiarity with the trails and woods of Delphi. *Credit: Courtroom Exhibit.*

After identifying Richard Allen as a suspect, Tony Liggett and Steve Mullin took photographs of Allen's car at the CVS parking lot to determine if his vehicle was in the vicinity of the crime scene. *Credit: Courtroom Exhibit.*

After police found Richard Allen's gun during a search of his house, they were able to link it to an unfired round discovered at the crime scene. *Credit: Courtroom Exhibit.*

Police recovered a large trove of knives while searching the home of Richard Allen. *Credit: Courtroom Exhibit.*

ABOVE AND BELOW: Members of the public crammed inside one of Carroll County's small courtrooms in order to observe the trial of Richard Allen. *Credit: The Authors.*

Indiana State Police Superintendent Doug Carter became the public face of the investigation. *Credit: The Authors.*

Carroll County Prosecutor Nicholas McLeland took on one of the most high-profile trials in recent Indiana history. *Credit: The Authors.*

CHAPTER FIFTY-FOUR

Brian Harshman's face was sorrowful as he took the stand. The time had finally come to testify to a jury about his grim task. The state's plan was to play a series of recorded phone calls between Allen and his wife and mother, in which he confessed to the murders.

The sky outside was dark. One of the bailiffs wore a bright pumpkin-colored tie. Allen's transport team donned orange shirts and black ties. They hatched the plan while securing the basement one morning. Two of them realized they had orange shirts ready to go. The others ordered theirs on Amazon. They were curious if anyone would notice and realize it was Halloween.

Rozzi had tried to argue that the state was picking and choosing the phone calls too much. He pointed out that on April 3, 2023, Allen had made three calls to his family. In the first, he said nothing incriminating, and in fact emphasized his innocence.

McLeland pushed back. "The defense has the absolute right to call Mr. Allen." In fact, he very much hoped they would. He had been preparing to cross-examine the defendant for some time. He was ready.

"I think it's one of those situations where we play them all or we play none," Rozzi said.

Gull complimented the defense attorney's argument as "novel," which is a judge's way of saying something is creative but completely off-the-wall.

But she let the state proceed with Harshman, the self-described "phone guy" of Unified Command.

"I sort of appointed myself as the person who would keep track of his communications," he said.

By that time, he had listened to nearly seven hundred total phone calls. Then he had relistened to all of them.

The first call of interest came on November 14, 2022. The prosecution played it over the big TV. The courtroom heard Allen introduce himself as Ricky. His voice sounded ragged, and identical to that of Bridge Guy.

In the defense row of seats, Kathy Allen cried as she heard her husband's voice. Zentner-Calderon rubbed her back. The call was not a bombshell confession. Allen's words offering to tell the detectives "anything they want to hear" could be heard as an offer to come clean. Or they could be the words of a man desperate enough to wrongfully implicate himself.

The call to Janis on April 2, 2023, was also innocuous, out of context. Jurors listened to mother and son check in on one another and describe their newfound religiosity.

On April 3, 2023, the recorded confessions really got underway. Allen called his wife and confessed. She cried and wheedled and hung up on him. On May 10, 2023, he called again and did the same. That time, Kathy Allen told him to stop talking about the case. Later that day, he called back to beg her to love him despite the fact he had killed two children. Her reaction did not give him the assurance he wanted. On May 17, 2023, Allen confessed to his mother once more. On June 5, 2023, he complained that his family was drawing back from him. On June 11, 2023, Allen's wife told him to stop calling her and confessing.

At one point, the prosecution continued their streak of technical errors by playing the wrong call. A boring family discussion about golf clubs filled the courtroom. Strangely, Allen's tone sounded the same, whether he was talking about golf clubs or about murder.

But aside from that mistake, the calls were gripping, a sordid family saga played out in audio installments before the whole court. The story started with Allen eager to come clean. He wanted to tell the truth about the awful thing he did. He needed his family to love him anyway. He turned to the two most important people in his life, his wife and mother. Perhaps his pivot to religion was sincere, or perhaps it was a ploy to garner sympathy with them. Either way, it was ineffective, because his chief enablers did what they always did. They jumped in to protect their little man from the consequences of his own actions. They cried and pleaded and interrupted and snapped. They did not listen. They remained incurious. They spouted nonsense about his food being poisoned, his medications being tampered with. Everyone was to blame except their Ricky.

As Allen despaired, Janis offered her son banal blandishments about her eternal love. But he wanted more than assurances from his mother—he wanted to know his wife was still with him. And Kathy's pledges were unconvincing. Perhaps she could not love a child killer. That only seemed to redouble her efforts to believe her husband was the victim of a vast conspiracy. She had apparently submerged whatever part of herself fretted about Allen's lies about walking the High Bridge, or his overbearing insistence that she not help with the search for the girls, or his history of erratic behavior. Or the lumbering walk on the video, and the hauntingly familiar voice that urged two children: "Down the hill."

Allen was left reeling. His true self was being roundly rejected. He was left with no one. Nothing but a mailed-in Bible with verses that failed to improve his circumstances. His wife and mother started ignoring his calls. They did not soothe him. There was no room for that. The unspoken message was clear: Little Ricky needed to sit back, shut up, and let the adults fix his mess, once again. It was for his own good.

Outside, the day grew darker. When McLeland handed Harshman some documents to review, he needed to switch on his phone's flashlight just to see the papers in the dim courthouse. He explained he had investigated the white van angle after learning of Allen's detailed confession. There were no mentions of that in the case file. But he was able to determine from BMV records that Weber owned a white van at the time. When asked his opinion on the voice of Bridge Guy, Harshman was terse: "It's the voice of Richard Allen."

Rozzi tried to spin and spin on cross. "Mr. Weber might have been involved with the circumstances had his van been there at that time."

He brought up the defense's contention that Allen had admitted to inaccurate things, such as shooting the girls or raping them.

"That came through an inmate companion," Harshman said. "There's no recording or video of [Allen] saying that."

Then Rozzi got into Harshman's hopes about what incriminating things Allen might say next—as if the trooper was sitting around eagerly awaiting Allen's latest conversations to come through.

"I don't wish for him to say anything," Harshman said. Truly, after months and months spent hovering over a sick man, he felt done. On some level, he regretted ever trying to get involved in the case.

Rozzi brought up the possibility that Allen suffered from psychosis.

"It would not afford him the opportunity to have knowledge only the killer would know," Harshman said.

The jurors liked Harshman. He was subdued and solemn on the stand. He came across like a professional. He was also sharp, in a subtle way. When Allen's behavior came up, he managed to slip in that the defendant was far from the harmless innocent the defense portrayed. He had spat on at least one prison staff member. When correctional officers ignored him, he would start banging his head on the wall.

"I think Richard Allen struggles to be alone," Harshman said. "He does things for attention, and he gets upset when no one pays him attention."

And the outbursts continued after his move to the Cass County Jail, that brand-new facility with its fresh paint, clean cells, showers, and kiosks. The place where the defense team insisted Allen would be safe and well. That was where, of course, Allen had pantomimed slitting his own throat while threatening to kill correctional officers out of nowhere.

McLeland knew the defense was angling to bring in footage of Allen's miserable life at Westville. If that was allowed in, he argued, his team ought to be able to put in the haunting Cass County footage. That would damn Allen for sure.

But Gull held firm. Again and again, she ruled against admitting the Cass County video. Such footage did not include any confessions. It might raise questions about the legitimacy of Allen's claims around his mental health issues being linked inextricably to prison. But whatever value was far outweighed by the video's prejudicial nature.

Deflated, the prosecutors realized that the quest for the Cass County video was likely futile. The jury would never see Allen's violent fury. The prosecutors only hoped the jurors had seen enough.

The state rested.

CHAPTER FIFTY-FIVE

The defense's theory of the case came out haltingly over the course of days. It was not their first choice, of course. Gull had thrown out Odinism, the thrilling tale of the murderous cult in the woods with far-reaching powers. It was also not their burden. The defense had no obligation to explain what happened to the girls. They could have simply focused their energy and resources on the mistakes made by law enforcement.

The attorneys never spelled it all out. Not in their opening statement, nor in their closing argument. That was possibly because it sounded better piecemeal, as incisive comments or devastating questions.

But stitched together, the theory seemed to go as follows. Libby and Abby made it to the end of the High Bridge. Bridge Guy followed them, but the real killers were waiting just out of sight, uncaptured by Libby's video and uncommented upon by either girl. The Bridge Guy himself might be involved in the murders. Or he might be an innocent dupe. Nobody could say for sure.

Either way, the defense agreed with the state's contention that the girls were then kidnapped. Only, in the imagination of the defense attorneys, the girls were not forced down the hill and across the creek. Instead, they were brought down to the seldom-used Weber drive. From there, they were taken away. The defense seemed to argue that the reason Libby's Apple Health data showed no movement after 2:32 P.M. was because the girls were moving in a vehicle. That contention did not offer much of a robust explanation; after all, the moment the girls got out of any vehicle, the health data would have presumably shown more movement. Baldwin would later suggest Libby's phone might have been ensconced in a Faraday bag, a container designed to block electromagnetic fields. But if he thought that, then he certainly made no mention of that at trial.

By that logic, the girls were held as prisoners in an undetermined location for approximately fourteen hours and two minutes, perhaps moving all the while in a vehicle. During this captivity, the girls made no moves to fight back. They were not bound or restrained. They incurred no defensive wounds. They were not sexually assaulted. Apparently, they just sat placidly for over half a day. Then, without Libby's phone registering any steps, their kidnappers ushered them back to the trails, right near where they had first vanished. That was despite the widespread, highly publicized search for the girls that continued at that point.

Without making a sound, without alerting any of the searchers that lingered unofficially in the darkness, the girls were brought down a steep ravine. Libby's phone was placed on the leaf-strewn ground. An unknown accessory was plugged into the headphone jack. Libby and Abby would have then been forced to strip, if they were not naked already. Some of Libby's garments were tossed in the river, while others were given to Abby to wear. Then, both girls had their throats slit. Abby's body fell atop Libby's phone and shoe.

That was the theory the defense was going with. They said the phone data told the story. That the lack of insect activity and predation from coyotes—all variables that could easily be delayed in the winter months—told them the girls had not been out for long. That the reason no one heard the girls scream was because they had been gone for hours before the murders.

Taken together, the defense's story of the crime read more like a true crime fanatic's rambling, late-night social media post than a thoughtful theory put forward by legal professionals who had access to all the discovery.

The defense eyewitnesses had not glimpsed much of anything at all.

Cheyenne Mill and Shelby Duncan had visited the trails the day of the murders to enjoy nature and smoke cigarettes. Shelby Hicks was an acquaintance of theirs who had also been there with her then-boyfriend, Daniel Pearson. All three women—now in their early thirties—appeared in court to testify about what they saw and heard. Or more accurately, what they did not see and hear.

The defense ostensibly brought them all out to attack the state's timeline. The problem was, they were all admittedly at the trails well after the state contended the girls were dead.

Diener was gentle with them all on cross. There was no sense in ripping apart everyday civilians dragged into the mess. She asked questions about the times they had arrived. She slowly teased out that they all had given depositions saying they had arrived at the trails closer to three, at the earliest. So the fact that none of them heard or saw anything unusual was no surprise.

On the stand, Mill was perhaps the most dramatic witness of the three. While she acknowledged that she had seen nothing unusual that day, she still harbored a grudge over the perception that law enforcement had not taken her seriously enough. Mill had also undergone the online gauntlet after posting about her presence on the trails on social media. From that day on, a troupe of "Facebook vigilantes" and internet sleuths hounded and threatened her. She felt that law enforcement had failed to protect her.

David McCain was another person who walked the trails that day. By the time he testified, he was seventy-nine, ruddy-faced in a red polo shirt. McCain made for a poignant witness, an elderly man who loved his community, who sought out history and beauty in nature. He recalled walking the bridge as a child, and as an adult, as recently as a month before. He remembered the "exceptionally nice day," the peacefulness shattered when he first encountered Derrick shouting for Libby and Abby. But his recollections had faded with time. Years ago, FBI special agents had taken the memory card from the camera he had that day, with all his pictures. They said they would return it, but they never had.

On cross, Luttrull talked about McCain's earlier statements to police.

"I would think that would be more accurate than what I remember now," McCain said.

Luttrull provided him with one such statement from 2017. In that, McCain said he got there around a quarter past three.

"Well, that sounds right," McCain acknowledged.

Brad Heath had not been on the trails on the day of the murders. He was a retired exterminator who had been driving around Delphi that morning, serving businesses like the Andersons grain elevator.

The seventy-year-old suffered a coughing fit on the stand. Bringing the witness a bottle of water, Rozzi quipped that all the cops gathered around would be glad to jump in and perform the Heimlich maneuver. That got a laugh from the courtroom.

Heath's story was simple. Driving near the trails that day, he had seen a mysterious car. Dark blue, faded, out of place, the vehicle reminded him of something he saw in the film *The Fugitive* with Tommy Lee Jones.

On cross, Diener got him to explain that the car was not parked in the old CPS lot. Heath did not remember seeing other cars in the lot or nearby.

"There could have been, but I wasn't paying attention," he said.

Several days later, the defense would bring in Blair. She had once told police that she saw a car in the old CPS lot. The color was nondescript, not bright red or yellow or anything flashy. It had sharp angles. She described it as a 1965 Ford Comet. No such car existed, and Blair acknowledged that she had made a mistake, and had been trying to refer to a Mercury Comet.

Diener knocked the defense's car angle down on cross. She asked Blair if hearing about Heath's memory of the blue car changed her recollection.

"I feel certain that that's the shape of the car at this time," Blair said.

In other words, she had not seen a car at the old CPS lot at all. The vehicle she had witnessed was a ways away, along the side of the road.

Still other witnesses were not from the trails or the roads. Theresa Liebert lived near the Webers, and she had reported seeing something unusual that day. A gray-haired elderly woman, she had a slightly vague and confused air, as well as a nearly inaudible voice. Baldwin repeatedly urged her to speak up, to no avail. When he pulled up a map on the big TV, she wandered in front of it, blocking the jury's view. After his verbal instructions failed, Baldwin gently took hold of her shoulders and guided her to a better position. At the defense side of the table, Rozzi's young assistant Max Baker held his head in his hands.

When asked, Liebert could not even identify Weber's home on the map.

Liebert's story was that hours before the girls disappeared, around 8:30 A.M., she and her husband had been driving back to their home. Along their road was a row of mailboxes for all the neighbors. Liebert saw a man there. She did not recognize him.

Luttrull asked Liebert if she remembered the man's face. She did not.

Smiling, his voice warm, Luttrull thanked Liebert for coming in. He had no further questions for her.

Moments like that left the prosecutors feeling genuinely bewildered. Even as professionals who had spent countless hours studying this case they simply could not figure out what the defense was trying to accomplish by calling some of these witnesses. Liebert said she had seen a man at her mailbox nearly six hours before the girls were abducted. It was difficult to imagine a connection between her observation and the crime.

The defense's answer to the deputies and civilian searchers came in the form of Darrell Sterrett, the former fire chief of Delphi. The goal there seemed to be creating the impression that the searchers could not have missed the girls' bodies.

Recent health issues had left Sterrett prone to confusion on the stand. At one point, Baldwin seemed to be ready to impeach his own witness. At other times, he kept apologizing and assuring Sterrett he was doing well.

But Sterrett did not give much ground. What he had to say was not helpful to the defense.

"There was not an organized grid type search," he told Baldwin.

After all, he and his firefighters had been looking for two lost girls. Not dead bodies.

All throughout the defense's case, the defendant visibly unraveled. From his seat, Allen would glower at Diener or McLeland or even roll his eyes at the judge.

Then his face would go slack. Allen's expressions were often void of any emotion. The defendant struck the prosecutors as a man trying to intimidate those around him. So once, Diener stared back at him, until he blinked and finally looked away. Then, Allen started gazing at a pencil organizer on the table in between the prosecution side and the defense side. A pair of scissors jutted from the little container. Allen seemed to be looking a lot at those.

"Don't take your eyes off this guy," Diener told Holeman.

Allen was small in stature, but he had nothing to lose. The pencil organizer was moved.

Other times, the defendant's behavior was less threatening, but more bizarre. Once, he scribbled something on a Post-it note and then popped that into his mouth to eat.

A few times, the defendant turned his head. His angry gaze fixed on Motta Jr., seated next to Kathy Allen. The façade of normalcy he achieved at jury selection was long gone.

CHAPTER FIFTY-SIX

The defense wanted Christopher Gootee to come in and destroy Brad Weber's story. A lieutenant with the Hammond Police Department, Gootee had worked extensively on the FBI's Gang Response Investigative Team, or GRIT. During the early weeks of the Delphi investigation, he and then-special Agent Adam Pohl had come down to help with canvassing and interviewing. Together, they had interviewed Weber.

Their interview contained an aberration. In all his other statements early in the investigation, Weber said he drove straight home from work. But the FBI statement had him checking on his line of automated teller machines first.

There was one issue though. The FBI does not typically record interviews. If Gootee remembered Weber's claim, that could help knock down the evidence about the van. Auger asked Gootee about the ATMs. Gootee did not remember Weber saying anything like that. His shrugging lack of recall was a blow for Allen.

Later that day, after the jury left, the defense would desperately try to bring in Pohl himself. By then, he was a supervising special agent. He was also far away in Texas, running security for the upcoming presidential election. Extracting him from the Lone Star State would not be easy. According to the defense, Pohl suffered from a medical issue that precluded him from hopping on a flight. Citing Allen's Sixth Amendment rights, the defense wanted the agent to testify through a remote video conference.

Gull sounded wary. "When was he subpoenaed?"

It came out that Pohl had only received his subpoena three to four weeks ago. McLeland objected, saying the defense was once again improperly attempting to impeach a witness. If the defense wanted to knock down the van story, they already had Pohl's report. They were also due to call Weber himself.

Gull did not believe she had heard good cause. Pohl was out.

All throughout his life, Allen was a closed-off sort of person. He did not have many friends. At work, he showed flashes of personality, but it was hard to truly get to know him.

To make an impression on the jury, his defense team was determined to give the court a glimpse into his mind.

They had never filed anything around Allen's competency to stand trial. Nor were they arguing that he was insane. Competency was only about whether Allen could assist in his own defense. Despite his historical preference for eating rather than reading his discovery paperwork, the defense apparently felt he was good-to-go in that regard. Legally, insanity had more to do with whether an offender knew right from wrong while committing a crime. The fact that Allen was accused of hiding his crime for years all but precluded an insanity defense.

For Allen's defense team, the goal was to introduce testimony around mental health in order to compel the jury to throw out their client's myriad confessions.

The first expert they brought in was Dr. Deanna Dwenger, the executive director of behavioral health at the Indiana Department of Corrections. She had never met with Allen, but she had worked with Wala and Dr. Ellen Keris in planning his care.

Rozzi had her go over Wala's status as a "true crime fan" who had disclosed her interest to her supervisors and pushed for Allen to have a visit with his wife in early 2022. Much of her testimony focused on Allen's sufferings in prison.

Diener handled the cross-examination. She asked the witness about the possibility of Allen feigning. Dwenger acknowledged that the possibility that the inmate was faking his symptoms had been the subject of much discussion. As time passed, though, that became largely irrelevant. An inmate might bang their head, forgo sleep, and starve themselves due to legitimate mental illness, or as a calculated ploy to get what they wanted. But at some point, those damaging behaviors would begin to affect the inmate, either way.

She also talked about the use of haloperidol, commonly known by its brand name Haldol, in Allen's treatment. The antipsychotic medicine is frequently used to manage acute psychosis. In Allen's case, he received several involuntary injections of the drug amid his worsening behavior.

The jury had plenty of questions for Dwenger. On the stand, she seemed to enjoy hearing from the jurors, praising a few of their questions in particular. Judging from the questions, jurors seemed interested in learning whether Allen was truly psychotic or faking it. Seeing an opportunity, Diener jumped in to encourage Dwenger to expand on her insights.

Dwenger explained that psychotic individuals are detached from reality. They suffer from delusions. Classic presentations of delusions largely fell into five categories. Persecutory delusions featured someone believing that certain individuals or groups were out to get them. Grandiose delusions centered around an ill-formed belief about one's own talents or exceptionalism. Delusional jealousy might involve somebody accusing their partner of infidelity without evidence. Erotomanic delusions were about thinking that one was irresistible, the object of lust or love. Another type might feature command hallucinations, where the sufferer might hear instructions on how to behave from a TV or radio.

Allen's claims about killing two girls certainly did not seem to fit into any of those categories. Dwenger also revealed that Allen had been evaluated for delirium, a confused mental state often brought about by a medical issue. The experts on his care team ruled out that possibility.

According to Dwenger, the signs of a psychotic episode included delusions, disorganized thinking that jumped from topic to topic, and moodiness. Dwenger had been called as a defense witness. Diener's nimble follow-up based on the jury questions flipped her in the public's eye, at least. Because what Dwenger had described as psychotic did not match what everyone heard on those phone calls. Diener had known Dwenger would be good for the prosecution side since deposition. By calling her, the defense indicated that they had not come to that realization.

Perhaps even more importantly, Dwenger's testimony rehabilitated Wala.

What Dwenger had to say was that Wala was a diligent, empathetic employee who properly disclosed her interest in the case and always went above and beyond to care for Allen and improve his time at Westville. For that, Allen and his team crucified her.

During the morning break, Allen lumbered around in the well of the court, gaping and pointing at members of the public present. Some of those seated in the gallery were there to support the defendant. One old woman showed up clad in a garment that appeared to be fashioned from a soiled white tablecloth. Glowering, she took a seat and rocked her body back and forth, as Allen himself swiveled and spun in his chair.

CHAPTER FIFTY-SEVEN

Leazenby was a great favorite of the defense team. After all, he had been the one to tell them in a deposition that he believed multiple killers were involved. He had even said he thought Liggett agreed with him. So Baldwin was deferential as he called the former sheriff up on the stand.

"I don't know what to call you—former sheriff Leazenby?" he asked.

"Tobe's fine."

But on the stand, Leazenby did not give the defense much. In some ways, he had functioned as one of the public faces of the case. But behind the scenes, Leazenby said his work was mostly administrative and managerial. His goal was to support his detectives, not investigate the murders himself. His statement about multiple killers had been based on outdated information. He had misspoken.

The direct and cross-examinations were a bit hard on Leazenby. He had to come out and say that he did not know much by way of the details of the case. But Leazenby was nonplussed. And the jurors loved him for his candor. Afterward, in the hallway, he enjoyed chatting with some of the deputies visiting from nearby counties.

As he walked around, he saw an old friend he had not seen for years. They almost did not recognize each other. They had both gotten older, and Leazenby had lost a lot of weight. "Tobe?" The man was only at the courthouse to pay his property taxes. "I thought you retired after being sheriff?"

Leazenby smiled. "Well, you know, that fine line between dedication and stupidity—I haven't found it yet."

The defense made a last effort to bring Odinism into the trial. For all their bluster, their final move was a quiet plea out of earshot of the jury, made at the end of the day.

Baldwin rattled through names. Olehy. Kohr. Holeman. State's witnesses who all mentioned sticks. Was that not opening the door? Could the defense not parade through that opening with their promenade of experts? Were Allen's Sixth Amendment rights not at stake?

Gull denied the motion. "There's no nexus."

A supposed rift between the FBI and the state police had somehow become a centerpiece of the defense's case. Baldwin had even alluded to it in his mini opening statement during jury selection, as well as his full-fledged opening statement during trial. Among the defense's online fans, the falling out was hugely important. For whatever reasons, the same contingent that expressed skepticism and often hatred of all law enforcement in the case came to regard the FBI as an exalted exception.

When the defense called Indiana State Police Superintendent Doug Carter, those in the courtroom expected to finally learn more about what happened between his organization and the FBI. Carter arrived in his blue uniform. He was slated to retire in just a few months. The Delphi case had lasted half his tenure as superintendent. At times, it consumed him. He had always wanted the girls and their families to get justice. But the conspiratorial circus around the trial got to him, too. Watching men under his command come under attack was also agony for Carter. He could not speak out in defense of investigators like Holeman. That would violate the gag order. The silence made him feel completely helpless, like a father forced to watch his children get beaten up.

Baldwin had Carter introduce himself. Carter acknowledged that the FBI was one of dozens of agencies involved in the case, but that they left in August 2021.

McLeland asked the judge if he and Baldwin could approach. When they returned, Baldwin asked Carter if it was his decision to have the FBI leave. Carter affirmed that it was. And that was the end of his testimony. Carter was only on the stand for a few minutes.

Due to a separation of witnesses, people who testified in the trial could not attend any other part of the proceedings while under subpoena, unless the judge granted a special exception. Carter wondered if the defense had made him a witness simply because they wanted to keep him away from the trial.

In the early days of the case, many in the media had made a big show of empathy toward the girls and the community. That soft-touch coverage had centered Abby and Libby and the families. Those pretenses dropped for some media figures when the defense launched their broadcast-friendly Odinism theory. The families were somewhat bewildered to watch the girls get lost in their own story, in favor of one-sided talking points centering their accused killer as the ultimate victim of a vast and shadowy conspiracy.

During one of the breaks, Becky found herself standing in line for the restroom with MacDonald, the Court TV reporter. Becky found herself fuming. She decided to say something.

"So when can we expect to hear that you were wrong about the bullet being found later?" Becky asked her. "Is there going to be a segment now where you admit you gave out false information?"

MacDonald just stared at her. The Court TV producer offered no explanation. Nor did she later issue a correction. Like so many YouTubers, she spewed out a major error and then moved right along without taking accountability.

Gull gave the defense what they wanted. Over the prosecution's objections, several hallway and in-cell videos were admitted as evidence. Not only that, but the attorneys would be allowed to skip around at will, curating the jury's viewing experience.

The defense wanted to show the jurors that Allen's confessions had to be tossed—that Westville had exacerbated his underlying depression and anxiety so much that he had slipped into psychosis. That what he said should not be believed. The lawyers believed the jury would see the state torturing a mentally ill man with major depressive disorder.

The big TV that gave the prosecution so much trouble was tilted toward the jury box, angled away from the gallery. The defense team did not wish the public to see Allen at his most vulnerable.

Allen's family members were not present that Saturday. As she often did on days of hard testimony, Kathy Allen chose not to attend. She presumably did not wish to witness scenes of her husband naked, ranting, and smeared in excrement. So Allen was left to exchange hand-heart gestures with Zentner-Calderon that day.

Up on the stand, Max Baker thanked the state for the assistance in helping him label each piece of footage with a specific date. The day before, the defense had attempted to introduce the videos, but Gull had told them to go back and determine the actual dates before they could be admitted. With his reddish beard and close-cropped hair, Baker was a youthful presence on the defense team. He had only just received his bachelor's degree from Indiana University. He had interned with Rozzi for two years. He had also interned at the Logansport law firm of Allen appellate counsel Mark Leeman.

In his capacity on the defense team, Baker had listened to hundreds of calls and watched hours of footage.

The hallway videos were all from 2023, covering April to June. From his seat, Rozzi clicked through portions of the videos Baker had prepared.

The hallway videos came first. Correctional officers shot those on a camcorder. They had audio, but the jury only saw the video. As far as the prison staff was concerned, the purpose was to document that Allen was not being abused, to protect the prison and its staff from liability. The footage followed Allen as he was shuttled to and from medical appointments or therapy check-ins with Wala. Sometimes he wore a lead, which looked like a dog leash. In one instance, he was pushed around on a wheelchair. In another, his face was swollen and bruised from his persistent head-banging. He often seemed vacant.

McLeland pulled up a chair next to the jury. Sitting beside an older juror, he watched the screen intently. Auger hovered behind him. As he watched the videos, Baldwin winced, blinked, and shook, the picture of a man experiencing pure horror.

CHAPTER FIFTY-EIGHT

That Monday, the in-cell videos came in. Those captured Allen in his one-man cell. He smeared his feces on his body and once ate a little. He banged his head against the wall, lightly but often enough that his face ultimately swelled. He was often nude, and occasionally masturbating. Baker had been tasked with organizing all the footage. Several times, he slapped nudity warnings on the wrong clips.

The jurors watched the muted footage. The gallery watched their faces. Members of the public and press read all kinds of emotions into their expressions: horror, sorrow, rage, and disgust.

The truth was that some of the jurors were underwhelmed. Others were outright annoyed. In a way, the remaining fifteen jurors and alternates were effectively prisoners in their hotel. Like Allen, they had been torn from their jobs and families and forced to shuttle around to a courthouse. They had more freedom, of course, but they could grasp the difficulties. But staring at Allen's antics, they could not muster much sympathy.

The defense had badly miscalculated. Had Rozzi, Baldwin, and Auger opted for a matter-of-fact description of the footage, the dehumanizing reality of prison life in a one-man cell might have resonated more. By spinning Allen's treatment as uniquely cruel, they had overplayed their hand. Prison was a harsh place, that was hardly breaking news. The correctional officers did not appear abusive as they ushered the inmate around. In fact, most of Allen's most disturbing moments appeared entirely self-inflicted.

McLeland stood off to the side watching the in-cell videos. Baker's selection seemed to favor dramatic moments. Jurors saw correctional officers tase Allen when he refused to remove his hands from his cell's cuff port. They saw him brought out to the showers. And they saw him conferring with Wala.

In McLeland's mind, the defense was trying their best to flip the narrative and paint Allen as the case's true victim. So when he got to cross Baker, he did not hold back.

"You've probably watched hundreds of videos. You said you chose these two because they were the most important. Why did you choose them?"

Smiling, nearly simpering, Baker politely responded to the prosecutor's brusque question. "They showed different aspects of Rick's life in prison."

"You wanted to curry sympathy for Mr. Allen with the jury, right?"

Baker's friendly smile faded. "Well, if that's your interpretation." Baker had toiled over the videos for some time. Forcefully, he told the court that he had "wanted to show more." Had McLeland wanted the jury to receive further context, he could have "not objected" to the defense playing even more videos. But as far as the prosecution was concerned, Allen's bizarre activities in prison had little bearing on the facts of the case.

McLeland accused Baker of wanting to portray Allen as the victim.

Baker was heated by then. So much so that he stumbled over his words. "I don't think I was trying to victimize him."

McLeland's question was quiet, but fiery all the same. "Richard Allen is not the victim in this case, is he?"

"No."

Gone was the sharp young professional. On the stand, Baker had been reduced to sounding like a whiny kid. The jurors did not have much use for him either. They joked about him always staring at one of the young women in their midst. They called him "Little Max." Their questions seemed to reflect a certain sense of dismissiveness. They asked Baker if the lawyers had put him up to picking the worst videos.

Baker pushed back. "They trusted me."

The women in Allen's life were always ready to defend him. Dutifully, some of them did so on the stand at his murder trial.

Kathy Allen did not testify on her husband's behalf. Allen was adamant about that. Putting her up as a witness could also open the door for damaging questions about his history of erratic behavior, or worse. Janis also did not testify. But the two relatives Allen claimed to have molested did speak out.

Jamie Jones breezed through her testimony. Clad in a coral cardigan, Allen's half-sister alluded to a somewhat distant relationship with her brother. She noted that he was five years older than her. Right out of high school, he had left early for basic training, and then married shortly after that.

Auger led Jones through a tight direct examination. Her task was a delicate one. She needed to keep the focus narrow, or else the prosecution might jump in with some tricky questions on cross. She also had to get into some sensitive and disturbing topics. She asked Jones if Allen had ever molested her or touched her sexually.

"No, he did not."

Jones went on to say that she loved her brother. But she would not lie for him.

Luttrull got up. He needed to be careful too. Needling Allen's relatives would come across like bullying and would likely alienate the jury. He asked Jones to recall growing up in Mexico, playing with the kids in the neighborhood. The question was deceptively innocuous. Luttrull was seeking to unravel the mystery of Allen's other alleged victims. He asked if one of the children was named Chris.

"Yes," Jones said, even as Auger belted out an objection that Gull sustained.

Allen's daughter, Brittany Zapanta, fared far worse on the stand. She plainly did not want to be there. Round-faced and pale with light brown hair, she strongly resembled her mother. Allen smiled at his daughter. She did not seem to return his gaze. Her smile was a miserable one. Brittany did not have much contact with her father in prison. She only made a brief appearance on calls that occurred when she happened to be visiting her mother. Allen's daughter never seemed eager to talk to him. And now she would have to testify under oath on his behalf.

Brittany described moving out of her parents' home in 2015. She went to work at an urgent care center, attended Ball State University, and later went to Indianapolis.

Gently, Auger apologized for her disturbing question. She asked Zapanta if her father had ever molested her.

"No," Brittany said quietly.

She said she loved her father, but she would not lie for him.

On cross, Luttrull asked Brittany if she visited the trails of Delphi often. Auger objected, and Gull sustained because the question was beyond the scope of the direct examination. But the judge did permit Luttrull to ask questions about Allen's appearance in years past. He wanted to know if Allen changed his appearance between when Brittany left college and 2022.

Nodding, Allen mouthed the words "it's okay" to his visibly anxious daughter.

Luttrull broke out several photographs of Allen. The judge and lawyers conferred in a sidebar. Alone on the stand, Brittany stared down at her hands. Allen pulled goofy expressions. He grinned. He mouthed the words, "I love you." He did anything to get his only child's attention. Try as he might, he could not get Brittany to look at him.

Coming back, Auger established that the precise dates of all the photographs remained unknown. Gull did not permit some of the pictures to come in. Others, she allowed. Luttrull showed Brittany the photographs. He asked if the images captured her father's appearance between 2014 and 2022.

"Yes." Brittany appeared to be trying not to cry.

The jurors wanted to know even more from Allen's daughter. They took Luttrull's stifled line of questions and ran with them. They asked her about visiting the High Bridge.

The facts came out haltingly from Brittany. Yes, she had visited the High Bridge as a teenager. Yes, she crossed it once or twice. Yes, she had done so with her father. Luttrull asked if she had been frightened. She said she was scared of the bridge.

Brittany left the stand crying.

———

Weber walked into the courtroom once more. His hair was wild as ever. When Baldwin got him on the stand, he immediately pointed out that Weber had gotten upset with him in their last interaction.

Calm but unapologetic, Weber replied, "Yes, you were trying to tell me what I did."

He went on to say that he believed he drove straight home on the day of the killings. He did not recall telling anyone that he checked his ATM machines that afternoon. In all but one of the law enforcement interviews he gave, he repeatedly said he just drove home. That was despite the fact that given his proximity to the crime—and given the focus on other neighbors like Ron Logan—such an admission was not necessarily in his interest.

Baldwin was less rough on Weber during direct, and the witness was far less cantankerous. The examination devolved into a lengthy discussion of the ins-and-outs of running a small ATM business.

When it came to his memory, Weber never wavered. "On the day in question I went straight home."

The vans sped up. Soon they were flying, going ninety miles per hour down the highway. The jurors began to murmur. Bailiffs drove both vans. They said nothing. The bailiffs had no radios, no way to communicate. All they knew was that they were tasked with following closely behind the police car out in front. And that cruiser had sped up significantly. The bailiffs each accelerated in turn, and the caravan of vehicles hurtled down the highway.

Unbeknownst to anyone in the vans, a car had been tailing the jury. A police officer spotted that, and saw the driver pulling out her phone to aim it at the windows of the vans. That prompted the escort car to speed up, to get the vans out of there. Meanwhile, another police officer pulled over the mysterious driver, a young woman. They confiscated her phone. As she and the officers waited on the side of the highway, the phone was transported back to Gull. The judge found no videos or photographs of the vans.

That corroborated the young driver's story. She claimed to be a student heading down to Indiana University. She had heard about a big trial and got excited when she saw the vans and police cars. She pulled out her phone because she wanted to tell her friends all about it. Fortunately, she was not one of the internet nuts, just a curious onlooker. The judge handed back the phone to the officers, who drove it back to the woman still waiting on the side of the highway. Then they let her go.

The jurors remained in the dark about the incident for some time. All they knew was that by dint of serving on the jury, they were liable to be chased down by unknown threats.

After the jury left for the day on November 4, Baldwin suggested it might be a good time to have an offer of proof. This was a process by which bits of information which were not permitted in the trial could be entered into the record so that an appellate court could determine if the trial judge erred in excluding them. On this occasion, Baldwin had a rather unique idea.

He was still obsessed over the idea that Elvis Fields's question about what would happen if his saliva was found on the girls' bodies meant something quite significant. So now he proposed that Holeman be made to get up on the stand and answer a question about it. "If Richard Allen made that comment about spit, would you be using that as evidence in this case?" After that, Baldwin said, he might very well ask Holeman about some of the alleged evidence against the other so-called Odinists.

It was a bizarre question, as McLeland pointed out. The spit question had not been enough to bring charges against Fields. It would not have been enough to bring charges against Allen either. But if there was a hypothetical situation where the spit question existed in addition to the other evidence against Allen, then perhaps it would be brought in. It was purely speculative.

Perhaps the key point, though, was that Holeman was an investigator and not a prosecutor. It was therefore not up to Holeman to determine who should be charged and what evidence should or should not be used against them.

Gull agreed with that point. "Trooper Holeman stays in his lane," she said.

Baldwin protested that he believed there was sufficient evidence to bring charges against the Odinists.

"You misunderstand me, Mr. Baldwin," said Gull. She told him there was no nexus. And then, a bit wearily, she added, "We've had this discussion a thousand times."

CHAPTER FIFTY-NINE

The defense ceded ground to the prosecution in the battle of the experts. In terms of most of the forensics, they left the field, failing to counter anything Cicero or the state police crime scene investigators said. But when it came to forensic firearms examinations, they would mount a full-scale assault on Oberg's findings. On that front, they deployed Dr. Eric Warren, a former special agent of forensic science with the Tennessee Bureau of Investigation who served on the board of the Association of Firemark and Tool Mark Examiners. Bald with a red beard, Warren had since gone on to start his own as-of-yet unaccredited laboratory. As he noted to the jury, he was not a big believer in accreditation.

Rozzi had Warren go through the basics of forensic firearms examinations. The expert said the defense had given him all the materials an examiner could want, from microphotographs to transcripts to depositions to other reports.

For some reason, they kept bringing up the Rhode Island State Crime Laboratory's suspension of firearms examinations in August. That continued until Luttrull threw out an objection that Rhode Island was not Indiana, and the closure of one lab in one state over nine hundred miles away had little bearing on the Allen case.

Rozzi and Warren went on to critique Oberg for using a fired round for her test. Then, despite her warnings about the use of photographs, they pulled out a few of their own. Blown up pictures of the cartridge with valleys and peaks were unveiled to the jury. Looking irritated, Luttrull moved his chair to get a better view.

Warren wanted to tell the jury about the consecutive matching striae technique, or CMS. He described it as an answer to criticisms about observing sufficient agreement. It was a method that allowed for examiners to seek out striations—either two runs of three or one run of six consecutive striations. He portrayed it as a better, more objective method for firearms examinations.

Based on CMS, Warren said he found insufficient agreement in the markings on the cartridge.

Warren did not mention that CMS was often critiqued for relying on the subjectivity of determining which striations truly "matched" and an overall lack of research about the findings. The ISP lab did not use it. Many of those who did favor CMS would not utilize it for all examinations. And while the CMS method allowed for the use of photographs in training, the technique did not train examiners to complete their evaluations based solely on pictures.

On cross, Luttrull hopped up with a simple question. Looking at Oberg's report from October 2017, he wanted Warren to say whether she indicated any concerns about finding subclass characteristics within the ejector marks. The presence of subclass characteristics would raise questions about whether anyone could even link the cartridge to a specific gun.

Looking at the report in front of him, Warren demurred. He gave a wordy response that did not provide a definitive yes or no.

"You didn't answer my question," Luttrull said. "Did she articulate any concern about subclass characteristics?"

Warren slammed Oberg's report, saying there was "no way to know" for sure based on what she wrote.

Luttrull sounded incensed. "I'm going to ask that question again."

When Rozzi came in with an objection, Luttrull snapped, "It has not been asked and answered."

Warren tried to wriggle out of the question once more with a lengthy opinion about the report. "He's giving a speech to the jury," Luttrull told Gull.

Finally, Warren gave his answer. "No." The October 2017 report contained nothing indicating that Oberg was concerned about subclass characteristics around the ejector marks.

Throughout the trial, Luttrull operated as a sort of invisible lawyer. He could elicit powerful testimony just by hanging back. Sometimes, people in the gallery would not even notice him as he crossed the room, turning their heads in surprise when he threw out an objection from near the courtroom door. He was the rare attorney who did not seem to be in love with the sound of his own voice. Luttrull had largely left his own ego behind in order to tackle the Delphi case. He did not feel the need to wow the crowds. He just wanted to guide his witnesses through their testimony.

But facing Warren, he sounded indignant. At one point, as he sat at the prosecution's side of the table, he had his hand pressed over his mouth, stifling a derisive, angry chuckle. He asked Warren about his years of experience.

"Would it surprise you to learn that [Oberg] had well over the amount of time you had?" Luttrull asked.

Throughout the rest of the cross, Luttrull would somewhat facetiously reference Warren's six years of experience with the TBI. He questioned Warren's decision to base his findings on photographs alone. Was that not wholly inappropriate? And given that CMS was all about striations rather than the impressed marks found on the cartridge, was that, too, not problematic?

Luttrull took Warren back to a case in which he had testified in Flagstaff, Arizona, in 2021. He said then in an interview that he did not use CMS methodology.

Quoting Warren's past statements, Luttrull asked why he had changed his mind that examiners "cannot render a conclusion on a result based on photographs alone." The deputy prosecutor then asked Warren about the most valuable tool in his lab. Warren said he considered himself the most valuable tool.

Sounding pleased, Luttrull retorted, "So it sounds like a comparison microscope, you can take it or leave it."

Luttrull pointed out that Warren could have had the opportunity to break out the microscope. The ISP lab would have shipped him the cartridge. He could have checked Oberg's findings for himself. The witness's response gave a good indication of why the defense did not ask him to conduct such an experiment.

"There's the potential I could've said, 'Hey, I agree with her,'" Warren said.

Most of the jurors came away favoring the state's interpretation of the cartridge. But Warren's testimony and Rozzi's cross of Oberg had been bewildering enough to prompt one of the twelve to throw the cartridge out altogether, as far as the evidence they would weigh.

Luttrull leaned back and grinned. But inside he worried. He knew how crucial this testimony was and he felt concerned he had not been as effective as he hoped.

CHAPTER SIXTY

The climax of the defense's theory came in Auger's presentation of witness Stacy Eldridge, who left the FBI's computer analysis response team in 2012 and ultimately became a private investigator. Eldridge claimed that somebody had inserted a device into the headphone jack of Libby's phone hours after the state said the girls were dead and the phone had stopped moving. Indiana State Police technology digital forensics experts Brian Bunner, Jeremy Chapman, and Christopher Cecil had not said that. After drawing out Eldridge's conclusion, Auger strutted away, with the satisfied air of someone who believed they had just blown the whole case wide open.

But her triumph did not last long. A quick Google search during a break provided Cecil with a counterargument. Moisture and dirt could cause an identical reaction, one far more likely than some late-night congregation around a murder victim's phone.

On November 6, 2024, the defense finally started to run out of things to say in court. That morning, figures from both teams walked in and out of the courtroom. Baker hauled in files. Jerry Bean, the former Carroll County deputy prosecutor who remained McLeland's trusted confidant even after losing his bid to be appointed prosecutor, came in holding a box. And finally, Holeman walked in, carrying Diener's white purse. Allen smirked at him. "Nice bag, Jerry."

After the jury filed in, Rozzi announced that the defense was resting.

The entire trial, McLeland, Diener, Holeman and the others had been waiting for Allen's team to pull some kind of big surprise. They had all worried they were missing something. Even when the trial got underway, no one relaxed. McLeland had spent hours preparing for arguments that the defense had not even thought to make. In the end, all that anxiety came to nothing.

The end of the defense's case came so abruptly that it nearly threw off the prosecution's plans. They had wanted to call in a rebuttal witness. Problem was, he was not yet there. Dr. John Martin, the former prison psychiatrist, was still in the process of traveling down from the Chicago area.

The defense resting also meant Allen would not get up to testify. McLeland had spent hours and hours preparing for that possibility. He had a list of incisive questions he wanted to throw Allen's way. All of that had been for nothing. As a former defense attorney, McLeland was not surprised. Having a client testify was often not worth the risk. Still, it could be a boon, a way for the jury to come to like and relate to a defendant. Without Allen testifying, all the jury had to form an impression of the man was his twitchy behavior during trial and his phone calls with his family, where he whined and groveled and manipulated and begged for their love.

The end of the defense's case also caught the judge by surprise. Through her glasses, she squinted at the six attorneys. "I didn't receive any juror instructions from either side. I wasn't anticipating having this discussion quite just yet."

She told both sides she would allot between two and two and a half hours for their closing arguments. As a former trial attorney herself, she sympathized with them. She wanted McLeland and Rozzi to have plenty of time. But if they started getting close to the time limit, she would let them know.

"I might be clicking a pen . . ." she said. "'Hey, can we wind things up here?'"

After a long break, Martin was brought in to provide a few mumbled insights on the possibility that Allen was feigning symptoms. The defense had one more piece of business to attend to regarding their offer of proof.

Baldwin wanted Gull to issue an arrest warrant for Elvis Fields. As Gull's expression turned baffled, the defense attorney explained his thinking. The defense had subpoenaed Fields. But he had not come in. They wanted to get the man on the stand and push him until he said something incriminating.

Gull looked stricken. "You have to know what someone's going to say for a legitimate offer of proof."

His voice strained, Baldwin explained that he wanted to see if Fields would break and say something that opened the door. Perhaps the defense could bring Odinism in at the last minute. He speculated that Fields might burst out with some major confession, that he might cry out that he was there but not responsible for the killings.

The judge was skeptical. She declined to order Fields's arrest. The Odinism theory was dead.

McLeland spent the whole trial thinking about the end. He was an attorney who loved closing arguments. Those were the moments to get a little dramatic and theatrical. Closings were a great time to bring in the emotional elements of a case. That was where McLeland felt most comfortable. He liked to be on his feet, pacing before a jury, unleashing all the intensity he had kept stifled during the rest of the trial.

When he was not questioning a witness, preparing to question a witness, or helping out one of his deputies with note-taking, McLeland had been hunched over his laptop typing out points for his closing argument. He wanted to have all the important notes close at hand for that.

For the Allen case, he sought to achieve a few different goals. He needed to emphasize all the evidence that would push the jurors to feel comfortable convicting the defendant beyond a reasonable doubt for each element of each offense. After that, the closing was all about touring through the high points of the case. Leading the jurors by the hand through the big pieces of evidence. On the rebuttal, he could knock down defense points and leave the jury with something to remember.

He strived to avoid the impulse to overstuff his argument. Dragging things out for two hours seemed excessive. Brevity helped a jury avoid feeling bogged down. So did clarity. He knew lawyers sometimes struggled to translate their lofty legal arguments for everyday civilians like the jurors.

So throughout the trial, McLeland sought to poll the non-lawyers in attendance. In preparation for closing, Luttrull's wife, Debbie, was one of those who listed out a few key points for the prosecution team. She even threw out the phrase "Bridge Guy starter kit" in quotation marks, to describe the litany of items pulled from Allen's house. McLeland liked that. It was catchy. Figuring she was quoting Luttrull, he added it to his notes.

When he entered the well of the court that morning, McLeland's priority was to ensure the jury could see the screen of the big TV. The prosecution team had finally mastered the device, but McLeland did not want to end with yet another technological failure.

In the gallery, Kathy Allen tossed down a pillow on her seat. Auger hurried over to pass along a blue sticky note to a defense-oriented YouTuber who had offered the team a legal sounding board. Among the girls' families, Anna was crying. Tara's wife, Amanda, headed over to comfort her.

Gull looked out at the gallery with some skepticism. "Yesterday you were very quiet." The trial was almost over. She did not want any eleventh-hour incidents. "I would appreciate your continued compliance."

When the jury came in, Gull read out the four murder counts. Kathy Allen shook her head and wiped her eyes. Then it was time for McLeland's closing argument.

He described February 13, 2017, as "a day this county will never forget." The day the girls were taken. On the TV screen, he pulled up the last selfie the girls had taken together. Libby's bright blue eyes stared out at the jury. Behind her sat a serious-looking Abby. McLeland described the disappearance, the desperate search.

"No one is looking for two dead bodies," he said. "That doesn't happen around here. Small community. Those kinds of things don't happen."

He described the video. "The video shows the moment Abby and Libby were kidnapped. You can hear the fear in their voices. You can see the fear in Abby's face."

Piece by piece, McLeland built up the circumstantial evidence against Allen, encircling him. He talked through the movement of Libby's phone, from exiting Kelsi's car to the walk across the bridge to the abduction, and the last movements before 2:32 P.M. He drew on a map of the woods. He led the jurors down the trails. He pointed out each of the key witnesses. They all saw a man. A creepy man, an angry man. A man walking with purpose. A man lying in wait. They had all seen Bridge Guy.

Then McLeland told the jury something the investigators had been saying to each other for years. "If we identify who Bridge Guy is, we can determine who killed Libby and Abby."

Fortunately, Allen had done a lot of the work for investigators on that front. Coming forward in 2017, Allen put himself on the trails at the right time. He dressed himself in an outfit identical to that worn by Bridge Guy. On the Hoosier Harvestore video, a car that looked exactly his zoomed by at the exact right moment. When police searched Allen's home, they found a mess of knives and box cutters, a blue Carhartt jacket, and a cartridge in a keepsake box the same brand and caliber of bullet as the one dropped in the woods. McLeland dubbed the finds a "Bridge Guy starter kit." He went into the cartridge, into Allen's bizarre manipulation of his wife in the interview, into the defendant's fleeting embrace of Christianity.

In the defense row of seats, Morse vigorously shook her head when McLeland asked the jury if the pieces were starting to fall into place.

McLeland played audio clips of Allen's confessions. Once more, the defendant's voice—so similar to that of Bridge Guy—filled the whole courtroom.

One of the girls had to watch the other die. But Allen was able to go back to his life "like nothing happened." For five years, he lived among the people of Delphi. But he was not the quiet retail worker he pretended to be. He was a killer.

"He gives details that only he could have," McLeland said. "Only the killer could have."

Rozzi handled the closing for the defense. In criminal trials, the state has the final word. Rozzi's closing was the last time the jury would ever hear from the defense. He needed to make it count. He started with a list of numbers. The trial had lasted seventeen days and featured over sixty witnesses, and somewhere between two hundred and three hundred pieces of evidence. Rozzi urged the jurors to focus on all of that more than the final arguments.

Rozzi outlined four main themes he wanted to hit: "broken timelines," "bungled ballistics," Allen's false confessions, and digital forensics. Despite that attempt at an outline, most of Rozzi's closing was like a patchwork quilt, scraps of fabric ripped out and sewn together. He landed solid points amid minor quibbles. Nothing flowed, and nothing seemed to follow. His argument was less a greatest hits album and more of a cobbled-together bootleg that sprinkled a few well-known radio singles into a series of scratchy recordings of songs from a band's poorly received experimental phase.

Topics that Rozzi chose to veer into included the state's refusal to rely on sketchy height analysis, Brad Heath's story—which Rozzi himself admitted "may not be the biggest piece of evidence in the case"—Kelsi's strands of hair, Allen's social drinking, and McCain's believability.

"You should question the credibility of this investigation," Rozzi said.

He brought up Libby's phone. He castigated the state for not considering the defense's preposterous phone theory viable in the face of more logical explanations like the presence of dirt or moisture in the headphone jack. He blasted Cecil for offering up "some fast food" with his Google search.

"Does that thing ever have stories to tell?" he asked. "The phone has no personality. It has no feeling. No emotion. No opinions."

He said that the state could not explain what he described as the phone's continued activity well after 2:32 P.M.

"There's no explanation because the phone is right," he said.

Rozzi returned to a favorite stock phrase he had used since the "***press release***," calling the cartridge "the magic bullet." The comparison to a bullet used in the assassination of President John F. Kennedy never made much sense, but that certainly never stopped Rozzi before.

Now he had another twist on the slogan for the jury. "The magic bullet is nothing more than a tragic bullet."

Rozzi was far from done. He threw out the FBI's withdrawal from the case without mentioning the fact that the ISP's decision to ask the agency to withdraw was instigated by the FBI falsely accusing Rozzi's own brother of a mistake that had actually been made by their own agents. He accused Oberg of talking a lot without seeming to consider his own endless cross-examination of her. He slammed Kohr for walking into his garage and—"tada"—deciding the murder weapon may have been a box cutter. He called Carbaugh "worthless."

All the while, Morse sat in the gallery, her head bobbing up and down.

"They say all of this is done by a five-foot-five man?" Rozzi asked.

The defense's contention seemed to be that a shorter-than-average adult male could not kidnap two children at gunpoint and murder them.

Late in the game, Rozzi included five helpful bullet points about all the things the state could not provide the jury: the lack of positive identification of Allen, the lack of digital evidence connecting him with the girls, the lack of fingerprints, the lack of DNA, and the lack of other forms of trace evidence. The sorts of points that could have made for a gripping closing were lost amid the rambling.

Rozzi himself acknowledged that for the defense team, the case had "been a long haul," although he conceded that it had been likely more difficult for Allen's relatives. And, of course, the girls' families.

Rozzi got fierier as he went on. He decried Allen's treatment in Westville. "Can you blame him for picking up that Bible?"

By that point, Rozzi's argument felt long. But his performance was in the realm of the acceptable. Then things twisted. On cue, Baker pulled up a surprising image on the big TV.

It was a long wooden table with chains and cuffs attached to both ends. Rozzi suddenly adopted a folksy cadence. "This here is called a rack."

He wanted the jurors to look at a torture device that dated back centuries. Once, authorities used such barbaric instruments to stretch bodies and cause excruciating pain, snapping ligaments and pulling bones from sockets. Next, Baker displayed the illustration of a bearded man. He was screaming, his hands locked in thumbscrews. Dating back to the early modern era, those viselike instruments were used to crush the digits of torture victims.

Rozzi explained that confinement in a one-man cell was just as much a form of torture as the cruel devices used in centuries past. He said that every now and then, the citizenry had to rise up and push back against the state's overreach.

"That time is now," he said.

Holeman wondered if the defense lawyer was on his way to becoming a sovereign citizen. Beside him, the deputy prosecutors shifted in their seats. Rozzi had his back to the prosecution. McLeland looked beyond him. He watched the faces of the jurors. He felt Rozzi was pushing his luck.

Baker put up an image of a big snake strangling its prey. The serpent was a metaphor.

"That's the power of the state," Rozzi told the jury. "It's the power of your government."

In disbelief, Diener and Luttrull looked at the snake, and then looked back at McLeland. The prosecutor just sat there. The rhetoric and images were clearly inappropriate and went far beyond the bounds of argument. Struggling to keep his voice at a whisper, Luttrull indicated he felt an objection was in order. Diener hit McLeland on the arm. But the prosecutor said nothing.

To McLeland, the argument was overwrought and ridiculous. But Rozzi had not even done a good job making his point: that the serpentine government had strangled confessions out of the blameless rodent that was his client.

McLeland kept his gaze on the jurors. They had asked sharp questions and always seemed determined to focus on the facts of the case. McLeland thought Rozzi had gone too far and lost them all by himself. Sitting there, he realized that if his gut was wrong, if the serpent's coils had snared even one of the jurors, he might regret the moment for the rest of his life. Still, he ignored his outraged deputies and put his trust in the jury.

"No man or woman should be treated like this—whether guilty or not," Rozzi said.

There it was. After all of the defense's bluster about actual innocence and corruption and Odinism, their last move was a transparent nod to jury nullification. Allen could be guilty of slaughtering two kids, and he ought to walk anyway. The jurors ought to pay no attention to the evidence in the case, and instead crush the serpent beneath their heels.

In that way, by at least tacitly acknowledging the possibility of Allen's guilt, Rozzi's closing argument featured a gesture to reality. But in terms of its bluster, it seemed a pure appeal to the online cranks. All throughout the case, the defense had operated in a bubble. When forced to choose between a reasonable explanation and a conspiratorial one, they always seemed to opt for the latter. Even when they had an opportunity to broaden their reach, they only seemed to have eyes for the case fanatics that already worshipped them.

On the way out of the courtroom for lunch, Diener leaned over to Buckley and said, "We're the snake." McLeland had all of lunch to hone his rebuttal. When he came back, he felt ready. For nearly seven years of his life, he had prepared for this moment.

McLeland went after the defense. Pointing back to Baldwin's opening statement, he accused them of throwing out claim after claim without proof. He told the jury he would not lecture them about how they should feel.

No one had heard the girls scream. That did not mean anything. Thanks to Cicero, investigators knew that at least Libby cried.

"Scared. Fearful. All because of Richard Allen," McLeland said.

The prosecutor kept gesturing at the defendant.

At some point that day, Allen leaned over to Baldwin and muttered, "If Nick points at me again, I'm going to do something about it."

That got back to McLeland during break. The prosecutor felt angry. Allen had used the threat of violence to control Libby and Abby. McLeland was determined to show the defendant that his menacing had no effect in the courtroom. So he made sure to point at Allen as much as possible. Allen sat there and did nothing. His box cutter was long gone, buried in a landfill. The courtroom was filled with people, not much like the wintry woods. The prosecutor was an adult man, not a little girl. Allen sat still and took it as McLeland pointed his way again and again.

As McLeland spoke, all the emotions that had come up over the course of the case roiled inside of him. The fear the girls felt must have been overwhelming. On the march down the hill, the race across the creek, in that hollow in the forest. McLeland was thinking about the two murdered girls. He was thinking about his own two girls. He choked up. For an instant, he found it difficult to get the words out, but he pushed on.

"There are two victims in this case: Abby and Libby," he said. "They're also heroes."

Libby was a hero for shooting a video of Allen. Abby was a hero for concealing the phone beneath her body.

"Those pieces of evidence helped law enforcement find Richard Allen," he said.

In the gallery, relatives of the girls began to cry. McLeland harkened back to a detail from Becky's testimony. Libby had wanted to grow up to help police solve crimes.

"That's exactly what she did," he said. "And she brought Abby along to help her."

CHAPTER SIXTY-ONE

The jurors had been away from home a long time. But they did not feel hurried. They faced a heavy task ahead.

After hearing the judge's instructions about the state's strict burden and the importance of disregarding Allen's decision not to testify, the jurors left and gathered in the designated jury room. The twelve jurors sat in the uncomfortable chairs around a large table. The three alternates remained off to the side, silent sentinels. After all that, they were not permitted to speak at all. The other jurors felt terrible for them.

There was no detailed guidebook on deliberating. The process was largely left in the hands of the jurors themselves. They knew they needed to select a foreperson. They decided to elect one. There were several candidates. They selected one of the older men. In time, everyone would agree that he was an excellent choice.

The jury did not vote that first day of deliberations. There would be time for that later. A man's fate was in their hands. They could not rush.

Gull advised the lawyers not to go far. A verdict could come in at any time. The parties each left their numbers with the court reporter, Jodie Williams.

Then it was time for both teams to wait. There was no rest for the prosecutors. McLeland and his deputies went down to his office and busied themselves working on the stack of arrests and traffic court filings that had piled up throughout the trial. To Luttrull, such mundane matters were a pleasant distraction. All the adrenaline and excitement from the trial faded away, leaving the attorneys with only nerves. They needed something to do as they all wondered if they had proven their case to the jury.

McLeland asked Debbie if she noticed that he included her quip about the "Bridge Guy starter kit." Nervously, she told him she had been quoting *The Murder Sheet* podcast. McLeland let out a dismayed laugh. All those months, the defense had actively courted the internet sphere. Now at the last minute, he had managed to give the conspiracy theorists fodder for the idea that he had his own online army.

A few blocks away from the courthouse, the defense lawyers headed out to a late lunch at the Sandwich Shop. They brought along Motta Jr. He had managed to go on Court TV no less than eight times to parrot defense talking points for a national audience. The group enjoyed their meal in the corner of the restaurant. The defense team projected an elated optimism. Given the stack of evidence against their client, an informed observer might be forgiven for assuming that a mistrial would be considered a big win for Allen. But the defense attorneys were giving people the sense that an acquittal might be in order.

Perhaps they had begun to buy their own press. The media spin throughout the trial had favored the defense. That was partly by design. The prosecutors did not leak. The defense did. Defense attorneys would chat openly with YouTubers and reporters in the court's foyer and outside on the sidewalk. Forging relationships and providing off-the-record insights was a good way of winning over the media.

The problem was also structural. Gull bore much responsibility for the often misleading coverage. Cameras or an audio-feed would have allowed the public to see or hear for themselves, although such measures hardly halted misinformation from spreading in other high-profile national cases. Perhaps more crucially, Gull had deprived news outlets of a place to stage and organize. Receiving sporadic media passes did not set up most journalists and organizations for success. A media overflow room could have provided reporters with a place to confer, to fact-check, to clarify, and to file copy or shoot broadcasts to meet their deadlines. Instead, through her restrictive rulings, Gull created an environment rife with spotty, error-riddled reporting.

As a result, the coverage was often confusing and skewed heavily toward Allen. Investigators and prosecutors were bombarded with texts from friends and family, preemptively consoling them on their upcoming loss.

Holeman considered himself a patient man. But the waiting was making him crazy. All he wanted to do was jump back into his normal life. Working for the state police was surreal enough, and he had seen all kinds of bizarre things in his career. But all of that was far more manageable than the dreadful quiet. He broke up the day by pacing all around.

The prosecutors hung out in McLeland's office on the second floor. The lawyers were working on other Carroll County business. The office television played *SportsCenter* and *Groundhog Day*, a film that the prosecutors had frequently quoted to one another throughout the trial. Holeman would go there. Sometimes, Liggett was there too. They would all talk about the case, go over all the facts, speculate about what the jury was considering.

When the restlessness struck, Holeman would wander out to the other war room on the second floor, where most of the detectives hung out. Downstairs, he would chat with the troopers and public information officers, who favored the break room, a space so filled with food and snacks that it resembled a convenience store. Occasionally Holeman would slip outside to a building across the street, where the girls' families waited. He wanted to keep checking on them.

When the apprehension got really bad, Holeman went outside and circled the courthouse. He saw all sorts of things on his walks. He took a picture with a woman holding a sign decrying him as corrupt. Once or twice, he ran into Baldwin with his foot propped up on an orange barrier, huddled up with reporters. During the trial, camera crews had taken to following along after Holeman, filming B-roll to spice up their evening broadcasts.

Harshman was aghast when Holeman asked if he and Mullin wanted to join him for a stroll outside. "What, you're going to walk through that?" During the defense's case, a small cluster of protestors had picketed the courthouse, holding handmade signs reading "Disbar Judge Gull" and "Holeman Is Lying!" But without any court sessions to attend, there was nothing for the crowds to do other than mill around and wait. The Carroll County deputies were always on alert, on the off-chance somebody's bombastic YouTube live sparked a riot.

But Holeman was numb to the true crime cranks by that point. "Yeah, don't worry about it."

Harshman relented, and the three investigators walked around the courthouse together. There were still lawn chairs lined up along the sidewalk. A few people cried out, begging to shake Harshman's hand. The positive attention was welcome in the face of all the harassment and threats. But for investigators like Holeman, the adulation was discomfiting in its own way. The true crime fandom had come to see real-life police investigators as celebrities. Something about that felt very wrong.

Turning the corner, Holeman ended up walking through the spot where the Richard Allen supporters hunkered. All along the wall, they had crude cardboard signs supporting the defense and the defendant weighed down with rocks.

One woman glared at Holeman. "Oh, my God." She added she wanted to go throw up.

He thought about asking her what she ate for lunch. But he kept quiet and paced back toward the courthouse.

The citizens of Delphi did what they had done at almost every step of the case. They sent food to those involved. Snacks, sandwiches, and hot meals for lunch or dinner kept appearing at the courtroom. Those had kept law enforcement, the prosecutors, and the families of the girls fed during the trial. But as the wait grew longer, many of those working the case lost their appetites. In the prosecutor's office, Luttrull switched between sitting in the different barrel chairs. McLeland remained at his desk. Diener now had her own desk, too. In July 2024, she had accepted McLeland's offer to join his office as the chief deputy prosecutor.

Reviewing police and traffic reports in other cases became difficult for McLeland. He still thought a not guilty verdict was highly unlikely. He felt a hung jury was a bigger threat.

All three prosecutors and the entire team of investigators put pressure on themselves. That pressure had been necessary to prepare for trial. Everyone wanted justice served for Abby and Libby and their families. But they each tried not to show it as the hours of deliberation seemed to grow longer and longer. They remained patient with one another, even as the exhaustion hit them. Diener and Luttrull saw McLeland as carrying the heaviest burden as the elected prosecutor—and as a perfectionist on top of that—and they did what they could to help him.

The jury finished their timeline that Friday. The foreman split everyone into four groups of three. Each one was assigned a topic to focus on. One handled the door sheet confessions from the suicide companions. Another did all the phone calls. Another focused on the confessions to Martin and Wala. The jurors wanted to take seriously the possibility that Allen was innocent but psychotic.

That day, they took a vote. No one voted for not guilty. Nine selected guilt. The remaining three were undecided. There was still work to do.

CHAPTER SIXTY-TWO

On Saturday, the jurors asked to review the two interviews, along with the edited video of Bridge Guy. Holeman thought that was a good sign. McLeland was despondent.

The jurors went into the courtroom to watch the edited version of Libby's video and the interviews with Allen. The attorneys came in and filed into the back row. Among the jurors, some had seen enough. Others needed to see more. They rearranged themselves in the seats, yielding the first row to a handful of jurors who each stared carefully at the interviews.

Some of the jurors really did not care for Holeman's style. They found him overbearing. Some were confused about why he started yelling. The edits to remove the questions about the polygraph examination made for a jarring jump. A tense back-and-forth morphed into a screaming match without warning. They were bothered that Allen kept denying his guilt, and the investigator just kept pressing him. Others did not care. They pointed out that police interviews were supposed to be tough and confrontational.

Still, after watching all the videos with Mullin, Liggett, and Holeman, some of the jurors remained uneasy.

The video evidence took a long time to watch. The jury stayed late and took a vote. The uncertain contingent gained a member that day. Now, the count was eight guilty, four undecided.

Everyone had their own ways of coping with the wait. Luttrull's wife, Debbie, texted him verses from Psalm 10. "Lord, you listen to the desires of those who suffer. You steady their hearts; you listen closely to them, to establish justice for the orphan and the oppressed, so that people of the land will never again be terrified."

Luttrull sent her back a picture he had received from Nathan Meyers. The investigator had seen something remarkable while driving. A deer stood in a field of harvested corn. Swooping down from the sky was an eagle. Among those associated with the case, all manner of things became good omens—birds, a gentle breeze, and the pink sunrise.

Stuck in McLeland's office, the prosecutors passed the time by working on more traffic court filings. Each of them agonized over their performance in the trial.

All week, Holeman had dreaded Saturday. He thought if the deliberations did not come to an end by then, he would break down. He waited until the jury left. Holeman did not collapse, but he felt exhausted. His early optimism was gone. The jurors had not sent any distress signals Gull's way, but that seemed imminent. A mistrial loomed.

After all those years with the Indiana State Police, he found himself questioning the justice system. The facts were clear in his mind. He did not understand how a jury could fail to see what he saw.

McLeland said very little that day. He was confident the jury had enough to convict. But the doubt had crept in. He wondered what he had missed.

The jurors sympathized with one another. Sometimes, things were said that led to hurt feelings. Opposing views were formed and voiced. At least one juror had to be asked to allow others to talk. But everyone understood, and nobody begrudged. They were all in a hard spot. Dragooned into service, taken miles and miles away from home. Missing work emails and birthdays and texts from friends. Ripped away from their parents, children, spouses, and others they loved. The jurors had all gone through that together. They bonded over the course of the trial. They took in a movie together one weekend, and bowled so often that they joked they ought to start their own league. Sometimes the bailiffs would grill for them in the covered stone patio outside their hotel. They respected each other, and they respected the process. They took the task before them seriously.

Sunday was the loneliest day.

"Everybody needs a day off," Gull had declared after the closing statements. The jury could choose to rest on Sundays. They did so. They huddled in their separate rooms at the Lafayette hotel where they stayed. Outside of the rush of the trial, away from the push and pull of the deliberations, they had a day to ponder. They collected their thoughts.

With the jury room empty, there was no reason for the defense and the prosecution teams to hang around the courthouse. They were all free to go home. During the week, those involved in the case had relied on one another during the long wait. Sunday saw them all ripped away from the only other people who could possibly understand what they were going through.

Afterwards, Liggett could not remember his movements that day. He might have gone to church. He might have stayed home. He might have watched a football game. All he could recall was that Sunday was ordinary, aside from the looming decision by the jury.

Luttrull did two things he had not done all month. He went to church. Then he watched the Indianapolis Colts play the Buffalo Bills. That did not help, because the Colts lost.

Diener sat at home on her couch. She watched something on one of the streaming services, but it did not hold her attention. She regretted being alone. She thought the prosecutors and investigators should have planned a group activity that day to pass the time. They could have all brought their families. That would have been far better than waiting in isolation.

McLeland went over the case again and again in his mind. He wondered about the delay. He tried to forget. He moved through life in a haze. He went to the gym. He watched a movie or two. He spent time with his daughters that day. They did arts and crafts projects.

Holeman tried to do work around his house. He decided he would put off abandoning all hope until the following day.

Rested from the weekend, the jurors gathered on Monday. That was a good day, as if everyone had come back ready. Civil discussion flowed. The foreman asked the undecided jurors to make a list of everything they knew, everything they believed, and everything they doubted. The undecided jurors did so.

The foreman asked them about the sum of those beliefs and doubts. Could all their beliefs be true, all their doubts be confirmed, and Allen still be guilty?

The undecided made their final choices. Then they voted. The guilty votes began rolling in. Some of the jurors knew it was over before the final tally. The twelve were unanimous on each count. Allen was guilty.

The foreman was awestruck. He had labored so hard and so patiently to keep everyone together. Now the work was done, just like that. "Are you serious? Unanimous?"

One of the jurors cried. The girls would stay dead. Another family would shatter. But they had an answer.

The jury had done its job, but the wait was not over. After delivering the news to the bailiffs, the jurors lingered in their room. The atmosphere seemed to stifle.

Word got out to the parties. Now they knew a verdict had been reached.

In most trials, once that happens, the process unfolds quickly. But not that day. Kathy Allen had left Delphi and needed to be summoned. The wait for the parties felt endless.

The prosecution and investigative teams fell into two camps.

Some, like Luttrull, were worried. He believed in the case's strength. But one could never fully anticipate a jury. There was always the possibility that they could acquit Allen. Others like Liggett and Holeman were convinced a decision meant only one thing: a conviction.

Outside the line formed in a hurry as the news spread. Those who waited jostled and fumed. Accusations of cutting were hissed about one of the *Dateline* producers. Others hung back, content to wait outside. Local deputies requested that the crowd leave room along the sidewalk for passersby. Julie Melvin loudly sang hymns.

Inside the courthouse, ascending the stairs with his colleagues, Luttrull came to a few conclusions. Lawyers were always invested in the outcome of a case. Winning fed a sense of accomplishment and triumph. Losing could shake an attorney's sense of self-worth. Heading up to the courtroom, Luttrull was struck by the sense that he did not matter. His feelings on the case did not matter. All that mattered were the girls, their families, and their community. He only hoped the jury would deliver justice for them, not to mention for the investigators who had toiled over the case for so long.

Altogether, between arranging the security and gathering everyone and admitting the public, the wait lasted a few hours. But then it was time. Gull gazed at those in the gallery. In stern tones, she urged everyone to refrain from raging about the outcome. "Be angry outside, not in here."

Then it was time for the foreman to read the verdict. Allen was guilty on all counts. McLeland grabbed Diener's arm. They had done it. They had won. Holeman felt a great weight lifting off his chest.

Allen did not react. He said nothing. He did nothing. His face was empty of all emotion. The transport team snapped the cuffs on Allen at 2:32 P.M., the same time Libby's phone stopped moving forever. Then they escorted him out of the courtroom, as his wife cried. His defense team marched down the courthouse steps, crestfallen. Miles away by then, the transport team drove their client from the courthouse back to Cass County for the last time. Allen was silent the whole way.

Other officers urged on the jurors. The remaining fifteen fled down the slippery marble steps of the courthouse. Together they rushed outside, through the tent, one last time. The fear was that members of the media—or the nuttier online fanatics—might chase them down. The jurors and alternates piled into the vans and sped back toward Fort Wayne. The vans hauled away from the courthouse. Then a block or so away, the bailiffs hit the brakes. Lights flashed before the windshields. A long, slow train chugged across the road. Delphi would not give up the jurors that easily.

Not every investigator was in the courtroom, of course. Vido was back working another investigation when he heard about the guilty verdict. Later on, he would not remember who rang him first. He only recalled a flurry of calls back and forth between his fellow investigators. He was sitting in his car. He was working on a different case. He had since moved on to so many other investigations, officer-involved shootings, child molestations, and rapes. He was no longer the detective stuck on Delphi, going nowhere. There was no celebration, just a moment's relief for the families. He took a breath. Then he went back to work on the next case.

Back in the courtroom, the mood was a peculiar blend of relief and sorrow. Holeman turned to McLeland. "I feel like I just want to kiss you on the lips right now."

McLeland smiled. "Don't." He was not a man who cared much for hugs. He had grown up in a family that preferred handshakes. But he did not protest when Holeman and later Diener embraced him. The trial was over. They had won.

Holeman went around hugging Diener, Luttrull, Mullin, Meyers, and the relatives of the girls. Turning to Anna and Mike, he said, "Thanks for believing in us." The families could have easily turned on the investigators long ago, amid the years of frustration. But they had stuck together, just as Abby and Libby had on the bridge.

In the very back of the courthouse, Liggett observed the rows and rows of people. He felt grateful that few could see him in the corner. A tear rolled down his cheek.

The prosecutors lingered with the family. Sunlight streamed in through the courthouse windows as they all embraced. McLeLand thanked the relatives, then he stood back and let them ask questions and say whatever they wanted to say. Then the expressions of gratitude and happiness and grief dwindled, and they got to talking about practical matters. The sentencing was set for December 20. Finally, after seven years, the relatives of the girls would have the chance to confront Allen face-to-face. After that, the prosecutors returned to the second floor and packed up their files. All kinds of emotions tore through McLeland. He could not bring Abby and Libby back, but he had done what he could do.

McLeland left. He went to get his two girls and took them home.

Though Allen had stood accused of committing two murders, McLeland actually filed four murder charges against him. This was to give the jury options. If they stood convinced that the state had proven that Allen had "knowingly or intentionally kill(ed)" the girls then they could convict him of the two charges under Indiana Code 35-42-1-1(1). If, on the other hand, they merely believed that the girls had been killed during Allen's attempt to kidnap them and were not certain that it had been intentional then they could convict him of the two charges filed under Indiana Code 35-42-1-1(2), which was Indiana's felony murder statute.

As it happened, the jury found Allen guilty on all four charges. Gull would vacate two of them before sentencing him. But in the meantime some felt confused by the situation. Even Allen—who perhaps had not been briefed on this point by his attorneys—expressed bafflement. After his conviction, he was heard telling someone at Cass County that he did not understand why he had been convicted of four counts of murder when he had only killed two people.

Allen swore he would harm the judge if he did not get what he wanted. He did not wish his family to see him at his most vulnerable, shackled and awaiting to learn his fate. He told his relatives that if he saw them at the hearing, he would hurt Gull.

Before the sentencing hearing, McLeland stood at the railing, staring down at the gathered crowd. Deputies ushered in the press and members of the public. Then, Allen's transport team brought him in. A sheepish expression on his face, the convicted murderer wore orange bottoms and a gray shirt. His hands were cuffed in front of him to a leather belt. Reading glasses perched on his head. The convicted murderer glanced over to where his family usually sat. His wife, mother, stepfather, daughter, and sister were all absent. Allen's SIG Sauer was boxed up in evidence, but he could still control others with his threats of violence.

Before the sentencing hearing, Allen had the chance to cooperate with the pre-sentencing report. The report would allow probation officers to document the convicted killer's entire life. It was not for the public, it was simply to help Gull determine a fair sentence. Before the sentencing hearing, the defense team advised their client not to participate in the pre-sentencing report.

After years of silence, investigators, as well as those closest to the girls, were finally ungagged.

Holeman testified first. He was there to speak on behalf of law enforcement. He confronted the defense, saying that Richard Allen had allowed them to use the "unethical strategies" of falsely accusing the prosecutor and the police of corruption, withholding evidence, and lying.

He argued why Gull ought to give Allen the maximum sentence. "This one was very brutal. Mr. Allen laid in wait, he stalked the girls, he kidnapped, he humiliated them, he treated them like animals, he used a gun to control them."

Holeman said one of the girls would have had to witness her best friend die.

"I can't imagine the fear and anxiety that they went through to watch that," Holeman said. "And then he covered them with sticks and left them there alone and went on to live his life like it never happened."

Relatives from both families spoke next, reading their victim impact statements. Libby's cousin Josh Lank Jr., her mother Carrie Timmons, and her grandparents Mike and Becky Patty all took to the stand. So did Abby's grandparents, Eric and Diane Erskin.

The family members thanked the investigators and the prosecutors. They talked about their loss. They also slammed the defense team, focusing on the leak in particular.

Through tears, Timmons expressed pride in her daughter, her sunshine. "While there will never really be justice or closure, and nothing will bring my daughter back, I am so very proud of her for not only exposing her and Abby's killer, but also bringing much needed attention to so many cases near and far."

Lank asked for the maximum sentence for Allen, expressing anger on behalf of his family and his cousin. "God doesn't have a place for sick, twisted minded individuals like Richard Allen. The devil has a special place in hell for him and I hope the prison community can get him there quicker than the sentencing. He is a dead man walking."

Mike Patty confronted the defense directly. "I understand the role you needed to play, but I cannot connect the ways of our legal system to allow so many things to interfere with the truth and facts to simply be brought before a jury," he said.

Eric compared the loss of Abby to an amputation that could never fully heal. He asked Allen, "How could you continue to go about your daily routine like it never happened?"

Diane spoke about listening to Libby's video, hearing Abby ask her friend not to leave her. Those words rang in her head all throughout the trial, whenever she wanted to walk away. "Libby didn't leave, so I didn't leave." Diane talked about life after Abby's murder. She wondered how many great grandchildren she lost that day. She said she felt cheated out of her old life, the one she could share with her "sweet Abigail." Diane shared her granddaughter's favorite question: "Do you need any help?"

Choking up, she replied, "Yes, Abby. I sure need your help right now."

Becky Patty talked about February 13, 2017. "I live every day with the burden of the choice I made that fateful day—I can never change the results of my choice of letting the girls go to the trails—and I take responsibility for that." She paused, staring at the man who slit her granddaughter's throat. "What about you, Richard Allen? Will you ever own up and take responsibility for the choices you made that day?"

With the victim impact statements done, McLeland argued for Allen to get the maximum sentence: one-hundred and thirty years. Sixty-five years for Abby and sixty-five years for Libby, to be served consecutively. That would be an effective life sentence for the middle-aged Allen. McLeland cited factors like the devastating effect of the murders on the community, as well as the fact that one of the girls would have had to watch her friend die.

Before Gull got to sentencing, Rozzi rose and asked her to disregard all commentary related to Allen's defense team.

Then the judge spoke. She told Allen she had presided over many "hideous cases" in her career. But Allen's crime ranked up there.

"These families will deal with your carnage forever," Gull said.

Allen chose that moment to roll his eyes at the judge.

"You sit there and roll your eyes at me like you have done through this entire trial," she said.

In a calm, cold voice, she sentenced Allen to sixty-five years for each murder, to be served consecutively. Once again, he did not react. The transport team marched Allen away, and he was gone.

When the hearing was over, Auger stormed over to the prosecution side of the table. She snapped at Holeman, taking umbrage with his statements criticizing the defense team. She was upset that she had essentially been called unethical before a judge. McLeland chimed in that he agreed with Holeman's assessment. When Holeman told Auger he would say whatever he wanted, she fired back, "Screw you!" Holeman advised her to do the same. Diener interjected, saying that the courtroom was no place for such a scene. After all but openly declaring the prosecutors and police corrupt and evil—directly and through their back channels on social media—the defense attorneys reacted to any sort of response with utter shock.

After hearing the jury convict her husband of the murders, Kathy Allen had walked out of the courthouse and past a line of television cameras. Motta Jr. was at her side, his arm draped over her shoulder. "This isn't over," she said to the media. "This isn't over at all." In that same spirit, the defense team had no intention of stopping. They did a round of interviews with YouTube channels and television news outlets, during which Rozzi downplayed the leak of images of murdered children and suggested that the blame fell on police for spurring interest in the murders by asking the public's help in identifying Bridge Guy. The pictures of Abby and Libby lying dead on the forest floor continued to pop up on Reddit, Facebook, and blogs, forever displayed for the benefit of the morbidly curious.

But before they really renewed their work, Baldwin's firm threw a Christmas party for their employees and even gave them gifts. Brian Alvey, one of the team's investigators, proudly posted what he received on Facebook. The defense team had inexplicably presented him with a framed photo of the Monon High Bridge; this was, of course, the site from which their client had been convicted of kidnapping two young girls and leading them off to be brutalized and killed. Each of the three defense attorneys had inscribed the image with jokey messages attesting to things like Alvey's "death defying bridge crossings" and making optimistic references to what they saw as the likelihood that not only would Allen get a second trial but they would all once again get the opportunity to work on it together.

To make that happen, the team pinned their hopes on a convicted meth dealer named Ricci Davis, who was serving a fifty year sentence. During that time, Davis claimed, he had gotten to know Ron Logan and, according to Davis, Logan had confided in him that the girls had been killed with a box cutter. But that was not all the suddenly loquacious Logan had allegedly revealed.

According to Davis, Logan also divulged the girls' bodies had been moved several times and that the battery from Libby's phone had been removed. Those details completely contradicted the physical evidence. Davis also took and failed a polygraph examination.

Perhaps most significantly of all, none of this information had been concealed from the defense team. Andrew Baldwin had even had an interview with Davis months before the trial. After that meeting and (presumably) after an assessment of Davis's tale, the defense chose not to call him as a witness in the three-day hearing where they had had the opportunity to present an argument that Logan had been involved in the murders. Clearly they had not placed much value on what Davis could bring to the table.

But, after the trial, that all changed. Baldwin had another meeting with Davis and left it with new revelations. Davis now claimed he had also become friendly with Kegan Kline and that Kline had also confessed to him about his role in the murders. According to this latest version, Kline and Logan had done it with the assistance of a third man. Davis had supposedly spelled it all out in a series of letters to prosecutor McLeland, letters which the defense angrily insisted they had never received. These letters, they contended, would exonerate Richard Allen and therefore should have been turned over to them as part of discovery.

Davis also provided a new detail. He said Kline indicated that the girls had been handcuffed. None of the many qualified experts who had carefully examined the evidence in the case had seen any sign to support that contention. But, after speaking with Davis, Baldwin, Auger, and their investigator Hoffman pawed over photographs of the dead girls, staring at images of their lifeless wrists until they convinced themselves they saw something everyone else had missed—marks indicating the girls had indeed been handcuffed.

Baldwin proudly noted this observation in a filing—and even declared that Logan and Kline were the most likely suspects in the murder. He did not bother to explain why—if that was the case—he, Rozzi and Auger had instead focused on the Odinists. He demanded that the Davis letters be released.

Soon after, McLeland published them in a filing. They were not what Baldwin had expected. Instead of exonerating Richard Allen, the letters implicated him. In the letters, Davis identified Richard Allen as the third man allegedly involved in the killings. Not only that but Davis went on to denigrate Andrew Baldwin and even claimed that the attorney had hinted that Davis should lie. Since Davis had no credibility and his entire story had been false from the beginning, it was difficult to take seriously what he had to say about Baldwin. But still it could not have been what the attorney wanted.

Yet he claimed that it was. In a subsequent filing, he maintained that the letters which incriminated his client actually could be used to exonerate him and crowed about how McLeland had been "forced to turn over the letters, perhaps out of fear." Baldwin acted convinced that the publication of the letters—which implicated his client and suggested that Baldwin was not above suborning perjury—was a tremendous boon for him and his client. Remarkably, the YouTube crowd he catered to rushed to agree with him.

Richard Allen had fans. Case obsessives who saw nothing strange about their fandom around a convicted child murderer and his defense team. They said that Allen would soon be free. They made it clear that they would support Allen forever, no matter what they saw, no matter what they heard. They said that they would never stop fighting the evil at the heart of the case, the true villains, the police, the judge, the prosecutors, and even the families of the dead girls. They spread ridiculous rumors about Holeman attempting to have a crank killed. They suggested that Kathy Shank was herself a willing agent of some shadowy conspiracy. They wished death and misfortune against all those who stood against Allen.

As long as Andrew Baldwin or anyone who came after him could endlessly dredge up matters that had been long before adjudicated, as long as they could hop from one theory to another with abandon, as long as they could try to desperately spin losses into successes, Kathy Allen would be correct. This was not over.

Maybe it never would be.

In the garage, Becky worked alone. There were so many things happening for her family. So many things to look forward to. Cody had gotten married not long ago. Kelsi was pregnant with her second child, another daughter. Soon she would have two girls of her own. The new arrival would keep the family running around, just as Kelsi and Libby had kept them busy so many years ago.

The problem with those wonderful occasions was that they came with a jarring reminder. Someone was always missing. Libby's family tried to keep her present, though. They planned events and parties and vacations with her in mind.

Other milestones were missed entirely. The classmates that Libby and Abby had attended middle school with had grown up. Some moved away for college or work. Others married and had babies of their own. That was hard to see.

Tucker trotted around the floor. He had only been a tiny puppy when Libby disappeared. He was an unusual dog in some respects. There was something so reserved about his nature, as if he was still waiting for his girl and her best friend to come back from the trails.

Becky supposed that in a way, so was she.

APPENDIX

In the course of our research and coverage of this case, we also consulted a variety of court documents. We are listing some of the most significant here.

State of Indiana v. Kegan A. Kline (2020)
Probable Cause Affidavit
Videotaped Statement of Kegan Kline

State of Indiana v. Richard M. Allen (2022)
Probable Cause Affidavit
Order Re: Sheriff's Request for Safekeeping
Emergency Motion to Modify Safekeeping Order
Response to Defense's Emergency Motion to Modify Safekeeping Order
Motion for Public Access to Court Records
Verified Motion to Disqualify
Verified Information of Contemptuous Conduct
Motion to Dismiss for Destroying Exculpatory Evidence
List of Witnesses and Exhibits for Contempt Hearing
Motion for Early Trial
List of Additional Witnesses and Exhibits for Contempt Hearing
Motion to Compel and Request for Sanctions
List of Additional Witnesses
Motion for Parity in Resources
Verified Petition for Public Funds
Motion in Limine
Motion to Correct Error (2024)
Motion to Correct Error (2025)
State's Response to Motion to Correct Error

Defendant's Verified Motion to Strike the State's Response to Motion to Correct Error
Defendant's Verified Motion to Preserve and Produce Specific Evidence
Addendum to Defendant's Verified Motion to Preserve and Produce Specific Evidence
Response to Motion to Preserve Evidence
Richard Allen's Verified Reply Memorandum to State of Indiana's Response to Preserve and Produce and Request for Sanctions
Motion to Reconsider

State of Indiana ex rel. Richard M. Allen v. Carroll Circuit Court, et al. (2023)
Record of Proceedings Volume 1 (includes Emergency Motion to Modify Safekeeping Order, Franks Memorandum, Letter to Court from Attorney Rozzi, and Memorandum Regarding Possible Disqualification or Sanctions and Motion to Disqualify)
Record of Proceedings Volume 2 (includes Transcript of hearing held on October 19, 2023, Transcript of hearing held on October 31, 2023, Affidavit from Mitchell Westerman and Affidavit from attorneys Brad Rozzi and Andrew Baldwin)
Record of Proceedings Original Action Supplemental (includes transcript of In Camera Proceedings October 19, 2023)

State of Indiana v. Ronald E Logan (2017)
Information Filed

State of Indiana v. Todd Click (2024)
Probable Cause Affidavit

Sue Wright, Angela Sadlowski v. Carroll County, Indiana, Carroll County Board of Elections, Sharon Milburn et al (2022)
Complaint
Motion to Dismiss- Carroll County
Motion to Dismiss- Carroll County Board of Elections
Motion to Dismiss Granted
Order Issued- Plaintiffs to Pay the Fees of Defendant

Thomas v. Carroll County, Indiana et al (2022)
Complaint

ACKNOWLEDGMENTS

We would like to thank everyone who had a hand in publishing this book. Thank you to our wonderful literary agent, Gideon Pine of Inkwell, whose encouragement, enthusiasm, and patience we relied on throughout this whole process. Thank you to Jocelyn Bailey, Julia Romero, Lisa Gilliam, Maria Fernandez, and Jeremy Chase, whose thoughtful feedback and work helped us immensely. And thank you to our editor and publisher Jessica Case for her tireless efforts and understanding.

We would like to thank those associated with the case who spoke to us on the record on our podcast, *The Murder Sheet*: Courtney Alwine, Steve Buckley, Doug Carter, Pat Cicero, Stacey Diener, Michael Hobbs, Jerry Holeman, a juror, Roland Kohr, Tobe Leazenby, Tony Liggett, James Luttrull, Nicholas McLeland, Brian Olehy, Becky Patty, Lori Sustarsic, and David Vido. Thank you to all of our anonymous sources. We thank you for trusting us. Thank you for taking a risk and providing us with the truth. We appreciate you so much.

We would like to thank the following people for their friendship, assistance at trial, compassion, or thoughtful conversations: Eric Askren, Sarah Elrod Ausbrook, Ted Bartlett, Mallory Bitterman, Jayson Blair from *The Silver Linings Handbook*, Sierra Bowman, Lindsey Bramlage, KC Claybourne, Kathy Clendening, Coffee and Waffles, Anna Cooper, Jim and Jackie Cramer, Lauren Crow, CT, Eileen DeBararac, Alie Dillon, Duchess, Thomas Eidson, the Espinoza family, Lydia Fiedler, Thomas Frost, Tony Garner, Nancy Grace, Ezra Gray and Christina Langsdorf and Stuart and Sheldon, Barb Griffith, Gwen, Susan Hendricks, Julie Heise, Nicole Holeman, Trevor Hyde, Mark Inman, Michelle Jensen, Jinx, Sadie and Greg Johnson, Justice Served Daily, Courtney Kennedy, Kelly Kennedy, Shane "Frankmeister" Kersage, Aimee Kiptoo, Jason Klinker, Tammy "Turbo" Kirby, Susan Laughlin Kisinger, Bart Kraning, Alice LaCour and Brett Talley from *The Prosecutors*, Debbie Luttrull, Christina Mack, Paul Mannion, Jennifer "Marv" Marvin, Joe Massey and Amanda Philips, Lauren and John Matthias, Liberty Maxwell, Sheryl McCollum, Danielle Michael, Juli Middleton, Aaron Murdoch, Jane Myers, Beth Neilson, Nic and The Captain from *True Crime Garage*, Seana Pappas, Jeremy Pion-Berlin, Elle Reagan, RescueAllTheDogs, Sarah Rosenberger, Michelle Roth, Nora and David Schambers, Karen Shank-Chapman,

Mark Siblisk, Tim Sledd, Kevin and Angela Smith, Tiffany Smith, Gail Stanley, Michael Stanley, Cristlyn Swinford, Ted and Redd, Jeff Townsend, Josh Traxler, S. Uebersohn, Emily Wallace, Tom Webster, Alan Wieder, Julie Wood, and Grayson Yohr. Thanks to our listeners, the members of our Facebook group, our patrons on Patreon, and all those who emailed and texted us kind messages over the years, including during the trial. We are grateful for all of you. There are so many of you. Your correspondence and kindness kept us going. Thank you.

We want to thank the journalists and media figures who made us feel welcome in this space: Colin Baillie, Audrey Conklin, Noah Crenshaw, Jamie Duffy, Richard Essex, Camila Fernandez, Kody Fisher, Angela Ganote, Brady Gibson, Sierra Gillespie, Clark Goldband, Ruthanne Gordon, Hannah Grace, Amy Graham-McCarty, Julie Grant, Jason Hammer and Nigel Laskowski, Cyndee Hebert, CJ Hoyt, Marina Hutchinson, Marguerite Incardone, Annie Kate, Jacara Jackson, Demie Johnson, Maura Johnson, Kaitlyn Kendall, Luke Kenton, Jen Leong, Angenette Levy, Emily Longnecker, Laura Ingle, Janet McGowan, Russ McQuaid, Drusilla Moorhouse, Alex Null, Alexa Reghanti, Kyla Russell, Vic Ryckaert, Rafael Sanchez, Bob Segall, Rachel Sharpe, and Danielle Zulkosky. We are sure there are many more and we appreciate the hard work done on this case by all journalists and media personnel.

Thank you to the deputies and other law enforcement officers who provided security during the trial. Thank you to the court staff and county personnel in Carroll County and Miami County. Thank you to the citizens of Peru and Delphi for making us feel so welcome. We would like to thank the employees at the following businesses for their hospitality: Bill's Rock Shop, the Buttermilk Biscuit Company & Coffee Shop, the Delphi Food Mart and Phillips 66 gas station, The Flower Shoppe II, Healthies Delphi & Delphi Depot, McDonald's, Jacob's ReDesigned, the Sandwich Shop, and the Shell gas station. We would like to thank the staff at the following libraries for their support and assistance: the Danville Public Library, the Delphi Public Library, the Greenwood Public Library, the Hamilton East Public Library, the Indianapolis Public Library, the Kokomo-Howard County Public Library, the La Porte County Public Library, the Logansport-Cass County Public Library, the Peru Public Library, and the West Lafayette Public Library. Thank you to the teams at Art19 and True Native for allowing us to dig into crimes.

We wish to thank our parents: Charles and Mary and Ken and Jeanne. Thank you sincerely for supporting our work and for your love and care. Thank you to Áine's sisters, Mary, Catherine and Máiréad for their love and support. Thank you to Áine's uncle David, and her late grandparents Vincent and Nan. Thanks to our wider extended family for their well wishes. Thank you to the talented Siddhartha Mahanta who allowed Áine to do a crime feature and changed her life. Thank you to all our teachers and editors and friends and neighbors. Thank you to Áine Cain, Frank Sinatra and Mort Weisinger for keeping Kevin going. Thank you to Kevin Greenlee, St. Francis De Sales, St. Michael the Archangel, Mary, Mother of God, and God for keeping Áine going.

We would also like to thank the families of Abby and Libby for their kindness and strength. Our hearts go out to you forever.